MW00788237

THE JUDAICA IMPRINT
FOR THOUGHTFUL PEOPLE

Searching for belief and meaning in today's turbulent world

FINGERPRINTS ON THE UNIVERSE

by Louis Pollack

Foreword by Rabbi Berel Wein

First Edition — First Impression / October 1994

Published by **SHAAR PRESS**
Distributed by MESORAH PUBLICATIONS, LTD.
4401 Second Avenue / Brooklyn, New York 11232 / (718) 921-9000

Distributed in Israel by SIFRIATI / A. GITLER BOOKS
4 Bilu Street / P.O.B. 14075 / Tel Aviv 61140

Distributed in Europe by J. LEHMANN HEBREW BOOKSELLERS
20 Cambridge Terrace / Gateshead, Tyne and Wear / England NE8 1RP

Distributed in Australia and New Zealand by GOLD'S BOOK & GIFT SHOP
36 William Street / Balaclava 3183, Vic., Australia

Distributed in South Africa by KOLLEL BOOKSHOP
22 Muller Street / Yeoville 2198 / Johannesburg, South Africa

ISBN: 0-89906-613-5 Hard Cover
ISBN: 0-89906-614-3 Paperback

Printed in the United States of America by Noble Book Press
Custom bound by Sefercraft, Inc. / 4401 Second Avenue / Brooklyn, N.Y. 11232

הרב לוי יצחק הלוי הורוויץ
דער באסטאנער רבי
Grand Rabbi Levi Y. Horowitz

מוסדות בוסטון בארה״ק
בנשיאות האדמו״ר שליט״א
מעלות האדמו״ר מבוסטון 1
הר נוף, ירושלים Israel

ב״ה

At a time when this generation is discovering the deepest mysteries of the Universe and is reaching billions of miles to the most distant planets, man is still at a loss to discover himself.

This volume brings closer to discovery that which is "more to life" by portraying some aspects of Torah that reach into the innermost parts of our being. By using the development of scientific thought as a means to appreciate the depths of Torah and its education, the author provides the reader with a true insight into the significance of Torah in our generation.

Rabbi Levi Y. Horowitz
Bostoner Rebbe

The manuscript was reviewed and warmly praised by two prominent scientists, both of whom have published books on the subject of Torah and science. They wrote the following comments:

Fingerprints on the Universe by Louis Pollack makes an important contribution to contemporary Torah literature. This book demonstrates the remarkable harmony that has emerged between recent scientific discoveries and the eternal message of the Torah that was revealed at Mount Sinai several millennia ago. Writing in a lucid style that is readily understandable even without a scientific background, Pollack has provided an excellent introduction to the Jew who seeks to correlate the Torah viewpoint with the ideas of modern science.

Professor Nathan Aviezer
Professor of Physics, Bar Ilan University,
Fellow, American Physical Society
Author of: *In the Beginning: Biblical Creation and Science.*

In science, we search for the 'how' of the universe. We study the world and hope to learn the laws by which it functions.

But at the end of the day, the question we all ask relates to "why," the why of existence. Is there meaning to our lives that transcends the splendor we see about us? Something that goes beyond the physical? And if so, how do we probe that meaning? Louis Pollack, in *Fingerprints on the Universe,* clarifies the difference between the search for the how and the need for the why. Citing developments in the physical and social sciences, the author maps the steady trend of science away from a position of confrontation with Torah to one that falls within the worldview first revealed at Sinai 3,300 years ago. Then, in contemporary language, Pollack develops a body of knowledge based on the traditional commentaries which for centuries have expanded our understanding of Torah, and makes this available for persons searching for meaning in their own lives or eager to help others find that meaning for themselves.

Dr. Gerald L. Schroeder
Physicist
Author of: *Genesis and the Big Bang:*
The Discovery of Harmony Between Modern Science and the Bible.

Table of Contents

Acknowledgments

Initially, I wish to convey my appreciation to Rabbi Aryeh Rottman, of Jerusalem, Israel, and to Rabbi Berel Wein, of Monsey, New York, each of whom has played a significant role in my life as rabbi, as rebbe, and as close friend.

Most of the Torah background and understanding which I possess I owe to them. As to this book specifically, I am greatly indebted to Rabbi Rottman for having originally conceived its theme and direction and to Rabbi Wein for his continuing encouragement and for his counsel, improvement of the manuscript and invaluable assistance in guiding it to publication.

During the book's development, there were times when I wondered if and when it would ever see the light of day. In these skeptical periods, I found support in recalling to mind one of this century's great rabbinic leaders, HaRav HaGaon Yaakov Kamenetsky, of blessed memory, who long ago had expressed assurance that I should pursue the book's purpose.

A special and most deserving note of appreciation goes to my wife, Elaine, for her keen insights regarding the book's thrust and for her consistent patience, understanding and support during the book's progress. Another heartfelt family thank you is due to my son, David, who oversaw the processing of the manuscript and who frequently alerted me to new research material and to means of achieving wider readership.

I also wish to express my especial gratitude to Rabbi Nachman Bulman, Rabbi David Gottlieb, Rabbi Shaya Cohen and Rabbi Aharon Feldman for their constructive recommendations and valuable advice. Professor David Luchins, Rabbi Joshua O. Haberman and Rabbi Hershel Billet also contributed a number of clarifying ideas and suggestions. Other good people who contributed practical comments are Rabbi Yitzchak Schlomo Zilberman, Rabbi Chayyim Yaakov Bulka, Yaakov Lavon, Chaim Billet and Ben Gasner.

As to those portions of the book relating to physics, I received most helpful advice and constructive suggestions from Professor

Nathan Aviezer and Professor Avi Greenfield, and I am obliged to them for their generous time and interest. I am quick to acknowledge, however, that any inaccuracies or errors which may appear in the book's scientific (or non-scientific) content are to be attributed to me alone.

I also wish to note the valuable assistance I received from Maria Diaz, who, with skill, patience and care, typed the several drafts of the manuscript.

A singular debt is also due to various members of the ArtScroll family for their splendid publishing and editorial support. Specifically, I wish to mention Rabbi Nosson Scherman for his early-on assessment that the book could serve a worthwhile educational purpose and who, together with Rabbi Meir Zlotowitz, provided exceptional helpfulness in bringing the book to publication. My encouraging and wise editor Rabbi Moshe Lieber merits a very hearty hug for his warmth, competency and help in eliminating more rough spots in the manuscript than I care to recall. The cooperative and time-consuming word processing and advisory efforts of Shmuel Blitz are also greatly appreciated, as are the graphic, proof-reading and other fine production endeavors of Eli Kroen, Avrohom Biderman, Yehuda Gordon, Fayge Silverman, Bassie Gutman, Udi Hershkowitz, and Leah Bracha Lasker.

But primarily and most importantly, I wish to express my deepest gratitude to the Almighty, blessed is He, for having enabled me to undertake and to complete this writing.

Foreword

From our earliest conscious moment we are assailed by basic, unrelenting questions. Who am I? What is the purpose of my life? How can I judge success in life? And perhaps most depressing of all, who cares? The numbing quality of modern life is that instead of attempting to deal with these questions, it ignores them and substitutes meaningful analysis of life with rapid and unrelenting pursuit of things and pleasures. Nowhere is this disastrous course of modern human behavior as evident as in the Jewish people of today. The overwhelming majority of modern Jewry rarely ever give serious thought to their heritage, value system and lifestyle. Having thrown out the baby of Torah with the bathwater of medieval Eastern European habits and mores, the modern Jew is defenseless in the face of the realities of life. Not knowing where he has been, he has no clue as to where he is supposed to go.

What can one say when the doctor tells us "I don't know" or "I can't help"? What of a world order still so cruel and dangerous that the tens of millions of murdered victims of this most advanced twentieth century seemingly have died in vain? What about marriage, children, family, community? Are they important? And most chillingly, what about life and its inevitable partner, death? We may be able to run from all of these questions, but we cannot hide from them. Western man has sought refuge in valium and alcohol, palaces and luxury automobiles, sports leagues without end and entertainment without conscience. And nevertheless we still all return to dust.

Judaism has from its inception at Sinai over 3,300 years ago dealt directly, honestly, compassionately and wisely with these issues. It is a faith centered on man and his problems, weaknesses and greatness. However, it is foremost a faith posited in the rock-firm belief of a Creator who has fashioned us all, guides us, gives and takes our lives, and has demands upon us for the proper use of our gifts of time, talent, wealth and opportunity. Western society, in removing the Creator from the equation of life, has doomed itself to the depressing state that has become its hallmark. In order for us to find ourselves, we must be able to analyze and redefine who we are and to see some connection to the faraway past and the even more distant infinite.

This book is meant as a primer for thinking people to enable them to begin the search for their Creator and themselves. It explains lucidly how the search for meaningful existence can be realized by Jews in examining their Torah and tradition. It points the direction to the wisdom of old in the new and ever-changing world of ours. It is not argumentative nor intimidating. It is not dogmatic. It is informative, understated, entertaining and very challenging. It will cause the reader to think about his life and being. It may therefore force us to use mental and spiritual muscles that we may have long considered to be atrophied.

The book is also a necessary explanation of modern concepts and theories in astronomy, physics and the world of nature. It explains the harmonious relationship between nature and its wonders and man and his soul. It informs and teaches without boring us. I am confident that the reader will leave this book wiser and more knowledgeable than when he began.

My friend of decades, Louis Pollack, has himself lived much of this book. I not only refer to the years of research and writing that have gone into this finely crafted book but also to his own personal life and search for meaning. Louis Pollack, who holds degrees from Cornell, the Cornell Law School and the Harvard Business School, is a lawyer, executive and now an author. But more importantly he is someone who has pursued his own life's meaning tirelessly and with tenacity. From this book not only facts, theories, anecdotes and good writing emerge but also the struggle and triumph of a modern-age Jew who, by dint of his own intuition, honesty and efforts, has found his answers to the mysteries of human life and existence. I am gratified that he has chosen to share himself with us and that he has allowed me these words of introduction.

Rabbi Berel Wein

". . . do not let a day be lost without secluding yourself and thinking of the meaning of your life."

— letter from R' Nathan of Bratzlav to his son (1830)

Introduction

There are times when many of us sense a lack of meaning in our lives. In occasional quiet and reflective moments, we find ourselves struggling with frustrating questions:

What is life's purpose?

Why was I put on this planet?

Is this daily monotony all there is to life?

Isn't there something more?

How can existence have meaning if nothing endures?

If having all the things I want is supposed to make me happily fulfilled, how come I'm not?

When these quandaries well up within us, oftentimes we react by concluding, "There really are no answers. I'll just make the best of things without getting involved in such insoluble mysteries." Still, as the years go by, these inner challenges do not go away. It is not unusual to find oneself still awake at two a.m. wondering, What's it all about? For it is in the nature of man to attempt to unravel the perplexities of his life. There is in most of us a strain of Indiana Jones seeking the Lost Ark of Understanding.

The profile of the average American Jew is one of a fairly successful person, with a respectable family, satisfying social relationships and few major complaints. Still we do not know why it is not enough. The nagging riddles remain. We continue to seek "something more" to our existence. More often than not, that existence has become routine, even boring, despite our contrived attempts to freshen and enliven it with distant travel, different lifestyles, various innovations and new possessions. After fifteen thousand miles of driving it, the Porsche or Lamborghini often tends to lose much of its original thrill.

The search for meaning and fulfillment is shared by a very large segment of mankind. Viktor Frankl, one of the world's preeminent psychiatrists, concluded early in a lifetime of research that the prime moving force in man is "striving to find meaning in one's life." The noted Swiss psychiatrist Carl Gustav Jung made a similar observation about his practice, pointing out that his patients' most frequently asked question was, "What is the meaning of my life . . .?" A professional study conducted several years back by Daniel Yankelovich Associates confirms that the search for self-fulfillment involves "in one way or another, as many as 80 percent of all adult Americans."[1] In an interview not long ago in *Life*, tennis star Chris Evert spoke of being unfulfilled despite her fame and money. "There has to be more," she confided. Remember, this is *the* Chris Evert, idolized by fans throughout the world and the winner of 157 tennis singles tournaments — more than any other player in history.

For some of us, the yearning for significance in our lives begins early. Jonathan Netanyahu, who was to become a legend through his exploits and martyrdom as the intrepid Israeli commander of the daring rescue at Entebbe of the hijacked Air France passengers, wrote, at age eighteen, that he wanted to "hold on to something," to discover some "meaning and reason" to life, but could not.[2]

For others, the yearning for a more meaningful course for our lives begins late — sometimes it starts after we're forty or fifty, even beyond. In July 1993, the Harvard Business School addressed this increasingly prevalent life-challenge by instituting its "Age of Options" Program, designed specifically to answer the "nagging little question" besetting a growing number of even highly successful graduates: *Is that all there is?* This eleven-day workshop explores this question in depth, with the participants considering the possibilities of "new, more fulfilling goals" or re-committing "to a current path in a more meaningful way."[3]

Recently, *Apollo 9* astronaut Rusty Schwieckart reminisced over a special moment in his life which occurred as he was floating outside the spacecraft, testing equipment. His fellow astronaut, Dave Scott, had been photographing him when the camera jammed. Scott had to return to the capsule to repair the camera, leaving Schwieckart dangling alone for a few introspective moments. What does he recall thinking about while traveling at seventeen

---

1. Yankelovich, Daniel, *New Rules: Searching for Self-Fulfillment in a World Turned Upside Down,* New York: Random House, 1981, p. 3.

2. Netanyahu, Jonathan. *Self-Portrait of a Hero: Letters from Jonathan*, New York: Ballantine Books, 1982, p. 21.

3. *Beyond the Pot of Gold,* Harvard Business School Bulletin, December 1993 issue.

thousand miles per hour in an absolute silence, looking down on our beautiful, blue earth? "Questions," he replied. "What does this mean? How did I get here? Who am I?"[4]

This book is an outgrowth of my own search for answers to such questions. It was a varied search. At first, I busied myself with a serious study of the writings of a number of well-known philosophers of the past, from Socrates to William James. I was impressed with their intellect, but I found that most of their papers offered more theory than practical solution. At other times, I found that their writings were tedious or difficult to penetrate. Frequently, they came across as having been written more for fellow philosophers than for people with average minds. After much investigation, I discovered little in philosophic literature to resolve my questionings or my dilemmas.

It was then that I turned my attention to the world-view of the scientific establishment. In the twentieth century the scientist became the hero of society. He was lauded as the creator of a dazzling array of technological and medical achievements. And the more man relied upon the scientist, the more science influenced man's thinking and direction. Twentieth-century man soon became willing to entrust his future to the men of science.

In the late nineteenth century, science and technology overtook and replaced social reform as the principal forces in the continuing emergence of the Enlightenment. Among the sciences, physics was especially intriguing, even to the common man. True, its complicated theories were mostly beyond his understanding. But physics bore a comforting resemblance to religion, which the rationalist Enlightenment philosophers had influenced man to devalue and jettison. Like religion, physics was seen as dedicated, purist, lofty, and it probed the mysteries of the universe for concealed truths.

This probe was markedly accelerated soon after the turn of the twentieth century by Albert Einstein's publication of his two great Theories of Relativity. These remarkable discoveries brought about a stunning advance in theoretical physics and earned worldwide recognition and esteem for the modest scientist. At a 1930 dinner in London to raise funds for needy East European Jews, George Bernard Shaw toasted Einstein as "the greatest of our contemporaries."

Man now seemed poised to make the final leap toward the most

---

4. Lemle, Miche, *Review*, June 1990 (reprinted from *New Age Journal*), p. 48.

exciting and passionate of scientific goals: that of "reality," which was deemed to represent the true meaning of the universe. Science assured us that if we could only discover reality, everything could be understood, and then there would be enough life-meaning to go around for everybody.

But this dream was soon shattered. Within a dozen years after Einstein published the second of his theories, a revolution in physics called the "Quantum Theory" took place. This theory partially overturned the Principle of Determinism which had previously shaped the "classical" physics of Einstein and all other scientific thinking for over two centuries. This principle held that every event is predetermined and the outgrowth of a chain of cause-and-effect, making every event exact and certain.

In the late 1920's, however, quantum physicists made the revolutionary discovery that there is an inherent *uncertainty* in nature. They found that the reliability and exactitude encountered in our vast, visible physical world do not carry over to the ultra-miniature, invisible world of atoms and particles.

Because of the uncertainty present in this latter, unseen world, it cannot be measured precisely. And since the scientist's goal of discovering physical reality cannot be achieved except through exact measurement of *both* the visible and invisible worlds, this meant that science never could totally fulfill the grand hope it held out, that the discovery of physical reality would provide man with universal understanding.

Consequently, when the quantum revolution established that science would not be able to provide us with a full understanding of ourselves and our universe, many of those who had relied upon science to do so turned instead to other thought systems. One was the new, fascinating discipline of psychiatry, brought to world attention by the startling theories of Sigmund Freud. Like physics, psychiatry also held out a promise: It would unlock many of the secrets of man's mind and personality and thus achieve the Enlightenment's aim of a rational society.

Yet, as was the case with Einstein, Freud's genius was praised highly, but some of his theories were seriously challenged by colleagues and fellow scientists. They criticized his overall tendency towards determinism, his strong reliance upon the value of self-knowledge, his slighting the importance of man's fear of death and his denigration of spiritual beliefs. Because of these flaws, they held, Freudian techniques could only partially resolve man's dilemmas. To this day, serious professional criticism of Freud's work continues.

Another thought system which attracted both American intellectuals and blue-collar workers was Marxist socialism, with its determinist-oriented beliefs of economic and social equality. It trumpeted that a classless society could achieve the goals of the Enlightenment more effectively than either science or psychology. Yet seventy years of Marxist-Leninism ended with its collapse throughout Europe. This was its final denouement, coming after gradual betrayal of millions who had surrendered their hopes and lives to a cause upon which they earnestly had depended for solutions to their personal problems and those of a troubled world.

But, by far, the largest segment of twentieth-century society was attracted not as much to science, psychology or politics as to the centuries-old enticement of money and materialism. Alexandre Solzhenitzyn, the famed Russian author, has observed that the materialistic overemphasis we see today was brought about by Enlightenment man's reaction against the dire material poverty of the Medieval Age. That the drive toward materialism characterized the earliest beginnings of the Enlightenment is evident from the writings of the sixteenth century's famed Jewish Italian sage, Ovadia Ben Yaacov Sforno (1475-1550): "Our people . . . concentrate their efforts on the accumulation of wealth, feeling this will protect them from the exigencies of their time." Regrettably, this reliance upon monetary protection and its disillusioning outcome continue into today's world, and most signs indicate that they will continue into tomorrow's as well.

When quantum mechanics discredited determinism to a large extent and enabled man to understand the inner structure and power of the invisible, non-material atom, we came to recognize that intellect, not matter or resources, would shape our future. Consequently, to the extent that they were based on the dogmas of determinism and materialism, Marxist theories, pre-quantum economics, Freudian psychiatry, classical physics and Darwinism were discredited as well.

The triumphs of quantum atomic energy, computers, instant telecommunications, fibre optics and many others demonstrated the victory of "mind over matter." Quantum physics largely defies common understanding, but, without question, its philosophy must be dealt with as an important element in our search for answers to the true purpose of our lives.

When I delved into the philosophy of quantum, I recognized that it established a most significant insight: pre-quantum physics had sought only a physical, limited version of reality; quantum demonstrated that, if we are to approach total reality, we must focus beyond the material world and look to the domain of the spirit and mind.

This insight triggered my recall of a basic tenet of Judaism, found in the Ten Commandments. In my thinking, "Judaism" is that system of Jewish law and belief which originated at Mt. Sinai and which has been passed on, intact, from generation to generation in a direct line to the present time. Its first two commandments proclaim the existence of an invisible, single God and admonish man not to serve or deify anything created. Nothing alive or inert, no infallible human being, no plaster saint is to stand between the Jew and his God, Who can only be conceived intellectually. Judaism, I realized, is the nonpareil "religion of the mind."

Like quantum, Judaism proclaims "mind over matter," with one significant difference: Judaism's message had been delivered to the world 3,300 years earlier. It then became clear to me that my own religion, not some newer, less tested or less authentic route, offered the very pathway to true meaning and total reality that I had sought for years.

Still, all too many intelligent people, to their spiritual detriment, continue to remain hobbled by their misplaced reliance upon the sciences and materialism as havens of meaning and understanding. They still persist in the conventional confidence that technology and what our five senses can perceive will provide all we need to know about truth and life despite recognition by many first-class thinkers, ancient and modern, that ultimate truth lies beyond our physical world. No wonder so many of us lead hollow lives. No wonder so many of us who have long been engaged in a search for values and significance are still asking, "What's it all about?"

Happily, there are wise and satisfying answers to this cry for comprehension. And it was my discovery of such answers within Judaism which led to the writing of this book and which shaped its principal theme. This theme can be stated in one sentence: We Jews can find real answers to our dilemmas of purpose and meaning through the wisdom of Judaism's spiritual heritage rather than through interaction with the other value systems or the material world.

Through Judaic wisdom, I am convinced, we can derive *both* of man's most sought-after reassurances:

(1)That there is a great store of meaning in the world which is available to each of us, and

(2)that the remembrance of our once having existed need never disappear.

And it is most important to know that wisdom and these reassurances are accessible to *every* Jew, whether his identification with Judaism is strong, nominal or even non-existent.

A few words should be said about the historical accounts, in the early chapters, of four sciences: astronomy, evolution, psychology and physics. What, you may well ask, are such accounts doing in a book about the search for meaning?

One reason is that the history and philosophy of modern science provide a helpful setting against which one can discern the marvelous difference which connectedness with Judaism can make in the lives of Jewish men and women seeking purpose and fulfillment.

A second reason is that, in the light of science's exceptional contributions to mankind, many people came to look to the sciences for answers beyond the purview of technology, to the deeper questions of life. Consequently, for many decades the foregoing four disciplines have exerted major influences in the formation of man's thinking as to the purpose of existence and his role in the world.

In the last seventy years, however, several basic beliefs of these disciplines have been substantially revised or outmoded by new findings of scientists in their continuing search for truth and accuracy. Since many of us still mistakenly adhere to such previously held but now-altered beliefs, I felt it important to trace why such beliefs arose and how they came to be superseded by recent, astonishing discoveries which can help us gain better understanding of ourselves and our universe.

We begin with the emergence of the Enlightenment Movement, which three hundred years ago began to shape the world in which we live: a world in which man ever since has struggled to find his place.

FINGERPRINTS ON THE UNIVERSE

1

The Unfolding of the Enlightenment Movement

"Me thinks . . . [the Heroes of this Age] . . . will leave the world better provided than they found it . . . they'll fill the world with wonders."[1]

— Joseph Glanville (1661)

1. Glanville, Joseph, *The Age of Dogmatizing*, London: 1661.

The Enlightenment Movement revolutionized medieval society as drastically and permanently as atomic energy has revolutionized the art of warfare. Historians disagree as to when the movement began. Some maintain it started as early as the fifteenth century, with the invention of the printing press. To others, it first gained momentum with the seventeenth-century scientific findings of Galileo, Leibnitz and Newton. Another view dates it from the latter half of the eighteenth century, with the impact upon society of the writings of the philosophers of the Enlightenment: Voltaire and Rousseau in France, and Paine and Jefferson in America.

Spreading from France to other Western European countries, the movement set off an avalanche of reaction against the poverty and repression of the Medieval Age. It attacked the decadence of the nobility, the belief in the divine right of kings and the infallibility of the Church. The results of this upheaval were extraordinary and far-reaching.

The main doctrines upon which the Enlightenment rested were the beliefs that human reason could solve all problems and that the rights of the individual were supreme. These great issues were debated and their expression polished in the literary salons of Germany and France, which were hosted by influential and charming ladies who welcomed into their stately mansions the new liberal, literary and philosophic minds of the age.

It was this new spirit of thinking which inspired such history-shaping documents as the French Declaration of the Rights of Man, the Virginia Statute of Religion and the Declaration of Independence. This initial phase of the Enlightenment, lasting till the end of the nineteenth century, focused upon the eradication of social ills. Secular humanism occupied center stage and the "common man" was assigned the leading role.

Medieval society's mainstay, the belief in an omnipotent God, was replaced by belief in the innate goodness of man. The most eminent of the Enlightenment philosophers, Immanuel Kant, proclaimed in his famous work, *The Critique of Pure Reason*, that man is endowed with an inner "moral law." This, Kant asserted, enabled man to do what is inherently good and to bring meaning to his life from "within himself," without reliance upon any "outside" teaching or belief.

For many centuries prior to the Enlightenment, man had little need to seek meaning. True, poverty and oppression were common in the medieval world, but man was able to capture a fairly satisfying degree of life-meaning through religion, pride in his daily labors, the comfort of a close-knit family and an uncomplicated rural environment. Emancipation's sweeping winds of change, however, virtually dismantled these societal underpinnings. In their place, it was promised, man would discover greater rewards through the social and economic gains of his new freedoms. But the Enlightenment, preoccupied with social and economic emancipation, did not address itself as religion had for ages to man's most perplexing challenge: What is the purpose of existence?

When it became apparent that this challenge would not be met in this phase of the Enlightenment, the modern search for meaning began in earnest.

Between the mid-eighteenth and mid-nineteenth centuries, a new phase of the Enlightenment began. It was initiated by a shift from an emphasis on the blessings of human rights to the blessings of technological benefits. This shift was fueled by the Industrial Revolution, which brought to the era improved technology, increased production, management efficiency and a harvest of exciting new inventions. Still, these innovations had unwelcome side effects. The individual's pride of workmanship was replaced by the monotony of mechanization. Higher wages encouraged the migration from the cottage to the city, causing an accompanying breakdown in the once central influence of family and home. Urban slums and overcrowding proliferated.

On the other hand, the increase in the availability of education, the widening of communication, the expansion of new markets and the heightened demand for goods contributed to the growth of the natural sciences. Exceeding even the far-reaching political and humanistic changes initiated by the earlier phase of the Emancipation, in this latter phase the sciences would alter the world beyond the dreams of earlier generations. Joseph Glanville, a member of the Royal Society and one of the exceptional visionaries of the seventeenth century, gave a startlingly accurate prediction of the future when, in 1661, he wrote:

> It may be some Ages hence, a voyage to Southern unknown Tracts, yea possibly the Moon, will not be more strange than one to America. To them, that come after us, it may be as ordinary to buy a *pair* of *wings* to fly into remotest Regions; as now a pair of Boots to ride a Journey. And to confer [sic] at the distance of the Indies by Sympathetick [sic] conveyances, may be as usual to future times, as to us in a literary [sic] correspondence. . .; And the turning of the now comparatively *desert* world into a Paradise, may not improbably be expected from late Agriculture.[6]

As we know from hindsight, each of these wonders and many more came to pass, as a steady stream of astounding discoveries and benefits poured out of scientific minds and research laboratories. As early as the turn of the seventeenth century we began to see the emergence of scientific disciplines which would exert an amazingly dominant influence upon society in the centuries to come. The most exciting and influential of these disciplines and each of their goals were:

Astronomy — to explain how the universe came into being
Evolution — to explain how man came into being
Psychology — to explain how man's inner self functions

6. Ibid.

Physics — to explain how both the huge and the minute aspects of the universe operate.

Each of these branches of science, then, saw as its ultimate goal the uncovering of segments of "reality." Science believed reality could be isolated and identified through investigation by our five senses and through the full discovery of the ultimate mathematical theories and physical laws governing the universe. Once reality would be identified, science postulated, man would be able to understand the underlying causes of all events, predict the future of the universe and comprehend his own role in it.

The next four chapters will explore this fascinating but unrealized ambition. It was unrealized because science failed to recognize that it sought a physical reality, which is only a portion of total reality. Until the late 1920's science did not take into account that a search for *spiritual* reality also must be pursued in order to discover total reality.

Astronomy took an early lead in the quest of science to understand our world. So let us begin with astronomy, the oldest science, in our account of the four most influential branches of science to emerge in the Age of Enlightenment.

2

Astronomy and the "Big Bang"

"Every Jew must know and believe that there exists a first Being ... who brought all things into existence and continues to sustain them. This Being is God ... Through such scientific disciplines as physics and astronomy, clear evidence for these concepts [can be] deduced."[1]

— Rabbi M. C. Luzzatto (1707-1746)

"In the beginning God created the heaven and the earth."

— Quoted from *Genesis* by U.S. astronaut on the first sighting of planet earth from outer space

1. Luzzatto, Moshe Chaim, trans. by Aryeh Kaplan, *The Way of God*, Jerusalem: Feldheim Publishers Ltd., 1977, p. 31.

The cosmos always has fascinated man, from ancient times when he could only peer up at the heavens to his contemporary, sophisticated search for evidence of intelligent life beyond our planet. And when we begin to muse that "there must be something more to life" to make it truly fulfilling, we usually think of that "something" as originating "somewhere out there" in the boundless cosmic "beyond."

What do we really know about this vast, silent space? How far away does it stretch? Recently, Cal Tech built a new telescope atop an extinct 13,600 foot-high Hawaiian volcano. This remarkable instrument, the Keck telescope, can "see" fifty percent further than any other earthbound telescope. It has a light-gathering power four times that of our previously most powerful Mt. Palomar instrument. (Keck can observe a candle flame as far away as the moon.) Recently, it spotted a quasar, the brightest class of objects in the sky, almost fourteen billion light-years away, close to the edge of the known universe, which is estimated to be fifteen billion light-years distant.

To gain a very vague idea as to how distant fifteen billion light-years are from, say, the Statue of Liberty, we should first grasp the extent of a "billion." A good way to start is by keeping in mind that it would take thirty-one *years* for a watch to tick off a billion seconds.

The next step is to try to think in terms of "light-years." We need to use the astronomer's measuring rod of light-years because the distances in space are so astoundingly great that they cannot be translated in terms of our conventional "mile." A "light-year" is the distance that light travels in a calendar year at light's speed of 186,000 miles per second. To express this in terms of our miles, the sun is ninety-three million miles from earth; this distance is covered in ten minutes by the sun's light traveling to earth.

Another way of gaining an idea of the enormous distance represented by a light-year is by recognizing that someone driving a car on an express highway at sixty miles per hour would need to stay behind the wheel for twelve million years in order to drive the distance covered in *one* light-year. Then we must multiply the immense number of miles driven during these twelve million years times *fifteen billion* (the estimated distance in light-years to the edge of the universe) to arrive at the incredibly great distance in our conventional "miles" between the Statue of Liberty and the known limits of the universe. That is why the word "vast" falls far short of describing its dimensions.

Now for a glimpse into what is contained within the mainly empty, airless black void of that universe. Until a hundred years ago it was thought that the universe consisted only of the great galaxy of stars which we call the Milky Way. But, early in this century, astronomers discovered that our Milky Way is only one of *billions* of similar galaxies. Our large telescopes are powerful enough to confirm that there are some one hundred million other galaxies just within the bowl outline of our Big Dipper! And *each* of these galaxies contains approximately one hundred billion stars or suns, making such an enormous, cumulative total of stars that even a trained scientific mind finds it difficult to deal with such fantastically huge numbers.

What we call the cosmos is simply too overwhelming in size for finite man to conceive. We live on a planet which is a mere speck in a galaxy which itself, in turn, is a mere speck in the enormous expanse of the heavens. Man is left to ponder how puny he is in the mysterious, swirling, immense system which we call the universe and which God probably calls His workshop.

The U.S. Space Program and the exploits of the astronauts have captivated the minds of peoples on every continent. About one-sixth of the earth's population watched the live broadcast on July 20, 1969, when U.S. astronaut Neil Armstrong took the first human step on another celestial body. We experience vicarious feelings of adventure and drama in following such explorations.

Landing a frail, retrievable machine on the surface of the moon is a form of tapping on the window of the cosmic mystery. We support the space effort for its geopolitical and military values but no less because it satisfies our curiosity to learn what lies on the "dark side of the moon." Despite the shadow of sadness which the Challenger disaster cast over the nation, America is moving forward with its space program. Something deep within us, more than just curiosity, moves us to peek beyond our earth to learn what lies beyond Main Street and above Mt. Everest.

Some thirty kilometers east of Mayaguez, Puerto Rico, is the site of Cornell University's Areceibo radio-radar observatory. The world's largest and most sensitive, with a diameter of 305 meters, it monitors cosmic radio signals reaching earth, seeking signs of intelligence in extraterrestrial space. When I visited Areceibo a number of years back, the staff allowed me to listen in on some of these radio waves. To me, they sounded like just so much static. But to the staff scientists, they were the subject of keen, technical analysis for hints of intelligent signals from possible civilizations beyond our own.[2] This is not H.G. Wells or Star Trek fantasy. It is motivated by a fierce drive within serious, dedicated radioastronomers to pierce into star space for signs of other worlds created with life-supporting systems.

On the 500th anniversary of Columbus' discovery of the New World, October 12, 1992, the U.S. National Aeronautics and Space Administration (NASA) launched "SETI" (Radio Search for Extraterrestrial Intelligence), the most intensive, coordinated listening search yet. Its scientists employ both the Areceibo and the Mojave Desert Goldstone Tracking Station radio telescopes, aided by widely-spaced powerful computers capable, when fully operational,

---

2. In January 1992, Alexander Wolszcan, a resident astronomer at Areceibo, announced the finding of the strongest evidence to date of a planetary system other than our own. It is reported to be orbiting the star PSR1257+12, some seven quadrillion miles from earth.

of searching fifteen million radio channels every second and sorting out those which have any possibility of originating from outer space. In the initial hours of NASA's program, more signals have been scanned than in all past years of investigation. This sophisticated search will continue for ten years in the grand quest of someday possibly tapping into a radio channel at the other end of which has been placed a long long-distance call to "anyone out there who might be listening." That would be the electrifying moment when man would learn that we are not alone in the universe.[3]

The man in the street shares this infatuation, as shown by the record-breaking popularity of such films as *Return of the Jedi* and *E.T.* A hundred million patrons stood in line to pay 350 million dollars to view *E.T.* in the first year of its release. To date, it has grossed over eight hundred million dollars more than *Gone with the Wind* earned in its day.

One can detect more than a science-fiction attraction in this exceptional response of the public. For such films do more than display slick cinematography. They have a moral and spiritual side as well. The Star Wars duel between Obi-Wan Kenobi and Darth Vader portrays a moral Armageddon between good and evil, between the wicked "imperial dark lord" and the goodness and light of "the force." And in teen-age Elliot's human affection and E.T.'s reciprocal creature feelings we see portrayed the theme of universal love and the belief that all creation emanates from a *single* source.

We find an interesting parallelism to this "single source" concept in that the Periodic Table of Elements, an undisputed scientific discovery, demonstrates that all matter in the universe, on earth as well as in outer space, can only be composed of the chemical elements listed in the Table. Two hundred fifty years earlier, Isaac Newton had postulated that our planet Earth and all the heavenly bodies are linked together by a common origin and the same physical laws. This conclusion was but one of Newton's spectacular findings. No other scientist before or since (although Albert Einstein came close) possessed Newton's remarkable, intuitive gift for scientific discovery.

But this scientific genius had a matching philosophical side. To Newton, the principles of physics demonstrated an origin, an order and a harmony to the universe which could be attributed only to a

3. Regrettably, however, federal budgetary reductions overrode SETI's worthy ambition, and late in 1993 Congress canceled the project.

supernatural Creator Who is beyond and independent of the universe. Like the great pre-Newton scientists Kepler and Leibnitz, Newton was convinced that the material and the divine must be viewed together to understand the meanings of human existence and the universe. These greatest of the early scientists believed that science and reason standing alone never could capture such meanings.

For centuries, man had accepted Aristotle's theory that the universe is eternal, that it had no beginning. Newton believed, however, that Aristotle was wrong, that the world had not existed forever but had a beginning at a single instant of time, just as described by the opening words of the Bible, "In the beginning . . ." Newton, although a loyal member of the Church of England, held that the world was so created by the "God of Jews." This belief was in part derived from Newton's lifelong reliance on the interpretations of Judaism's sacred writings set out by the twelfth-century Jewish sage, Moses Maimonides.

Maimonides is universally recognized as Judaism's preeminent legal authority, philosopher and codifier. His towering scholarship and leadership earned him the accolade of his contemporaries: "From Moses [the Lawgiver] to Moses [Maimonides] there was none like Moses [Maimonides]." In his philosophical writings, he supported a number of other aspects of Aristotle's thinking, but eventually Maimonides rejected the eternal universe theory, concluding that it was speculative and not provable. This issue was and still is a critical consideration in Jewish belief because faith in a Creator is not valid without faith in His creativity. To the Jew, unless the first words of Genesis are indisputable truth, the thousands of words which follow become considerably compromised. That this truth has now been substantially confirmed by science is the thrust of what follows in this chapter.

In the early twentieth century, almost every astronomer and physicist held fast to what is called the "Steady State" Theory, further advanced in 1948 by Herman Bondi, Thomas Gold, and also Sir Fred Hoyle. The theory held that new matter was continually being created and that, in effect, the universe is eternal and had no specific beginning — a proposition similar to that of Aristotle. Even Einstein continued to stand by this theory despite the clear demonstration by the brilliant Russian mathematician Alexandre Friedmann that Einstein's own General Theory of Relativity indicated a contrary finding. To counter this, an unyielding Einstein tried to modify his own theory to fit a Steady State condition (later calling this modification the "biggest blunder of my life"), but eventually he conceded the accuracy of Friedmann's conclusion. In the mid-1930's, the work of Edwin Hubble cast serious doubt upon the Steady State Theory and not long thereafter, Steady State was replaced with the once-opposed but now widely accepted "Big Bang" Theory. "Big Bang's" outstanding contribution was that it demonstrated that the universe did not always exist but rather came into existence within one split second of time.

Why did most of the leading astronomers and physicists of the early twentieth century oppose "Big Bang" so strongly? Robert Jastrow, founder of NASA's Goddard Institute for Space Studies and now Director of the Mount Wilson Institute, has published a fascinating volume on this subject entitled *God and the Astronomers*.[4] Dr. Jastrow notes that opposition to "Big Bang" stemmed from a reluctance by many earlier leading astrophysicists to align themselves with a scientific theory that was congruent with the Biblical account. Their acknowledgment that creation had a beginning would contradict what science had maintained from the start of the Enlightenment. To concede that the universe did not always exist but was created in a single instant of time would be tantamount to scientific apostasy.

Yet, in the late 1920's and early 1930's, the work of Edwin Hubble led his fellow astronomers and physicists to subsequently reject Steady State and to support "Big Bang." His brilliant work at the Mt. Wilson Observatory established the fundamentals which have since become the astronomer's "standard model" of the origin of the universe.

It is Hubble for whom the remarkable ninety-four-inch space telescope was named. This extraordinary device weighs twelve tons, is the size of an average room, cost 1.5 billion dollars, and was eighteen years in the planning. Scheduled to have been launched by the ill-fated Challenger space shuttle, the telescope was finally lifted into space in April 1990. It operates 381 miles above the turbulence of the earth's atmosphere, enabling it to see seven times deeper into

4. Much of the remainder of this chapter is based on Professor Jastrow's most interesting account in *God and the Astronomers* (New York: Warner Books, Inc., 1980) of the "new story of *Genesis*," and I wish to express my reliance upon this very helpful source.

space than previous instruments. Although some serious viewing difficulties developed soon after launching, technicians recently made a very expensive house call to Hubble to replace, among other items, the telescope's mirror. Sighting results since the corrections were made have left NASA officials jubilant, and there is great optimism that in the future Hubble will indeed reveal secrets beyond the reach of all present telescopic instrumentation.

Edwin Hubble was an exceptional man of many talents. In his youth, he was a collegiate basketball star and boxer.[5] Following his undergraduate days, Hubble was awarded a Rhodes Scholarship and studied law at Oxford. After his discharge as a major in the U.S. Army at the end of World War I, he began his study of astronomy and developed into a world-class astronomer. Handsome, patrician and articulate, he devoted the remainder of his days to a study of the speed and distances of stars.

Hubble's interest in this aspect of astronomy began with a lecture he heard delivered in 1914 by Vesto Melvin Slipher of the Lowell Observatory. This lecture's impact on the fledgling astronomer and the extraordinary results that followed Hubble's subsequent investigations have been interestingly detailed by Dr. Jastrow in *God and the Astronomers*.

Slipher's work provided Hubble with the clue to the seemingly impossible clocking of the incredibly fast speeds of stars and the enormous distances they flew into deep space. Slipher's clue lay in the differences (viewed through a spectroscope) of the color of light emitted by a star moving away from the earth (reddish) and that of a star moving toward the earth (bluish). The further away a star moves, the more the reddish hue increases in intensity; in this way the star's speed can be measured.

Building on Slipher's findings, Hubble set to work at the one-hundred-inch Mt. Wilson telescope, then the world's largest. Night after night (spectroscoping just one galaxy took an entire night), he monitored the galaxies to determine their distances from earth and the speed at which they traveled. He and his collaborator, Milton Humason, spent over a decade in the late 1920's and early 1930's

5. Baseball fans will be interested to know that one of Hubble's relations was the New York Giants famed pitcher Carl Hubble, who holds the fifty-five-year-old record for the most consecutive victories — twenty-four — and the All-Star Game record of five consecutive strikeouts (tied in 1986 by Fernando Valenzuela).

viewing hundreds of galaxies and stars, recording, collating and analyzing the data that flowed out of telescope and spectroscope.

Milton Humason had no previous training in astronomy and no education beyond grade school. He came to know the staff at Mt. Wilson through his employment as the supervisor of the mule teams that transported equipment, materials and people up and down the mountain during the construction of the observatory. When it opened, he remained on, doing menial work but all the while developing a keen interest in the imposing and sophisticated devices around him and in the bright, investigative people who were operating them. Soon he became fluent in the language of astronomy and gained a clear perception of what telescopes were seeking to discover. Before long he caught the attention of the staff through the care and devotion with which he handled the delicate equipment. Soon afterwards, he was invited to become an official member of the observatory personnel. In the years that followed, Milton Humason developed into the leading spectrographer in the world, contributing exceptional and unique findings which have greatly enlarged our understanding of the cosmos.

When the data that Hubble and Humason had discovered was fully analyzed in the mid-1930's, Hubble was able to publish what is regarded as "probably the most important discovery in astronomy ever made."[6] Known as Hubble's Law, it stated that the universe was expanding at speeds in excess of one hundred million miles per hour in all directions. Moreover, the more distant a galaxy, the faster its speed.

Why was Hubble's discovery such a cosmological triumph? Because it established that the universe, space, and time originated in a white-hot, multi-trillion degree explosion of unimaginable force and energy which took place in a *single instant of time*. Hubble further revealed that all of the exploding celestial bodies throughout the universe originated from a *common source*.

These findings closely paralleled the ancient Biblical description of the creation. Edwin Hubble, after centuries of dispute, had pioneered the way to the subsequent invalidation of the Steady State Theory and had confirmed that the universe was created at a precise point in time. And, while not all details of Hubble's findings and

---

6. Cornell, James, ed., *Bubbles, Voids, Bumps in Time: The New Cosmology*, Cambridge: Cambridge Univ. Press, 1989, p. 25.

those of the Bible match perfectly, his discovery also furnished powerful support for the "In the beginning" account of *Genesis* as stating a valid, believable theory of the origin of the universe!

Thirty years later, a fortuitous, extraordinary discovery by radio-astronomers Arno A. Penzias and Robert W. Wilson provided significant further confirmation of Hubble's earlier findings of an enormous explosion that took place in the very remote past. The work of Penzias and Wilson was so significant that it earned them a Nobel Prize.

In 1964, the two men had been conducting experiments in a Bell Telephone laboratory in New Jersey to measure the intensity of radio waves or "noise" emanating from our own galaxy, the Milky Way. They were astonished to learn that their antenna was receiving waves very much different from what they had anticipated. At first, they suspected that the noise might be the result of droppings left inside the antenna horn by nesting pigeons. This theory was found untenable once the pigeons were dislodged and the antenna cleaned.

What greatly puzzled Penzias and Wilson was that the noise was coming from *all directions*, and that it did not vary from day to day or week to week. Moreover, it did not appear to originate from the earth, the sun, the Milky Way or from any particular cosmic source.

Sometime afterwards, they learned from a colleague of work at Princeton, especially that of P. J. E. Peebles, which theorized that there was a glow of radiation throughout the universe which had remained from the huge explosion which took place at the beginning of the universe. This theory had been advanced since 1948, but neither Penzias nor Wilson was familiar with it. When they described their findings to their Princeton colleagues, it became evident that Penzias and Wilson had come upon the most important contribution since Hubble's work toward understanding the formation of the universe. For they, indeed, had located the radiation left over from the original "fireball" that generated all universal matter and energy!

Still further confirmation of the "Big Bang" Theory is noted by Professor Jastrow in his book *Until The Sun Dies*.[7] There, he describes

---

7. Jastrow, Robert, *Until the Sun Dies*, New York: Warner Books, 1977.

the fifteen-year investigation by astronomer Allan Sandage of the changing rate of the expansion of the universe.

In his youth, Sandage was an assistant to Edwin Hubble until the latter's death, and he is regarded by many as Hubble's successor. Known as today's grand old man of cosmology (the study of the nature of the universe), Sandage established through his findings that the expansion of the universe was of greater velocity in the "early" universe than in the present. The speed of expansion is slowing down, therefore, as the gigantic force of the explosion at creation gradually becomes spent. Jastrow observes that Sandage's investigation, together with the Penzias-Wilson discovery, confirmed the validity of the "Big Bang" creation theory "beyond a reasonable doubt." For his findings, Sandage was honored with the 1991 Crafoord Prize by the Royal Swedish Academy of Sciences. In astronomy, this prize is of equal stature to the Nobel Prize.

Thus we see coming to a close the three-hundred-year controversy among scientists over whether the universe had always existed, as Aristotle maintained, or whether it came into being in a single moment of time, as Isaac Newton had believed. Newton must have smiled wryly in his Westminster Abbey resting place over his eventual vindication by most of the leading astrophysicists of the twentieth century.

Still, the vindication belongs no less to Moses Maimonides, whose writings played such a vital role in Newton's thinking and who, five hundred years before Newton, held fast to the belief that we are part of a universe the existence of which is not eternal but which began, as Genesis relates, with one colossal stroke of its Creator.

3

The Theory of Evolution

"There is still considerable difference as to the means, such as how far natural selection has acted ... or whether there exists some mysterious innate tendency to perfectibility."[1]

— Charles Darwin, 1878,
twenty years after publication of his *Origin of the Species*

1. Cohen, I. Bernard, *Revolution in Science*, Boston: Harvard University Press, 1985, p. 296, quoting Darwin's 1878 letter.

Cose by Newton's honored place in Westminster Abbey is that of Charles Darwin who, in the mid-nineteenth century, initiated the most far-reaching scientific revolution since that of Newton. Darwin's Theory of Evolution seriously challenged the Newtonian concept that the universe is governed by a mechanism designed to function with order and harmony. Darwin postulated that creation's governing cause is chance, not design. Inevitably, Darwin directly attacked the Biblical accounts of creation and of the divine origin of man.

Darwin's *Origin of the Species*, published in 1859, had the near-immediate effect of altering the principal religious and social views which society had held for many centuries. And to this day, it continues to dominate the philosophy of both the intellectual and the man in the street, exerting powerful influence within the schools, the laboratories and the legislative halls of the Western World.

This influence becomes understandable when we recognize that Darwin's theory fit almost perfectly into the anti-religious, humanistic principles of the then-unfolding Emancipation Movement. The philosophers of the movement had declared that God is no longer to be enthroned as Sovereign of the world. Henceforth, man is to be his own master and in exclusive control of his own destiny. Darwin's findings neatly buttressed these views. All happenings in nature, he maintained, were without any pattern or plan. They were purely random, devoid of any trace of divine stamp. Man was not created in the image of God but evolved through the complex processes which Darwin called "natural selection" and "survival of the fittest." While this anti-Creator position may not have been Darwin's primary agenda, he certainly was adopted as a convenient fellow traveller by those seeking to deny God as the Creator.

There were only two possible approaches to the beginning of life: divine creation or "spontaneous generation." Since the training and philosophy of the scientist excluded the possibility of supernatural forces and since science believed that all answers were to be found in nature, the evolutionist was left with no choice but to select spontaneous generation as the rationale for the origin of life.

The opening salvo in the struggle between the evolutionists and the religionists was fired at the beginning of the nineteenth century by geologists who attacked the religionists' literal reckoning of the age of the earth as found in Genesis. Subsequently, with the publication of Darwin's famous *Origin of the Species,* a veritable fire-storm broke over the Biblical view of creation. The ensuing tug of war for man's mind was enacted in the meetinghouse, schoolhouse, courthouse and legislative house.

Darwinism became (and still is) a faith in itself. From its inception, its adherents crusaded for the teaching of evolution to the new generations. Among them was Sir Julian Huxley, who campaigned for the teaching of evolution "as the central core" of the educational system. (To this day, the ideological struggle continues. Not long ago my own university, Cornell, announced the formation of a "Committee of Evolutionary Biology" to stimulate enrollment in a course of evolution by students other than biology majors.)

But not every evolutionist has been comfortable in asserting that all human development is the sole result of the random mechanics of the evolutionary process. Alfred Russell Wallace (who is credited by history with having conceived the theory of evolution independently of Darwin but who failed to publish it before Darwin did) felt that natural selection could not have produced the human mind. He posited that a Creator must have played a major role in man's physical and mental development. Darwin was greatly distressed by

Wallace's conclusion but was forced to admit years later that the exact role of natural selection was unclear and that, as stated in the quotation at the head of this chapter, there may be "some mysterious innate tendency to perfectibility."

In the *Origin of the Species*, Darwin had already commented on his especial hesitancy to identify the human eye as one of the end results of natural selection:

> To suppose that the eye with all its inimitable contrivances for adjusting the focus to different distances, for admitting different amounts of light and for the correction of spherical and chromatic observation could have been formed by Natural Selection seems, I confess, absurd in the highest degree.[2]

He was later to write to his friend Asa Gray that he went through a stage when he would feel "cold all over" at "the thought of the eye."[3]

As marvelous as the eyes' capabilities are in scanning, tracking, locking onto and transmitting intelligence to the brain, it is a wonder that Darwin's misgivings did not extend beyond the eye, as did Wallace's. That the development of man's intelligence, his ability to conceive abstractions, to philosophize, to speak, that all of these wondrous qualities are the outgrowth of a random process which began in a "primeval soup" seems a belief far more difficult to accept than Judaism's opposing belief, that of the divine imaging of man.

Today, some scientists continue to contest the validity and soundness of evolution's premises. In his recent (and characteristically controversial) volume *The Intelligent Selection*, the prominent astronomer Sir Fred Hoyle attacks Darwinism on a number of fronts. He contends that natural selection could never have brought about the two thousand enzymes necessary for life. Further, he argues, man possesses many characteristics that are totally unconnected with survival. He cites, as an example, man's belief in religion, which often defies personal risk and even danger to life itself. Although he is a self-declared "non-religionist," Hoyle concludes that man's creation was not accidental and that our source of origin must be sought beyond this planet.[4]

---

2. Darwin, Charles, *Origin of the Species*, C. VI.
3. Letter to Asa Gray, April 3, 1860.
4. *Newsweek*, Jan. 11, 1989.

While Hoyle's position may be debatable, recent developments have begun to raise serious questions about Darwinism even among evolutionist biologists. Thus, Darwin had maintained that natural selection is powered by a fierce rivalry among the species for food and mates. Those species with specialized traits which increase their adaptability to the environment have better chances of survival. Eventually, the lineage which is best adapted survives, while those which do not adapt become extinct.

But this theory presents major difficulties. Even Darwin conceded that there were a number of "missing links" within certain species without which it could not be demonstrated that there was, as he theorized, a gradual transition of the evolutionary process from a lower to a higher stage of development. Darwin maintained that over the years we would discover the "missing links" in the then-still-incomplete fossil chains of many species.

Yet, in the 130 years that have passed, the search for the missing fossils to support Darwin's position has proved so disappointing[5] that paleontologists generally have abandoned this pursuit, turning instead to other approaches. Many believe, contrary to Darwin's description of an almost imperceptible and continuous evolution, that many new species came into being through abrupt "jumps." And within the past few years, gaps of millions of years have been uncovered in the evolutionary chain envisioned by Darwin.[6]

Darwin seemed to have laid a foundation in the *Origin* for such future difficulties. For he stressed that he had "...two distinct objects in view; to show that species had not been separately created and secondly that natural selection has been the chief agent of change..." But he went on to acknowledge that he had possibly "exaggerated" the influence of natural selection.

Thus, Darwin's approach in the *Origin* is one of occasional candor. Whenever he had little to support his position he was frank in admiting it. On the other hand, he frequently asserted' that views contrary to his own were simply wrong even though his own also

5. For example, paleontologists investigating the evolution of insects have not found evidence of any fossil to which the insect can be linked.

6. In Wisconsin several years ago, tiny skulls were unearthed which evolutionists consider were the ancestors of apes and humans. Yet paleontologists claim that these primates parted from other primates some fifteen million years earlier. Paleontologists do not deny that this leaves a break of millions of years in the evolutionary description of human development.

lacked convincing, objective scientific proof. (Interestingly, a similar position is taken by both sides in today's ongoing dispute between evolutionists and "creationists.") And although the *Origin* contains an orderly presentation of evolutionary theories which are frequently quite persuasive, the scientific proofs he submitted were considerably less so.

One of the most unconvincing of evolution's theories was the postulate that individual and racial competition together with natural selection are the mainsprings of socially desirable progress. In the light of the history of the last fifty years, marked so tragically by the regimes of Hitler and Stalin, it is obvious that evolution's thesis of "pitiless struggle" can hardly be viewed as a desirable means of achieving enlightened social advance.

Within the same historical context, we Jews can clearly detect that our own survival throughout the past four millennia demonstrates a marked incompatibility with the claimed validity of Darwin's "fittest" theory. For our survival has been that of the weak, the few, the powerless, the different and the hunted quarry of numerous "tooth-and-claw" pursuers ever since Abraham left his father's home in ancient Mesopotamia. Yet, "we are here" to tell the story.

While Darwin's explanations of natural selection and survival of the fittest are developed at length in the *Origin*, it would seem necessary for there first to have been in existence a broad range of alternatives and variations — the "initial conditions" — any one or a combination of which would determine those destined to become "the fittest." Consequently, one can make the strong argument that no matter how far we go back in time, such a set of alternatives and variations must have existed *before the evolutionary process began*. However far back Darwinism pushes the time frame of when and how evolution itself began, the issue of initial conditions remains.

Specifically, how does Judaism react to the Theory of Evolution? Not too nervously. Why is not Judaism seriously perturbed over evolution's postulate, which directly disputes one of Judaism's basic teachings, the creation of man by God? Why is not Judaism as militant and vocal in opposition to Darwinism as are Bible-belt fundamentalists?

While not all of Judaism's commentators are in strict agreement, a respectable segment of our sages does not view evolutionary workings *within* an evolutionary process as necessarily incompatible with or hostile to Judaism. They point out that the purpose of creation is to enable man to rise through successively higher levels of accomplishments and morality to the ultimate level of human perfection. Indeed, the account of Genesis is a model of transition from matter to vegetable, then to animal and finally to human. But, these sages caution, the point that must always be kept foremost in one's mind is that Judaism views these stages as the products of *divine ordering and purpose*, not of chance.

The problem with Darwinism, many Judaic authorities make clear, is that it does not even begin to clarify what Force accounted for the appearance of the so-called "primeval soup" and its bubblings in the first place. Evolutionary theory may attempt to explain *how* the processes of life evolve and change, but it does not ever address the fundamental question of *why* they evolve and change. And nowhere do Darwinists account for the mysterious Force within an evolutionary chain which ignites the development of a human being into someone able to reason, imagine and be possessed of an inner soul.[7]

It is Judaism's position that only a Creator in His purposeful act of creation established what the scientist calls the "initial conditions" which must exist to bring about any and all human and physical processes, whether the colossal explosion of the "Big Bang," the creation of man or even the seemingly mundane germination of a tiny seed in a Montana wheat field.

But what of the human sciences, particularly the "science of the mind," psychology? Do psychology and psychiatry accept Darwin's basic premises, so enthusiastically hailed by the Enlightenment as a major scientific breakthrough?

By the turn of the twentieth century, astronomy and physics were well on their way toward explaining many of the mysteries of the physical world. The next discipline to appear on the scene was the

---

7. Cultural anthropologist Ernest Becker, whose work is discussed at length in the next chapter, expressed a similar thought. Strongly questioning modern psychology's belief that man's inner self can be understood by "scientific analysis," without taking the soul into account, he pointed out that "we still haven't explained the inner forces that have led to the development of an animal capable of self-consciousness, which is what we still must mean by 'soul' . . . " (Ernest Becker, *The Denial of Death*, New York: Free Press, 1973, p. 191.)

new science of psychiatry, with its remarkable and previously unknown approaches, innovated by the genius of Sigmund Freud. His theories electrified the world of psychology, which saw in his work techniques which might explain the mystery of man's mind. Freud's startling conclusions held out the promise that through deeper understanding of the human personality, man could attain even greater maturity and strength than he had once found in pre-Enlightenment religious attachments.

Was that promise of psychiatry fulfilled?

4 The Emergence of Modern Psychology

"God, the Source of life, has placed in our nature the blessed hope of immortality, by which we may console ourselves for the vanity of life and overcome the dread of death."

— Yedaiah HaPenini (1270-1340), Jewish poet and philosopher

"Everybody has got to die, but I always believed an exception would be made in my case. Now what?"[8]

— William Saroyan, American author, 5 days before his death

"[Man] ... cannot achieve meaning in his life without regaining his religious outlook."[9]

— Carl Gustav Jung (1875-1961), Swiss psychiatrist

8. Statement called in to Associated Press by Mr. Saroyan.

9. Jung, Carl G., *Modern Man in Search of a Soul*, New York: Harcourt Brace, 1957, p. 264.

The subject of death has never been a comfortable one. Still, I have dealt with it at some length in this chapter because I believe it is a critical key to understanding why we think and behave the way we do. To make more sense out of the lives we lead, we must force ourselves to learn more about the near-universal dread of dying and how this fear may be diminished, even defeated.

As we shall note in this chapter's discussion of the work of psychiatrist Otto Rank, much of our behavior is influenced by the fear that our lives must end. Once we become aware that we are very mortal, we reach out for protection to insulate us from our fragility. It is terrifying to accept that when we die, all we are, all we have accomplished and all of our unfulfilled hopes will simply disappear, like the wisp of carbon curling upward from a blown-out candle.

Although the dread of our demise may not surface frequently, it is almost always deep within us. George Bernard Shaw called it "that great problem which we all must face." Very few of us are lighthearted enough to consider for ourselves what W.C. Fields once said he wanted chiseled on his tombstone: "I'd rather be here than in Philadelphia."

Among the earliest modern psychologists to deal with man's terror of dying was Soren Kirkegaard, one of the great minds of the nineteenth century and considered to be the "father of existential psychology." He had no formal training but was a brilliant investigator and analyst of the human condition. Kirkegaard recognized that man's greatest dilemma arises through his inability to resolve the baffling contradiction that man is capable of reaching sublime heights on the one hand and yet, on the other, is destined to perish like an animal of the forest. To know that we must die, Kirkegaard concluded, causes man's greatest anxiety.

As Shakespeare expressed it:

> The weariest and most loathsome worldly life
> That age, ache, penury and imprisonment
> Can lay on nature is a paradise
> To what we fear of death.

There is a legendary tale which describes man's futile attempt to escape from what terrifies us the most. It was touched on by John O'Hara in his early novel *Appointment in Samarra*. It is related also in Viktor Frankl's *Man's Search For Meaning*.

Frankl's version is that of a powerful prince who is being attended by a faithful servant. Suddenly, the servant cries out that Death has just appeared and has alarmed him. The prince comforts him and agrees to his plea for a fast horse to carry him off to Teheran, where he could lose himself in the crowded city and escape Death. The servant obtains the horse and speeds off to Teheran, a day's journey away.

Within a few moments, Death reappears and is now seen by the prince, who berates him for having caused the servant to panic. Replies Death: "I didn't menace him. I merely displayed wonder that he was still here in your palace, because I have an appointment with him tomorrow, in Teheran." [1,2]

How can man overcome his terror of death's certainty? Shortly before his untimely passing in 1974, the brilliant cultural anthropol-

1. Frankl, Viktor E., *Man's Search for Meaning*, New York: Pocket Books, 1963, p. 89.

2. Several thousand years earlier, Judaism's Babylonian Talmud described a similar incident involving King Solomon and two of his personal attendants who also feared the appearance of the Angel of Death. King Solomon arranges for them to flee to another city, Luz. When they arrive at the city gates, Death is already there and greets them with a reminder that "man's feet take him to the place where he must go" (*Babylonian Talmud, Tractate Succa*, p. 53).

ogist Ernest Becker published his Pulitzer Prize-winning *The Denial of Death*. It is one of the few books I have read four times. It contains a remarkably illuminating treatment of the difficult subject of man's search for significance and fulfillment in a topsy-turvy world.[3]

Becker's interpretations of the writings of Kirkegaard and the outstanding twentieth-century psychiatrist Otto Rank (Rosenfeld) made beautifully clear two critical findings of modern psychology:

> First, that our fear of dying causes us to indulge in childish self-deception and to cloak our personalities with artificial and shallow values, and,
>
> second, that we can learn to defeat this fear, and in the process, bring enhanced meaning into our lives.

Becker traced the direct line that runs from Kirkegaard's work to that of Rank, almost a century later. For many years Kirkegaard's work remained little known outside of Denmark because it had not been translated from Danish. Rank was one of the earliest psychologists to study and build upon the pioneering Dane's observations.

During his twenties, Rank had worked in a Vienna machine shop but later came to psychology through the influence of Sigmund Freud. He remained Freud's close colleague for twenty years and was brought into Freud's inner circle as a member of his "Secret Committee."

In those two decades, Freud gave to the world the basic principles upon which much of the science of modern psychiatry is based: Man's thinking and behavior are powered and shaped by forgotten events of our childhood, by "unconscious" drives and by our instincts. Freud held that once man is brought to recognize these causes through the "self-knowledge" that psychiatric analysis offers, he can grow towards overcoming the limitations of his personality.

Rank agreed that this approach was brilliant but argued that it was incomplete, for it failed to take into account, among other flaws, that we cannot reach full development through the process of self-knowledge, as Freud had theorized. For man needs more than to know himself. Moreover, Rank held, Freud gave little recognition to the concept that our behavior is influenced to a large degree by the

---

3. Many of my observations on psychology and psychiatry in this and later chapters are drawn from Becker's work, and I am quick to acknowledge here my sizeable debt to him.

terror we experience when we are confronted by the specter of the inevitability of our demise.

Rank left Europe in the 1930's to establish a practice in the United States. In this same decade, theoretical physics brought about a virtual revolution in the basic principles and philosophies of the "classical" physics of the preceding era (discussed at length in the following two chapters). In this revolution, classical physics' long-followed principles of certainty and positivism were undercut by new and opposing concepts of uncertainty and probability. Rank's work clearly shows a consonance with this "new thinking" in physics and with an equally new third force in psychology called "existentialism," which first emerged in Europe through the work of Viktor Frankl, Eugene Minkowsky and Ludwig Binswanger.

Existentialism was not to make any serious appearance in the U.S. until the early sixties through the writings of Rollo May, and later, of Gordon Allport, Abraham Maslow and Carl Rogers, among others. Until then, psychology had been dominated by two primary schools: the long-established behaviorism school and the more recent Freudian analysis approach.

Behaviorism held that the principle sources for understanding man's mental development are to be derived from his objective behavior and activities. Freudian analysis was somewhat less mechanistic and "animalistic," but it still relied to a great extent upon the influence of predetermining elements such as past events.

The existentialists felt that both of these approaches overlooked the valuable humanistic elements in man which can enable him to grow and achieve his potential more fully, through his capabilities of will, choice, affection, experience, creativity and finer values. May explained that existentialism "involves centering upon the *existing* person and emphasizes the human being as he is *emerging, becoming*."[4] Existential psychotherapy concentrates a great deal upon the "existential concerns" of man – such as the fear of dying, aimlessness and loneliness. It was one of Rank's singular contributions that, a quarter of a century before the emergence of existentialism in the U.S., he restored to the attention of his profession Kirkegaard's remarkable discovery that "death is man's peculiar and greatest anxiety."[5]

---

4. May, Rollo, *Existential Psychology*, 2nd Ed., New York: Random House, 1969, p. 11.
5. Becker, Ernest, *The Denial of Death*, New York: Free Press, 1973, p. 70.

Rank insisted that what men really crave is immortality[6] and that we need to latch on to a measure of such immortality if we are to rise above our fear of dying and instill purpose and significance into our lives. Becker, interpreting Rank, clarified that this reaching for immortality can lead man in either of two directions: toward the immature "cultural heroism" or towards the mature "cosmic heroism." The latter concept will be discussed towards the end of this chapter. First, let us explore "cultural heroism."

Cultural heroism, Becker explained, is the refuge sought by man when he is not able to face or escape from his perishability, his "creaturehood." Daily, man faces what appears to be a cruel, intolerable hoax: Capable of harnessing the H-bomb and conquering polio, gifted with the power of abstraction, man still must succumb inevitably to disabling age or destroying disease. All of his talents, intellect, dreams and ambitions are housed in a body worth about a dollar in chemical content and destined to decay and disappear.

Becker pointed out that too many of us cope with this fearful paradox by relying upon social and cultural "values" and upon devices which we mistakenly believe will make us "somebody special," a "hero," and thus distance us from the impermanence of ordinary folks. As Rank in the preface to his last work, *Beyond Psychology*, wrote, the "hero" needs to construct a life and a world which provide him with security from "destructive life forces." If we raise ourselves above the crowd, we become "a somebody" and feel this will insulate us from our mortality.

What are some of the devices we employ to gain such imagined invulnerability? How do we develop into heroes or become privy to heroes? By rubbing elbows with those who are affluent or prominent. Or through vicarious pride in the successes of our children. Sometimes, being a guest of honor at an annual dinner or having a room in a charitable institution named after us instills a feeling of "specialness" within us. At other times, it helps to have a powerful Ferrari Testarossa parked in our driveway. (I heard recently of one poor fellow who surreptitiously replaced the "230E" Model insignia on the rear of his Mercedes with a bogus "300E" plate.)

Perhaps the most widely employed defense against our finitude

---

6. Ibid., p. 271.

and fragility is the squirreling away of stocks, bonds and savings accounts. It is also thought to help if we own the neighborhood's most fashionable house, solidly built of brick and stone to last at least through the twenty-first century:

> They think their houses will endure forever, their dwellings for generation after generation . . . but man with all his honor will not outlast the night . . . (*Psalms* 49:12-13)[7]

From infancy on, we strive to become the centerpiece of our little world. As the eighteenth-century Torah sage Rabbi Moshe Chaim Luzzatto expressed it: "The desire for honor pulls at a person's heart more than any other yearning in the world."[8] Henry Kissinger in his *Years of Upheaval* records a lively dispute between himself and the then-Secretary of State, Alexander Haig, as to which of them would occupy the Kremlin suite nearest to that of President Nixon during the Moscow summit. Kissinger, to his credit, labels the incident "unworthy."

Just recently, a later Secretary of State, James Baker, made an incisive comment in relating a scene he had witnessed when he was Chief of Staff to President Reagan. It served, he said, as an example of how transient power can be. As his limousine was driven into the White House driveway, he saw a solitary figure walking on Pennsylvania Avenue whom he recognized as the man who had served previously as Chief of Staff to a president. Now he walked alone, Baker relates, without bodyguard, unheralded by the press, unnoticed by passersby. Baker noted that the incident reminded him of how fleeting prominence can be.[9]

I recall how, even as a child closeness to the seat of power attracted me. As a boy, I learned that New York Governor Franklin D. Roosevelt would stop briefly in our hometown enroute to the dedication of a nearby Boy Scout camp. When the governor's open touring-car arrived at our local inn, we boys surrounded the car. I managed to stand on the running-board, inches from the smiling, genial Roosevelt. He chatted with us and patiently signed autographs. To this day, I remember how thrilled and impressed I

---

7. Hirsch, Sampson Raphael, *The Psalms*, New York: Philipp Feldheim Ltd., 1960.

8. Luzzatto, Moshe Chaim, *The Path of the Just,* trans. by Schraga Silverstein, New York: Philipp Feldheim Ltd., 1966, p. 171.

9. Cal Thomas, *Has Baker Found New Meaning in Spiritual Values? Miami Herald* (*Los Angeles Times* Syndicate).

was to be close to that engaging, handsome figure, already then heralded as a leading candidate for the presidency.

Years later and long after Roosevelt had occupied the pinnacle of the world's power for almost a decade and a half, I came to regard him as a much lesser figure. My disillusionment stemmed from a conversation with Rabbi Abraham Kalmanowitz, one of pre-World War II Europe's most prominent rabbis. He was the last rabbinical head of the Lithuanian town of Titkin, in which Jews first settled in 1522.

In 1939, together with his colleagues, Rabbi Kalmanowitz had engineered the legendary and dangerous escape of hundreds of his students from the cauldron of eastern Poland. The escapees, blocked from traveling west, fled east across Russia and Siberia via foot, horse cart and the Trans-Siberia railway to Kobe, Japan, Shanghai and, finally to the United States. There, he became one of the most resolute leaders in the struggle to save European Jewry from Nazi extermination.

In a long talk with Rabbi Kalmanowitz in 1953, he related to me how he managed to gain an audience with President Roosevelt in the Oval Office in early 1944, to plead the case for rescue. He recalled that after a few minutes, he could sense from Roosevelt's bland expression that the interview was not going well. Heartsick over the cool reception, the rabbi fell prostrate on the rug in front of the President's desk, sobbingly imploring him to order as a minimum the bombing by the Allies of the railroad lines leading to the death camps. Roosevelt did not appear moved either by the pleading or the tears, and the interview was terminated shortly afterward.

The hero of my pre-teens, and in later years my commander in chief and leader of the free world, had rejected a realistic chance to save thousands from Hitler's crematoria.[10] Hero-worship may befit a

---

10. On a wall at the Yad Vashem Holocaust Museum in Jerusalem hangs an enlarged Allied Air Force reconnaissance photo of the I.G. Farber petrochemical plant. The photo was discovered in 1979 in the U.S. National Archives. The upper corner of the photo clearly reveals the entire infamous Auschwitz death camp complex and its railway lines, *just 6 miles'* distance from the I.G. Farber plant. The photo was one of a series taken between April 1944 and January 1945. During these nine months, I.G. Farber was the target of Allied bombers but Auschwitz's railway lines were not. In the same period, 500,000 Jews were cremated in Auschwitz's ovens.

Henry Morgenthau, Roosevelt's Secretary of the Treasury, confirmed in his *Memoirs* that in April 1942, the U.S. already knew of Hitler's extermination plans. A full and more completely documented account of the lamentable, detached reaction of the Roosevelt administration to the rescue of the beleaguered European Jews can be found in Arthur Morse's *How Six Million Died* and Walter Laquer's *The Terrible Secret.*

starry-eyed ten-year-old, but it is a slender reed upon which to lean in the real world of finite, fallible men. "Put not thy faith in princes," the Psalmist warns.

The need to paper over our mortality and creaturehood is often demonstrated in our fascination with a hero figure. Alexander Solzhenitsyn, in his famous Harvard address of a decade and a half ago, pointed out that contemporary society bases "Western civilization on the dangerous need to worship man and his material needs." Edwin Arlington Robinson, in his important poem *Richard Cory,* shocks us with his portrayal of such "worship of man":

> Whenever Richard Cory went downtown,
> We people on the pavement looked at him.
> He was a gentleman from sole to crown,
> Clean favored and imperially slim.
> And he was always quietly arrayed,
> and he was always human when he talked;
> But still he fluttered pulses when he said,
> "Good morning," and he glittered when he walked.
> And he was rich, yes, richer than a king
> And admirably schooled in every grace.
> In fine, we thought that he was everything
> To make us wish that we were in his place.
> So on we worked, and waited for the light,
> And went without the meat, and cursed the bread.
> And Richard Cory, one calm summer night,
> Went home and put a bullet through his head.[11]

Oftentimes we try to cloak our felt vulnerability with the power which we believe the possession of money can provide. The acquisition of bank accounts and real property camouflage and soothe our fear of extinction. They give us the satisfying feeling that we retain control of our lives. Still, as Becker emphasized in *Denial of Death*, when the devices we use to be "in control" fail us, such failures virtually "can cost us our lives or our sanity."[12]

We are not without our real-life Richard Corys. Every so often, we read a newspaper account of a successful executive

---

11. *Immortal Poems of the English Language*, ed. by Oscar Williams, New York: Washington Square Press, Inc., 1952, p. 498.
12. Becker, Ernest, *The Denial of Death*, New York: Free Press, 1973, p. 56.

who, generally facing severe corporate financial setback or loss of his corporate control, leaps out of a window or ends his life with a handgun.

In his last work, *Escape from Evil*, Ernest Becker made a well-known point, touched upon previously, that in the post-Emancipation society the religious symbols upon which man had based his hopes for immortality were replaced by the symbols of material success. But he added a telling insight. Modern society, he noted, brought on more than the desire to keep up with the Joneses. One's "specialness" in today's world is measured by how much one *surpasses* the Joneses. Man, he explained, no longer is willing to achieve economic "parity" with his neighbors; he is driven to accumulate more and more. And any diminution of his material holdings is regarded as a diminution of his invincibility.[13]

To be sure, man's craving for money is fueled partially by the thrill of the game and being able to enjoy the luxuries of the affluent. And few things gain more attention than money. But as psychiatrist Viktor Frankl capsulized it, money is the "most primitive form of the will to power" – power not merely to buy and enjoy but power to control, to manipulate. The well-known playwright George S. Kaufman once visited the newly built mansion of a colleague in fashionable Bucks County, Pennsylvania. The host explained how he had transplanted two giant oak trees at great expense to create a symmetrical frame for the main entrance. Kaufman is alleged to have reacted with the remark, "Can you imagine what God could have done if *He* had money?"

What else but power could have recently motivated a bright young Wall Street investment broker earning about two million dollars a year to chance a prison term by passing on illegal insider-trading information? What else would entice a super-rich, respected member of the community to use such information in a dangerous profit scheme which ballooned into a scandal with few equals in financial history? To believe that he simply wanted more luxuries in life prompts the question: What luxuries could he buy with three hundred million dollars that he could not buy with two hundred million?

The same question may be asked even more pointedly of a super-super rich Wall Street financier who gambled (and lost) the

13. Becker, Ernest, *Escape from Evil*, New York: Free Press, 1941.

risk of a jail term for securities violations while his annual salary alone approximated 650 million dollars, a sum which would require the combined year-long labors of one and one-half million Haitians to earn.

Ultimately, the futility of wasted "cultural heroism" becomes apparent. The heroes we venerate sooner or later prove unenduring or lose their stature. A recent survey of U.S. high school students established that less than forty percent knew who Franklin D. Roosevelt was only forty years after his death. Statues of Lenin and Stalin, whom millions once looked upon as veritable gods, recently came crashing down all over Eastern Europe.

And the reliance we place on money can prove to be most illusory. Among the finest motion pictures ever produced by Hollywood was *The Treasure of Sierra Madre*, starring Walter Huston and Humphrey Bogart. It portrayed man's greed for gold and the life-and-death risks he is willing to take to acquire it. In the final moments of the film, as a sudden Mexican windstorm carries off the hard-won gold dust before the helpless Huston and Bogart, they burst into hysterical laughter at the irony of their precious horde being blown sky-high.

I knew a man who lived in Cuba during the Castro Revolution. Through hard work over many years, he accumulated assets worth a quarter of a million Cuban pesos, a near-fortune for a storekeeper. Fearful that it would be confiscated, he converted it into cash and secreted the currency in a wall of his shop. Soon after, he fled Cuba, but by then, strict Cuban currency regulations prohibited his taking the money out of Cuba. Years later, he met a lady who had a shop next to his but who had remained in Cuba and was in the U.S. on a visit. She related to him that the entire building had been converted into a military warehouse. In the process of remodeling, Cuban soldiers broke open the wall of his shop. The now-worthless, replaced pre-Castro pesos fell into the street, where they were strewn haphazardly by the wind, much like the gold dust in the Huston-Bogart classic.

How, then, do we implement the thesis of modern psychology that one can conquer the dread of dying and bring genuine meaning into one's life as well? Becker, interpreting Rank, pointed out that we are able to achieve these twin goals only through *cosmic* rather than cultural heroism. Becker explained that in attaching oneself to a cosmic Supreme Power, "in place of merely social and cultural, historical value, . . ." one acquires "ultimate value" and is able to fashion a link with the "mystery of creation."[14]

Through this link, man is able to fulfill two of his deepest longings: overcoming his helplessness and gaining a measure of immortality. Rabbi Judah of Regensburg, poet, philosopher and mystic, anticipated Rank and Becker by five hundred years when he wrote of these two longings in the second verse of his famous composition, *The Hymn of Glory*,

> My soul desires Thy shelter,
> To know all Thy mystery[15]

Thus, Judaism has long known that man is, as Becker quotes Rank, not a "biological" but a "theological" being. This chapter's epigram by Yedaiah HaPenini spells out in one sentence what modern psychologists first came to understand seven hundred years later.

Even earlier, in the second century, the eminent Torah scholar known simply as Rabbi Yochanan, composed a prayer which Jews recite once every morning and several times in the Yom Kippur liturgy. In the few crisply stated phrases of this ancient prayer we find almost all of the wisdom that the science of psychology would first discover in the twentieth century about cultural heroism, cosmic heroism and man's quest for meaning:

> Master of all worlds! . . . What are we? What is our life? . . . What is our might? . . . are not all the *heroes* like nothing . . . for all is vain except for the pure soul . . .[16]

Rabbi Yochanan is telling us that through the "pure soul" — the divine spark within each Jew which links him to God, the "Ultimate Reality" — we Jews can triumph over cultural heroism, vanity and meaninglessness.

In a subsequent chapter, I deal at greater length with this potential triumph and with my assertion that it is through Judaism that we Jews are best able to approach the Ultimate Reality. But first, let us examine a fascinating parallel path which men of science have pursued for three hundred years to reach *their* version of "reality."

14. Becker, Ernest, *The Denial of Death*, New York: Free Press, 1975, p. 91.

15. *Daily Prayer Book*, trans. by Philip Birnbaum, New York: Hebrew Publishing Co., 1977, p. 416.

16. *The Complete ArtScroll Machzor, Rosh Hashanah*, trans. by Nosson Scherman, Brooklyn, N.Y.: Mesorah Publications, Ltd., 1986, p. 171.

5

Newton's Clock and Professor Heisenberg

"Thou hast set a boundary they cannot overstep . . ."

— *Psalms* 104:9

"The deeper we penetrate, the more restless becomes the universe, and the vaguer and cloudier."

— Max Born, Nobel laureate in physics[1]

1. Born, Max, *The Restless Universe*, New York: Dover Books, 1981.

Historically, the physicists' search for reality can be traced back almost four hundred years to Galileo Galilei, famous for his disputation with and trial by the Catholic Church over his belief that the planets revolved about the sun, and not vice versa. He is famous also for having demonstrated (according to legend, from atop the Leaning Tower of Pisa) that two objects falling from a height, although different in weight, size or substance, will reach the ground at the same time.

Equally important, Galileo was the first person to establish the standard method of scientific investigation. With this method of a controlled demonstration that showed *how* things happen, Galileo initiated the age of modern investigative science. And in 1609, when he invented a telescope powerful enough to view the moons around Jupiter and to gain a clear view of the surface of Earth's moon, he presented science with a remarkable and majestic tool in its effort to uncover the secrets of nature.

Galileo died in 1642. In the same year, Isaac Newton was born, a genius considered to be the greatest scientist who ever lived. The importance and scope of the discoveries which flowed from his intellect border on the incredible: the law of gravity, the universal law of optics and the three laws of motion, as well as the invention of the differential and integral calculus.

From these laws, men of science came to perceive the universe through the concept of "determinism," a term which will appear frequently in this chapter. Determinism, as the word suggests, holds that virtually every event in the world has been preordained; whatever happens can be traced to physical laws that initiate a chain of "cause and effect." The scientific world regarded these laws as fixed and universally controlling. For over 250 years, determinism and "causality" ruled physics and strongly influenced the physicist's world-view.

The Doctrine of Determinism, like the Theory of Evolution, also permeated the thinking of non-scientific intellectuals of the Enlightenment. Thus, an early (1755) work of famed philosopher Immanuel Kant was based on the existence of a causal, mechanical explanation of the workings of the universe. In the mid-nineteenth century, the Theory of Evolution clearly incorporated the Doctrine of Determinism. Espousing determinism, Karl Marx postulated that all of mankind's ills were the "effects," "caused" by the evils of capitalism. As late as the early twentieth century, Freud validated determinism and causality when he theorized that the choices, outlook and behavior of human beings are shaped by causes originating in the unconscious.

The concept of determinism was rooted mainly in what is known as the Newtonian Universe, briefly described in Chapter II on astronomy. Newton had theorized that the universe functions with a design and harmony that is flawless and unchanging — a sort of punctiliously accurate, huge clock, a comparison first made in 1644 by the French philosopher and mathematician René Descartes. All occurrences in our clocklike world were considered to have eventually traceable past causes which strictly "determine" all events. Hence, the universe is exact and "certain" in its functioning.

Given enough time and investigation, science predicted, all of the mysteries of the physical world could be explained. Scientific man would then discover the physical "reality" which underlies the "apparent" world of our five senses. We then would know the *real* meaning of everything. The goal of the scientist was no less than what the noted Oxford University mathematician E. A. Milne described as "to see into the mind of God." To the scientist who was committed to determinism, God was held to be, as French mathematician Laplace once commented to Napoleon, an "unnecessary hypothesis." God was viewed as divested of any role in a strictly deterministic universe but, nevertheless, was acknowledged to be the ultimate Repository of all knowledge pertaining to the physical laws which operate that universe.

Sir James Jeans once commented that before the advent of modern physics, classical physicists often mistakenly identified "appearance" with "reality." To distinguish the two concepts, it is important to recognize that virtually all of our knowledge is derived from appearance, registered through our senses. From the five senses we know that lilacs are fragrant and violet in color, that ice is cold, that lead is heavy, and that sound becomes louder as we approach its source. These are the sensations — which science calls our "sensory perceptions" — of light, shape, depth, color, touch and sound which identify the world to us.

Still, these perceptions are only *apparent*, not "real," because they differ from person to person and from time to time. The exotic scent of perfume or the melodic beauty of *Scheherazade* are subjective and personal experiences, rarely identical to different people, even to identical twins. Therefore, it is odd but true that such perceptions of scent, color and melody, because they are totally subjective rather than objective, have no existence except that which our individual senses attribute to them.

Centuries ago, Plato, in Book VII of *The Republic,* highlighted the contrast between the apparent and the real. In a famous allegory, he depicted all human beings as being imprisoned within a cave since childhood. We are seated, he wrote, facing the cave's rear wall and chained to the floor so that we cannot move our legs or turn our heads around towards the cave's entrance. Outside, a fire is blazing and people are passing between the fire and the entrance to the cave, casting their shadows onto the back wall of the cave. These shadows are all that those sitting inside can see. They cannot view the people moving back and forth outside or the fire whose light causes the passing persons' shadows to fall into the cave.

Plato explained that to the chained "prisoners within, the truth would be literally nothing but the shadows," for they can only see the "apparent." However, what is taking place outside, the people passing by with all sorts of goods, the blazing fire casting the shadows, is the "real." This reality is hidden from those within the cave because, Plato observes, they, "like ourselves," can only see the shadows of the objects outside; they cannot see the objects themselves.

Although modern science works mightily at penetrating beyond the apparent, seeking to learn the world's mysteries, it probes with impersonal (objective) tools: mathematics, abstractions, formulas. To the rest of us, this approach lacks any personal (subjective) element, for those tools are removed from our experience. They merely furnish information, devoid of feeling. The world man knows best is that of impressions and feelings, a world of the sounds of music and birds, of winter wonderlands and bursting renewals of spring. When science describes its version of reality, the cold, colorless, impassive, soundless world of symbols and theories, it can convey to ordinary man only a partial description of the reality (what is referred to as "physical" reality) which deals with "how" our world functions. As Chapter VI explains, to present a complete description, to conceptualize total reality, we must blend the scientist's physical reality with the *spiritual* reality conveyed to us by spiritual insights which cast light on "why" our world functions as it does.

No scientist since Newton contributed more to science's goals than Albert Einstein. His Special Theory of Relativity, published in 1905, and his later General Theory of Relativity astounded the world. They were giant leaps towards fulfillment of humankind's dream to understand, at last, how the universe works.

Albert Einstein was endowed with the uncanny gift of peering deeply into the functioning of the cosmos. His theories revealed a number of startling discoveries. Thus, he established that our three space dimensions are not independent of a *fourth* dimension. The combination is called "space-time." He also theorized that time runs more slowly in a clock that is traveling rapidly, say aboard an airplane, than in an identical clock on the ground. This phenomenon has since been confirmed.

Einstein theorized as well that when light travels from a star to earth, the light bends as it passes the gravitational field of a celestial body. This exceptional forecast was studied by a team of British scientists headed by the most prominent astrophysicist of his day, Sir Arthur Eddington. During the May 29, 1919 total eclipse of the sun over the Atlantic (which darkened the sky sufficiently to make visible the otherwise undetectable light rays of the stars), photographs were made which proved that light does *indeed* bend, fully confirming Einstein's prediction. The scientific community was delighted. Einstein's fame spread worldwide. He was hailed as the greatest scientific figure since Newton and lauded as the genius who had almost touched the very heavens with his towering discoveries.

Although Einstein's theories in some respects revise those of Newton, until his death Einstein fully supported the Newtonian belief that the universe operated predictably and faultlessly, within fixed laws and with the accuracy of the most precise of timepieces. Yet, within just a few years of the sensational confirmation of the reliability of Einstein's work, his never-surrendered deterministic belief in Newton's clocklike universe was being seriously challenged and soon undermined.

Credit for the initial discovery which led to the unseating of the long-held Principle of Determinism and the beginning of an enlarged view of reality belongs to a dignified scientific genius with an imposing name: Max Carl Ernest Ludwig Planck.

At the turn of the twentieth century, in the year 1900, while professor of theoretical physics at the University of Berlin, Planck discovered the famous measure of energy called the "quantum." He established that energy does not, as previously thought, flow steadily out, but rather in bits and pieces, or "chunks." The finding of the quanta was to lead to his formulation of "Planck's constant," which became the fundamental touchstone of a scientific revolution in physics called "quantum mechanics." Niels Bohr, the brilliant Danish physicist, said of Planck's discovery that it had "brought about a complete revision of the foundations underlying our description of natural phenomena."[2]

A few personal words should be said about Max Planck before describing the stunning impact of quantum mechanics upon the sciences generally and determinism in particular. Planck, who was forty-two years old when he published his quanta work, lived a long life, passing away in his ninetieth year. In Chapter II, it was noted that the properties of the radiation glow described by Penzias and Wilson were recognized as fitting precisely the pattern which could

---

2. Bohr, Niels, *Atomic Theory and the Description of Nature*, London: Cambridge Univ. Press, 1934. p. 98.

develop from a gigantic explosion. Interestingly, this conclusion was derived mainly from Planck's work on radiation some sixty years earlier. He was, indeed, the "grand old man" of the more than half-century-long "Golden Age of Physics." In a tribute to Planck, Einstein wrote, "His ideas will be effective as long as physical science lasts."[3]

During the years which followed the confirmation of Einstein's light-bending predictions by the Eddington party in 1919, Einstein, always the unrepentant idealist, clashed publicly over academic freedom with Philip Lenard, a Nobel laureate in physics and an early, ardent supporter of Adolf Hitler. Not long afterwards, Lenard and Yohanus Stark, another Nobel laureate in physics, were designated as the leaders of the Nazi movement's campaign to render German science *Judenrein*. Some courageous non-Jews (called by the Nazis "white Jews in science"), among them Planck, Max Von Laue and Hermann Weyl, opposed Stark and Lenard, but with little success. The campaign to vilify Jewish scientists, especially Einstein, gained increasingly anti-Semitic fervor, eventually causing Einstein, while on a visit to the United States in 1933, to renounce his German citizenship and thereafter to reside in America for the rest of his life.

In the same year, to his exceptional credit, Max Planck requested and, apparently in the light of his worldwide scientific prominence as Germany's most honored Aryan scientist, actually received an interview with Hitler in an attempt to dissuade the dictator from expelling Jewish academicians from Germany. Planck later told fellow scientist Werner Heisenberg that the meeting was fruitless, that Hitler ranted for one and a half hours, "lost all contact with reality" and was "no longer open to argument."

Planck thus had exposed himself to enormous risk in pressing his defense of Jewish scientists. Later, an even riskier self-sacrifice was undertaken by Planck's second son, Erwin. He was a German Wermacht officer who participated in the ill-fated attempt to assassinate Hitler in 1944. In the end, Max Planck a loyal, obedient and distinguished German all his life, whose older son had been killed in action at Verdun in World War I, had to endure the agony of knowing that Erwin was first tortured and then executed by the Gestapo in 1944.

When Planck died in October 1947, Einstein wrote to Planck's

3. Planck, Max, *The New Science*, Meridian Books Inc., Greenwich Edition, original, 1959, preface.

widow that "humanity needed more like him." Planck was buried at the University of Göttingen where he had spent some early fruitful years as well as his last few years after World War II.

In the late 1920's and early 30's, some of the most important advances in modern physics had taken place in this university, set in a small, picturesque German town with a medieval town hall and cottages dating from the fifteenth century. Among the great figures who taught at this remarkable research center of mathematics and physics were Max Born and Hermann Weyl. Nobel laureate Born's assistant at Göttingen was a young man named Werner Carl Heisenberg. Heisenberg had also studied under the university's famous James Frank and David Hilbert, and later came to know Niels Bohr following a number of visits to Göttingen by the highly honored Dane.

In 1927, Heisenberg discovered what came to be called both the principle of Uncertainty and the principle of Indeterminism. Sir Arthur Eddington (who, when he was characterized by an interviewing reporter as one of the three people in the world who then fully understood Einstein's Theory of Relativity, is said to have shot back at the reporter, "Who is the third?") declared that Heisenberg's discovery ranked in importance with Einstein's Theory of Relativity.

Essentially, Heisenberg's principle shook the foundations of the Principle of Determinism, the principle upon which the scientist had relied securely for over two centuries. After Heisenberg's discovery, determinism was no longer the scientist's all-encompassing rule of law, and the Principle of Uncertainty became a most essential feature of the "quantum revolution."

Exactly what did Heisenberg discover that caused such consternation among the followers of determinism? He found that in the invisible, ultra-tiny world of atoms and particles, unlike in the visible, physical world, nature is inherently uncertain, regardless of the precision of our measurement. Moreover, the measurement process itself affects the indicia of uncertainty.[4] Heisenberg's experiments

4. The late, prolific science writer Isaac Asimov, in his book *Please Answer,* gave several clarifying examples of this phenomenon, in non-technical, laymen's language. To paraphrase Asimov's explanation, he pointed out that if you wish to measure the temperature of hot water in a bathtub, you would go about it by inserting a thermometer into the water. But since the glass thermometer is colder than the hot water, it causes the water to become cooled by an extremely small fraction of a degree. Therefore the reading which the thermometer displays, while very close to an exact reading, is not *precisely* correct. So the very act of measuring altered, albeit almost infinitesimally, the

demonstrated that when we illuminate the electron (which performs the basic function of most electronic accomplishments, from the simple television set to the complex super-computer) in order to observe it and to measure its speed and direction, the stream of "chunks" of light which the illumination sends out so strongly bombards the electron that a radical change occurs in its behavior.

This change in the electron becomes very significant because it contributes to our inability to measure *both* the electron's speed and direction *at the same time*. Without such simultaneous measurements, it is not possible to achieve full knowledge of the ultra-minute world of the atom and subatom. Consequently, our knowledge of the universe must always remain with an element of uncertainty.[5]

Pre-quantum physics had hoped that what Einstein called his "golden eggs" would bring science tantalizingly close to its version of how reality works. But Heisenberg's principle put an end to this dream. It demonstrated that science is faced with being preempted from ever knowing with totality and exactitude why, or even how, all things occur. Heisenberg's discovery demonstrated that there is no perfect or absolute understanding.

It was almost as if pre-quantum physics, seeking to discover how the physical world works, had progressed down a long corridor which was divided into a series of interconnected steel compartments similar to the watertight compartments of a submarine. Each compartment had a vaultlike, combination entry door and a similar exit door leading into the next compartment. As each generation of scientists moved through successive compartments, the combina-

---

temperature of the water and gave you an unavoidably imprecise result. (In the tiny world of particles, even extremely small deviations are most significant.)

Again, Asimov wrote, if you try to check the air pressure in a tire with a pressure gage, you must allow a very small volume of air to escape from the tire in order to activate the gage. The pressure of the air inside the tire is then reduced by the tiny amount of pressure contained in the released air. Consequently, the reading on the gage is not 100% exact, an inescapable result caused by the act of measuring.

5. While the primacy of the Theory of Determinism was thus refuted, this did not disqualify its continued operation within the seen physical universe. For Heisenberg's discovery related only to the ultra-tiny, hidden realm of atoms and particles.

In the visible world of stars and galaxies, Newton's clock still ticks on with precise certainty, while the element of uncertainty characterizes only the world of the unseen, extremely minute, a relationship which Max Born described as the "dual nature of the world."

For further, more recent treatment of this intriguing duality surrounding us, see the observations of Professor Leo Levy on page 148.

tion of each entry and exit door became increasingly more complex.

Finally, in the early twentieth century, after a physicist named Einstein succeeded in solving the next exceedingly sophisticated entry and exit combinations, the scientist entered, walked through the compartment and swung open the exit door, hoping to find himself in the bright daylight of understanding of how physical reality works. To his dismay, he found himself in yet another sealed compartment; but worse still, where its exit door should have been stood a solid wall of steel plate, sprayed with graffiti reading: "Heisenberg was here." The stunned scientist had encountered the impenetrable barrier revealed by the Principle of Uncertainty.

A decisive battle in the conflict between Einstein as the defender of determinism and Niels Bohr[6] as the champion of uncertainty took place in Brussels in October 1927. The dramatic setting was the Fifth Physical Conference of the Solvay Institute. Einstein and Bohr engaged in vigorous and tense public debate over their conflicting positions, accompanied by complex blackboard and experimental demonstrations. It was then that Einstein made his famous remark to Bohr: "Do you really believe that God resorts to dice-playing?" Clearly, the remark intended to demean the conclusion that nature is governed by indeterminism and probability rather than certainty. Einstein insisted throughout the conference that the indeterminate element which Heisenberg demonstrated could and would in time be overcome through finer instruments and additional research. Bohr did not contest that such progress was possible. However, he pressed on, until science discovered an underlying framework which caused the seemingly uncertain behavior observed, we must accept that such a framework does not exist.

---

6. Niels Bohr was less well known than Einstein outside scientific circles, but he was one of the most brilliant and respected physicists of the era known as the "Golden Age of Physics." Also not well known are the exceptional contributions he made to the Allied war effort. One of Bohr's parents was Jewish and soon after the Germans occupied Denmark, he came under Gestapo surveillance. Worried, he escaped to Sweden and later to America. There, under an assumed name, he devoted his extraordinary talents to the "Manhattan Project," which oversaw the development of the first atomic bomb.

One of the great fears of Major General Leslie Groves, the man in charge of the Manhattan Project, was the very real and dangerous possibility that the Germans also were engaged in the development of an atomic weapon. To learn about Germany's intentions and capabilities, Groves and the OSS set up a special investigation unit code named the "Alsos mission."

The historic joust between these two highly honored knights of physics ended several days later with Bohr the clear victor, supported by Heisenberg, Born, Schrodinger, Lorentz and Dirac. Einstein stood almost alone in his position. Even Max Born, his lifelong friend and confidant, later wrote to Einstein that he found the remark about dice to be "completely inadequate," for the universe we observe is "not entirely mechanistic."[7] But Einstein remained adamant, commenting to Born many years later that at the risk of being called senile, he still did not believe in the "dice game," despite the almost universal acceptance then of quantum mechanics.

At the 1930 Solvay Institute Conference, the issues were discussed again but, as Heisenberg was to comment afterwards, "It was a particular triumph for Bohr,"[8] since he was able, through Einstein's own Theory of General Relativity, to discredit Einstein's objections. Einstein was left wounded but not vanquished. In the spring of 1935, he dispatched a strong challenging paper to Bohr in Copenhagen which, according to one of Bohr's colleagues, came down like a thunderbolt "out of the blue." Bohr is said to have pushed all other work aside to allow him to concentrate his entire time on a rebuttal paper. And so, the next and last great jousting match between these two illustrious minds was initiated.

The new and formidable gauntlet which Einstein threw down has been called the "EPR paradox," after the first initials of Einstein and his two Institute for Advanced Study at Princeton collaborators, Boris Podolsky and Nathan Rosen.

Now, the next few pages deal with pretty heady stuff, for even a brief summary of the EPR paper highlights perplexing scientific and philosophical concepts that go back to ancient times and deal with abstract conceptions such as "reality," "mind" and even what Einstein called "ghosts." Bohr once observed that whoever is not shocked by the Quantum Theory does not understand it, and I have run across the writings of a number of scientists who maintain that quantum mechanics can be awfully bizarre, bewildering and even spooky.

And yet, quantum mechanics is considered by many as perhaps

---

7. Born, Max, *The Born-Einstein Letters*, New York: Walker & Co., 1971, p. 156.

8. *Niels Bohr*, edited by S. Rozental, North Holland Publishing Company, Amsterdam, 1967, p. 108.

the most significant development in physics to date. It is certainly the most valuable approach yet discovered for dealing with the ultraminiature world and with those aspects of the universe which relate to that tiny world. Consequently, I feel that an attempt even to partially comprehend some of quantum's concepts is more than worth the effort. So I trust the reader will "hang in there" while reading the following layman's account of the 1935 Einstein-Bohr confrontation.[9] [Readers who wish may skip the next three pages without losing the overall thread of this chapter.]

As noted earlier, Einstein was a firm believer in the reality (in German, a "real state of affairs") of physical objects. Further, he argued, even miniscule subatomic particles, such as photons of light, possess such reality *whether or not* we subject them to observation or measurement. This position was in direct opposition to one of the most fundamental (but baffling) of quantum's principles, which holds that a photon is real (that is, it has an independent existence) only *after* it has been observed or measured.

Einstein challenged this seemingly absurd quantum concept. In effect, EPR was asking, can it be that a quantum subject such as a particle is brought into existence only because and after we measure or peer at it?

To prove that reality is not dependent upon either measurement or observation, EPR proposed an experiment. Assume, it said, a particle is exploded into two spinning parts, A and B, which then travel apart from each other for vast distances. Since A and B have a common source and each bears the original stamp of that source, one part (say, A) will spin clockwise and (in accord with Newton's third law of mechanics that for each action there is an "equal and opposite reaction") part B will spin counterclockwise. Einstein held that parts A and B both possess independent existence from the time they were exploded and began to spin, so they will keep on spinning in the same opposite but related manner (i.e., they will continue to communicate or "cooperate" one with the other) even while traveling in opposite directions and very far apart from each other.

On the other hand, quantum maintains that parts A and B *each* consist of *two* natures, or "ghosts," sort of ghosts A-1 and A-2, and

9. This popularized, condensed account is mainly drawn from a professional, scientific discussion of the EPR confrontation found in Professor Paul Davies' *God and the New Physics*, New York, Simon & Shuster, 1983, pp. 105-107.

ghosts B-1 and B-2. The two A "ghosts" will by their nature spin in opposite directions when exploded, as will the two B "ghosts." Which of A's two "ghosts," A-1 or A-2, is "real" will only be determined at the moment one or the other is measured or observed. If the observer elects to measure, say, a clockwise-spinning A-1, thereupon A-1 (rather than A-2) will be converted to "reality." Simultaneously, part B then has no alternative but to designate (again, in accord with the force and effect of Newton's law of equal and opposite reaction) its counterclockwise-spinning B-1 "ghost" to cooperate, i.e., communicate with the clockwise-spinning A-1.

How does quantum explain this mysterious communication? Bohr answered that this cooperation was able to occur (and do so simultaneously) because parts A and B remained a *single* entity even *following* their separation into parts and even *during* their distant, opposing flights into space. It is only *after* A-1 is measured by an instrument or viewed by a person that, Bohr went on to explain, A-1 and cooperating B-1 take on independent existences, *not before*.

While Einstein continued to resist what he called quantum's description of such "spooky actions at a distance," he conceded that Bohr's explanation was possible but insisted that it was in such opposition to his "scientific instinct" that he would not forgo his "search for a more complete conception."

The contest between Einstein and Bohr over the EPR paradox paper had to await advanced testing technology before the victor could be designated. In 1964, the Irish theoretical physicist John Stewart Bell expressed, in mathematical form, the nature of particle reality in a theory known as Bell's Inequality. It held that the amount of communication or cooperation between two separated photons cannot exceed a fixed limit *if*, as Einstein held, fragments A and B exist and are real *before* they are measured. Quantum mechanics, however, held otherwise, stating that in certain instances, Bell's maximum limit *can* be passed.

Bell's theory has been the mainspring of most of the experimental research in quantum mechanics over the past twenty-five years. Several years after the theory was published, physicist John Clauser (of the University of California) performed experiments based on Bell's work, the results of which indicated that separated fragments such as A and B do continue to be connected in some perplexing manner and are not independent of each other. Such findings tended to confirm quantum's position, but not as conclusively as the 1982 work of Alaine Aspect and his associates at the University of Paris.

By 1982, measuring and testing equipment had improved considerably. With these advantages, Aspect's measurement experiments established that if two subatomic fragments, such as photons A-1 and B-1, with parallel, correlated spins, are passed through filters which are also parallel in orientation, there is full and consistent cooperation between the traveling photons (e.g., if photon A-1 passes through the filter, B-1 does also; if A-1 is blocked, so is B-1). But if the filters are placed in an oblique position (and thus are no longer parallel in orientation to the photons), the cooperation between A-1 and B-1 is markedly less (e.g., at times A-1 emerges from the filter but B-1 does not). Nevertheless, Aspect established that even with the filters in the oblique position, a degree of cooperation still remained which was *in excess of that which could be expected* if, as Einstein theorized, the photons had independent reality before their measurement.

In effect, therefore, the results of the Aspect experiments overruled Einstein and affirmed Bohr's position. It was seen, then, that these Einstein-Bohr confrontations did not merely concern personalities or technicalities; they dealt with the basic foundations of the Quantum Theory and the Uncertainty Principle. Forty-seven years later, Aspect's work had confirmed Bohr's conclusion that in the atomic sphere, the property of uncertainty is "inherent and inescapable."

Still, Einstein's brilliant challenges were not totally answered, for while Bohr's explanations were confirmed experimentally, we still do not fully comprehend how these results came about. What quantum mechanics teaches us in respect of the behavior and properties of atoms and subatoms remains very complex and hard to follow, let alone believe. We yet need to learn a great deal more about quantum's interpretation of reality, an interpretation which we find so perplexing in the light of our everyday human experiences.

Yet, modern physics has introduced us to what Sir John Eccles, who shared the 1963 Nobel Prize for psychology and medicine, has called a "new cosmic world-view" [in which] ". . .mind and mental events have a status matching that of the material world."[10] Will it be found someday that the theories of quantum mechanics can apply outside the sphere of atoms and subatoms, perhaps to help in the investigation of mysteries which exist in the "twilight zone" between the micro and macro worlds? For example, can quantum assist in the search for how our thought processes develop and how the brain functions?

And if it is ever established "beyond scientific doubt" that a particle materializes (is "created"?) only after it is chosen for measurement or observation, will this establish as well that man (the "chooser," the "observer") is also a co-creator, with God?

The prospect of discovering answers to such matters is what makes physics an exciting study rather than the theoretical, intimidating science many regard it to be. We will discuss more on the subject of physical reality in Chapters VI and XI and on the subjects of man's freedom of choice and man as a co-creator in later chapters.

Considerably isolated from the scientific community in the last decade of his life, Einstein wrote that there is no doubt that "the day will come" when new discoveries will confirm his intuitive views. It has not. Max Born remains uncontradicted in his position that previously held scientific views such as "absolute certainty" and "final truth" are no more than "phantoms."[11]

Einstein spent the last years of his life attempting to revitalize the earlier work of Weyl and Eddington, aimed at discovering a "Unified Field Theory." Einstein's two great Theories of Relativity dealt with the working of the vast cosmos (the "macrocosm"),

---

10. Augros, Robert M. and Stancial, George N., *The New Story*, New York: Bantam Books, 1986, p. x.

11. According to some contemporary political and social scientists, the existence of uncertainty should be respected as a truth which impacts on facets of our society other than the sciences. They decry, for example, the fact that many decisions which are made in politics, the military and general society rely simply on inherently uncertain opinions, intuition or dogma.

Only occasionally, these scientists maintain, do many decision-makers recognize the need for alternative strategies that can be set in place swiftly, should uncertainties emerge which can render original expectations and policies obsolete. Society is ill served and poorly led, they warn, unless our leaders learn to apply scientific methodology to deal with the element of uncertainty present in our everyday lives. (The views of Professor Yaron Ezrahi in *The Peril of Ignoring*, *Jerusalem Post,* May 31, 1991, p. 10.)

whereas quantum physics involved the study of the unseen, minute world (the "microcosm"). Einstein theorized that if these two great systems could be harmonized and dovetailed into a single theory, science, at last, would be able to uncover the "really real."

His perseverance did not flag, but his efforts were unsuccessful. Nobel Prize winner Wolfgang Pauli, who along with Hermann Weyl became one of Einstein's closest friends in America, expressed the most widely held viewpoint of Einstein's fellow physicists when he urged Einstein to give up his insistent search, because "what God has put asunder, no man shall ever join." As to Einstein's refusal to recognize the inherent uncertainty of atomic matter, Pauli well might have added the words of *Ecclesiastes:* "A twisted thing cannot be made straight" (*Eccl.* 1:15).

Today, a generation later, the quest to unify the Theories of Relativity with quantum physics continues, especially with the work of the brilliant physicist Stephen Hawking, who is Cambridge University's current Lucasian Professor, a chair once occupied by Sir Isaac Newton. Yet Hawking, optimistic in his belief that a unified theory eventually will be discovered, concedes that, if formulated, it always will be subject to the restrictions which Heisenberg's Principle "sets on our powers of prediction,"[12] unless new discoveries radically change our current understanding.

Consequently, even the most advanced picture of the physical universe is grainy and out of focus to the extent that the Principle of Uncertainty blurs it. As Max Born observed, the deeper we penetrate into the universe, the cloudier it becomes. Where, then, can we find clear knowledge?

As noted earlier, pre-quantum physicists, in searching for understanding, had limited their concept of reality to a physical reality. They did not recognize that science cannot provide a total reality, for we must also seek out the reality which lies outside of and beyond our material world. As early as 1931, Sir James Jeans, famous for his work on radiation and stellar activity, pointed out that the "ultimate processes of nature are not to be found within our physical world."

Thus, quantum mechanics and the Principle of Uncertainty did more than undermine determinism. The recognition of a partially

---

12. Hawking, Stephen W., *A Brief History of Time*, New York: Bantam Books, 1988, p. 127.

non-determined universe motivated empirical scientists such as Niels Bohr, Werner Heisenberg, Sir James Jeans and Sir Arthur Eddington to turn their thinking toward the realm of the non-material. In the quest to understand how the universe works, these world-class physicists recognized that science would no longer be able to rely solely upon its instruments, theories and mathematics to predict the future. Hereafter, scientists would be constrained to direct their exploration beyond the limitations of the physical world.

Still, one may wonder how it came to be that the scientific Principle of Uncertainty, discovered in the rational, intellectual setting of Göttingen by an equally rational, theoretical physicist, should open the door to the possibilities of spiritual overtones in the functioning of the universe. Does this principle reveal anything about the domain of the spirit and the mind?

Moreover, what has all this to do with Judaism's ability to bring a Jew closer to a total understanding of our world than any other religion or thought system?

6

The Modern Scientist Turns Philosopher

"I do not know what I may appear to the world;
but to myself I seem to have been only like a boy
playing on the seashore . . . finding a smoother
pebble or a prettier shell
while the great ocean of truth rolls beyond me,
undiscovered."

— Sir Isaac Newton, shortly before his death

"All finite things reveal infinitude."

— Theodore Roethke, in his poem "The Far Field"

In the seventeenth-century world of Galileo, Leibnitz and Newton, the role of God in scientific events was axiomatic. These great men held deeply religious views and considered scientific discovery as the beneficence of an Omnipotent Being. In all scientific advances, man was the instrument, and God was the Source.

Newton, as he observed in this chapter's heading, felt that scientific advance is limited and that beyond the findings of science lies an "ocean of truth" which remains "undiscovered." Newton understood that the mathematical and physical laws he had discovered conveyed only a portion of the truth underlying the universe and our existence.

To the generations that followed Newton, the clock analogy represented the entire workings of the universe, but it was not so to Newton. To him the clock was of awesome design, but he always recognized that it was a product of God's design and was governed continuously by God's laws.[1]

---

1. Interestingly, Newton identified "God" as the God of Israel, writing, "We must believe that He is the God of Jews, who created the heavens and earth and all things therein as is *expresed* [sic] in the ten commandments. . ." (Manuel, Frank E., *Religion of Sir Isaac Newton*, London: Oxford Univ. Press, 1974. See also: Newton, Isaac, Sir, *Yahuda* manuscript, National Library, Hebrew Univ., 15.3 Fol. 46.)

It was a corollary of Newton's thinking that God is above nature and that nature is fully subservient to Him. And occasionally, he held, God intervenes in and varies the working of the universal order. This view has always been the belief of Judaism. In his classic *The Way of God*, the eighteenth-century sage Rabbi M. C. Luzzato stated a closely similar perception:

> In the vast majority of cases . . . God desires to maintain nature according to its natural laws . . . Nevertheless, this does not prevent Him from changing [them] for whatever reason He may determine . . . [be it] . . . to demonstrate . . . His providence . . . or for many other reasons that are not comprehensible to us at all.[2]

Over the two centuries which followed the Newton era, however, rationalist and anti-religious Enlightenment philosophy slowly captured the minds of many of the intellectual and scientific heirs to Newton's monumental discoveries. True, some outstanding scientific figures such as James Clerk Maxwell continued to recognize God's role in the operation of the principles they discovered. But by the end of the nineteenth century, concepts relating to the spiritual, to human consciousness and to creation generally came to be regarded as having no possible validity in the scientific process. Most centers of learning throughout the Western World embraced secular viewpoints and an unquestioned reliance upon the theories of determinism and of a perpetually existing, non-created universe.

Still, a specter always hovered over the scientist's shoulder. For whatever rarefied height of human thought he might reach, every solved mystery led to another which was even more complex and elusive. The goal of understanding always seemed beyond his grasp. With the publication of the Principle of Uncertainty, it became recognized that the ultimate knowledge he so ardently sought probably lay beyond the reach of his search and outside of our world.

And, as noted at the end of the previous chapter, in the late 1920's and early 1930's, a number of world-renowned scientific figures began to speak openly of philosophic matters such as religion, free choice and the human spirit — even of God. The scientist, like the rest of mankind, wrote Born, thirsts for "something fixed . . . in

---

2. Luzzatto, Moshe Chaim, *The Way of God*, trans. by Aryeh Kaplan, Jerusalem: Feldheim Publishers, Ltd., 1977, p. 397.

the universal whirl: God, beauty, truth."[3] Eddington, the leading astrophysicist of that era and much celebrated for his work on relativity and on the motions of stars, as well as for his collaboration with Weyl in the search for a unified theory, observed that the scientist now had a "much more mystic concept" of the physical world and that religion need no longer be regarded as "incompatible with physical science."[4]

In a lecture series given at Cornell in 1934, characteristically delivered with eloquence and brilliance, Eddington described this new approach of the physicist to life and its meaning in the following manner (paraphrased and directly quoted): When people are unable to comprehend why they exist, he said, and ". . . the cry goes up, 'What is it all about?'," we should not reply that the answer lies in the experience of our five senses. We must not say that existence is ". . . about atoms and chaos; . . . about a universe of fiery globes rolling on to impending doom. . ." Rather, we must become aware that there exists a "reality of spirit and consciousness," a concept which he clarified in language that the traditional, classical physicist might have considered heretical: ". . .I contemplate a spiritual domain underlying the physical world . . ." and while our sensory experience generally ". . . ends in a veil of symbols, there is an immediate knowledge in the minds of conscious beings which lifts the veil in places. . . ."[5] [6]

In two succinct sentences, Max Planck described this modern development of scientific thinking: "The essential point is that the world of sensation is not the only world which may conceivably

---

3. Born, Max, *The Restless Universe*, New York: Dover Books, 1981, p. 277.

4. Eddington, Arthur Stanley, Sir, *New Pathways in Science,* London: Cambridge Press, 1934, Chapter XIV.

5. All quotations and paraphrases in this paragraph are from Eddington, Arthur Stanley, Sir, *New Pathways in Science*, London: Cambridge Univ. Press, 1934, pps: 317-323.

6. Through light and our sense of vision, we achieve most of what we know of the physical order of the world. Yet, the range of light visible to man is but a small fraction of the "light" that exists in the universe. Our visible ability is confined to the spectrum of light that stretches from violet to red. But extending far beyond this "visible light" portion is the much wider spectrum of invisible light rays, which science identifies as ultraviolet, X-ray, gamma, infrared, heat, radar and radio.

It is worth contemplating that just as the X-ray machine enables man to utilize the great benefit of some of the light rays we cannot otherwise see, so too a spiritual approach to understanding may enable us to transcend the disabling restraints which the "prisonhouse of our senses" has placed upon our ability to explore the realm of the spirit for hints of the purpose of our existence.

exist but that there is still another world. To be sure, this other world is not directly accessible to us, but its existence is indicated, time and time again, with compelling clarity, not only by practical life but also by the labors of science."[7]

In Heisenberg's own writings, we can find a clear explanation for the unexpected philosophic implications of his work. In *Physics and Philosophy*, he traced the history of science, pointing out that reliance during the eighteenth, nineteenth and early twentieth centuries on the Theory of Determinism, on mathematics and on the five senses had saddled physics with a confinement and a "naivete" that gave it a limited view of the universe. For, he continued, this view which concentrated on matter and the physical did not "touch reality as do the age-old religious concepts of soul and God and mind," which have an "immediate relation to reality." (Interestingly, he commented in this discussion that the Jewish concept of God offers a "higher stage of abstraction" than that found in the various "natural gods" of the physical world.) These values of religious tradition, he went on, must be recognized because technology had slipped out of man's control and because such values, rather than theories, are the tools with which man must work if he is to truly touch reality.[8]

It was at this high point of the twentieth century's Golden Age of Physics that a number of its leading figures began to write and speak of a *philosophy* of physics. Max Born (under whom, at Göttingen, Heisenberg had discovered some of his most important findings) observed that he came to the realization that "theoretical physics is actual philosophy" and that, in his later years, he "tried to formulate philosophical principles derived from science."[9] And Heisenberg commented that the correspondence between Born and Einstein illustrated that although the subject matter of the scientist's work appears to be most distant from human matters, it is "fundamentally determined by philosophical and human attitudes."[10] Niels Bohr was among the earliest scientists to detect these unusual philosophical implications. It will be recalled that we met Bohr earlier, in

7. LeVan Baumer, Franklin, *Main Currents of Western Thought*, New York: Alfred A. Knopf, 1952, p. 602. Also see Planck, Max, *The New Science*, New York: Random Books, 1959, p. 156.

8. Heisenberg, Werner, *Physics and Philosophy*, London: Allen & Unwin, 1958, p. 19 et seq., p. 196 et seq.

9. Born, Max, *My Life and My Views*, New York: Charles Scribner's Sons, 1968, p. 55.

10. Born, Max, *The Born-Einstein Letters,*. New York: Walker & Co., 1971, Introduction.

the account of his famous debate with Einstein at the 1927 Solvay Conference. Occasionally, he was a guest lecturer at Göttingen in the late 1920's. There, he befriended the young Heisenberg. In long walks in the woods near Göttingen, the two men explored the new body of philosophic thought generated by the work of each, as well as of other physicists. Later, Heisenberg attended the Niels Bohr Institute in Copenhagen, where the philosophy of physics had become a significant line of inquiry.

In this period of his life Heisenberg may have developed a philosophical viewpoint which influenced his future outlook toward the second, exceptional role he was soon to play, an extraordinary undertaking with political repercussions as widespread as the scientific repercussions of his Uncertainty Principle.

This second role related no less than to the greatest mystery of World War II: Why didn't the Germans also develop an atomic bomb? The answer to that mystery is still not totally clear. Nor do we know much about the extent to which Heisenberg personally influenced this most decisive failure of German science.

What we did know before the war began was that the Third Reich was ahead of the Allies in nuclear fission by a three-year margin, having successfully split the atom in late 1938. Consequently, the very real and dangerous possibility that the Germans could produce a nuclear weapon became one of the great fears of OSS intelligence. German scientists who took refuge in the U.S. passed along much the same frightening concern, stressing that if any one person could bring about such a German feat, it was Werner Heisenberg.

Over the next three years, the U.S. and the Germans played out the ultra-serious guessing game: Was the other side working on a nuclear explosive?

U.S. Intelligence had learned that in 1942 Heisenberg was placed in charge of the German nuclear program under the direct authority of Hitler's Armaments Reichminister, Albert Speer. The Americans also received a report that Heisenberg had advised Speer that a bomb could be built but that it would take many years and an enormous amount of money. Still, this was only a report, and the specter of German capability, under the brilliant Heisenberg, of unleashing an atom explosion continued to spook the U.S. intelligence establishment until almost the end of the war.

The kidnapping of Heisenberg had been under consideration and study by the OSS since 1942. One of those who urged this strategy was physics professor (and later Nobel laureate) Hans Bethe, a German refugee who had joined the Cornell faculty in 1935, the same year in which physicist Robert F. Bacher also became a faculty member. (Prof. Bacher was my freshman studies adviser when I enrolled at the university a year later.) Both men were destined soon to become most vital to the Manhattan Project, Bethe as head of the Theoretical Physics Division and Bacher as head of the Bomb Physics Division.

The right circumstances for a kidnapping never materialized, and the OSS strategy was switched to a project calling for Heisenberg's assassination by an OSS agent. The man who was chosen for what is considered the most critical and risky intelligence mission of World War II was Morris Berg, a fascinating personality known as "Moe" to a number of the leading figures of the day, among them three outstanding men highlighted in previous pages of this book: Edwin Hubble, Franklin D. Roosevelt and Albert Einstein. The son of Jewish immigrants, Berg combined a rare cluster of talented accomplishments: He was a 600-plus game major league baseball catcher, a magna cum laude graduate of Princeton, a linguistic scholar proficient in over half a dozen languages ranging from Japanese to Greek and a Columbia University L.L.B. who practiced law on Wall Street.

Toward the end of 1944, Berg was dispatched by his superiors with instructions to attend a Heisenberg lecture in Zurich on December 18, 1944, to learn whether Heisenberg indeed was in the process of perfecting an atom bomb. (See pp. 397-399 in *Heisenberg's War* by Thomas Powers, Alfred A. Knopf, 1993, and pp. 202-207 in *The Catcher Was a Spy* by Nicholas Davidoff, Pantheon Books, 1994.) If Heisenberg let slip that he was working on the bomb, Berg was to kill him without hesitation then and there in the seminar hall, even though Berg's chances of getting out alive were almost nil. During the lecture, however, Heisenberg made no reference whatever to the bomb, and Berg aborted his mission.

In February 1992, more information was revealed about why Germany never built the bomb. The British government made public some three hundred pages of secretly recorded conversations among ten German scientists who were captured and interned in

England late in 1945. Professor Bethe has studied the transcripts carefully and in a lecture at Cornell in November 1993 concluded that the reason the Germans failed was that Heisenberg "did not at any time intend to build an atom bomb." The Germans, he stated, "never thought of building such an enormous project. . . They didn't think big enough."

We still have no certain answer to the mystery of why Germany never built an atom bomb in World War II. Perhaps such a project was not undertaken because — as Speer subsequently confirmed in his *Memoirs* — Heisenberg had represented that it would take too long and would be too costly. Perhaps it was simply because of Heisenberg's lack of personal interest and resolve stemming from his concern that this most fearful of technologies would slip, as he wrote in *Physics and Philosophy,* "out of man's control." We also know that he had once asked Niels Bohr whether a physicist could morally help develop a nuclear bomb. However, these insights remain only as possibilities since Heisenberg never disclosed his specific intent regarding a German bomb. Still, if future disclosures provide greater credibility to such possibilities, history may yet credit Heisenberg with having contributed to preventing the catastrophe that could have resulted had Germany built and exploded the bomb before the U.S. was able to do so.

In a strange footnote to history, Speer wrote in his *Memoirs: Inside the Third Reich* that Germany's failure to build the bomb "can be partly traced to ideological reasons." For, he revealed, Hitler was greatly prejudiced against the support of Germany's nuclear research program because, Hitler claimed, "Jews were exerting a seditious influence" through their involvement with nuclear physics (Hitler called it "Jewish physics," a term coined by the anti-Semitic, Einstein-vilifying German physicist Philip Lenard) and the Theory of Relativity.

Thus, in an ironic twist, while Hitler's obsession with Jews so tragically resulted in a near-total annihilation of European Jewry, that very obsession — by crippling German research — may well have foreclosed the early, successful development of a German atomic bomb, thus sparing the allied nations from the devastation which would have followed Germany's exploitation of such a deadly weapon.

As Heisenberg's mentor and one of the pioneers of quantum

mechanics, Neils Bohr had recognized early on that nature possessed a remarkable ability to select between alternatives. In those explorative years, J. J. Thompson had won a Nobel Prize for his finding that the electron is a "particle." Later, J. J.'s son George also was awarded a Nobel Prize for his proof that, at times, the electron behaves as a "wave." These alternating behaviors were described by Bohr as exhibiting a "*free choice* on the part of nature between various possibilities, a property of the physical world which is *inherent* and *inescapable*" (emphasis added).[11]

Bohr had an unusual feel for the mysterious insights implicit in the new Quantum Theory. Occasionally apologizing for what might be regarded as a touch of mysticism "contrary to the spirit of the natural sciences," he lectured and published brilliantly not only on nature's freedom to choose but also on man's free choice, a concept which until then scientists had viewed as contradicted by a deterministic world.

For Heisenberg's work had brought to light the ancient knowledge that man, too, has the exceptional ability to alter conditions surrounding him. When it was shown that the electron was caused to behave capriciously solely by the barrage of "chunks" of light shone upon it by a scientific investigator, it became clear that this modification was directly brought about *by reason of man's involvement*. It was now recognized that to some extent every observation of man affects what is being observed.

And it was in the context of this remarkable finding that Bohr and such other leading scientists of the day as Eddington, Jeans, Born, Schordinger, Weyl and Pauli affirmed one of the remarkable facets of quantum mechanics: that man, within limits, can influence events through his free acts and will. As Jeans wrote, man, by his presence alone, "can make the universe in some small degree different." Thus, Werner Heisenberg truly had uncorked the bottle long sealed by rigid determinism and from it emerged, among other concepts, the genie of "*free will*,"[12] that element in man which elevates him to a unique role in the world.

---

11. Bohr, Niels, *Atomic Theory and the Description of Nature*, London: Cambridge Univ. Press, 1934, p. 98.

12. See Chapter IX for additional development of this most significant and interesting concept.

But is there not somewhat of a paradox in these writings? Why would rational, lifelong, objective scientists such as Bohr and Heisenberg write of such matters as "mysticism" and "mind"? The best answer may be that they wished to give expression to their recognition, as Max Planck wrote above, that the results of their scientific investigations, especially in quantum mechanics, compelled them to reach out *beyond* physics for answers to the mysteries confronting science. They earnestly wished to make clear that classical physics had dealt with the shadowy, illusory world of Plato's cave and had overlooked that a more complete understanding of the universe required a search beyond the physical world of appearances and shadows.

While this core idea of quantum philosophy may not find frequent expression among post-1950 scientists, it remains alive and well. As our "Astronomy" update section (a few pages ahead) indicates, there are prominent, contemporary astronomers who detect the presence of non-physical implications in their studies of new, sophisticated probes of the cosmos; and there are physicists today who classify the abstract overtones of scientific investigation as "pure information."[13]

Apart from the subject of physics, what impact has recent scientific thinking had upon astronomy, biology and psychology, the three most important disciplines other than physics to emerge in the Enlightenment Era? Here again, paralleling revisions in the thinking of theoretical physicists, a number of new findings by astronomers, biologists and psychiatrists have helped to create new approaches towards resolving some of the unknowns in their respective branches of science.

To round out this chapter's tracing of the new developments in the philosophy of the scientist, let us summarize several recent revisions in the outlooks of the three disciplines of biology, psychology and astronomy, beginning with the former:

Evolution

Although Darwin had written in 1878 that "there is almost complete unity among biologists about evolution," this was not quite accurate. Even Darwin's leading supporters, T. H. Huxley in England

13. Pines, Elliot, *To the Editor, Jewish Action*, Spring 1992, pp. 8-9.

and Ernest Haeckel in Germany, differed with Darwin and with each other as to the functioning of evolution. This issue continued to be debated over the next six decades, but a relatively uncontroversial period ensued during the thirty years that followed the 1940's. In the 1970's, however, there was considerable challenge by some biologists as to the validity of natural selection. Thus, one group of biologists, the "neutralists" (or "non-Darwinians"), initiated dialogues to the effect that genetic change is not only the result of natural selection but also the result of "random genetic drift."

Other biologists, such as Stephen Jay Gould of Harvard, maintained that natural selection is not always the result of gradual change and that some evolutionary processes take place far more quickly than Darwin had theorized. Gould and Niles Eldredge of the American Museum of Natural History insist that their approach does not repudiate evolutionary theory, maintaining that the debate is simply a healthy, intellectual exchange of thinking. Although Darwin had postulated that the evolutionary process would be gradualistic and almost imperceptible, Gould and Eldridge (supported by a number of other respected paleontologists) hold to what they call "punctuated equilibria," a theory which describes the evolutionary process as taking place by "discontinuous leaps," that is, rapid starts following long periods of relative uneventfulness.

The "punctuated equilibria" supporters insist that they are only "reinterpreting" the concept of natural selection and that the lack of fossil support for Darwin's theory exists mainly in "fine-scale" transitions between species, not in "large-scale" transitions. They assert that there is considerable evidence of "large-scale" transitions, although they are "episodic" or "jerky." Moreover, they claim that "fine-scale" transitions are more "underrepresented" than "missing" in fossil remains. Today the "punctuated equilibria" approach and others similar to it are gaining increasing acceptance among paleontologists.

The appearance of the "punctuated equilibria" issue prompted another line of attack by the "creationist" movement upon Darwinism in general and the fossil record in particular. Creationism is the name given to the scientific-religious approach taken by Bible fundamentalists in the U.S., whose most visible and audible spokesman has become the I.C.R. (the Institute for Creation Research), established in 1963.

The major emphasis of creationism centers about legislative lobbying to prohibit the teaching of evolution and to permit the teaching of *Genesis* in the public schools. Attempts to achieve this legislative goal were quite common in the period 1921-1929, when some twenty states considered forty-five forms of such legislation, three of which became law. In the 1960's and 1970's, matters remained quiet, but, by the end of 1980, bills requiring the teaching of "scientific creation" alongside of evolution were introduced into the legislatures of eleven states. In 1981, two states, Arkansas and Louisiana, passed such bills, both of which were subsequently overturned by the courts. As of today, the tug-of-war between the creationists and the evolutionists has been characterized as a "Mexican standoff."

Evolutionary investigation in the field and laboratory has been accelerating during the past several years. U.S. and Russian scientists have discovered in northeast Siberia what are considered "perfect" rocks with which to date the happening of the "evolutionary big bang," in which period major animal groups are said to have first appeared. The rocks provide no evidence as to why this "big bang" occurred, but they revealed that the "evolutionary big bang" event took place over a startlingly shorter period of time than biologists had previously theorized. And new evidence was discovered very recently in China, findings which are considered "among the most spectacular in this century." These discoveries indicate that the transformation from single to multi-cell fauna and animals such as worms came about more suddenly and rapidly (even within thousands of years) than had been surmised.

In the past few years, geneticists have taken a strong lead in evolutionary investigation. Their DNA findings indicate that humans did not evolve gradually or in many areas, as Darwinism had long maintained, but rather in one place and in considerably more recent times than anthropologists and biologists had concluded previously.[14] Geneticists believe (and Gould agrees) that this establishes that people "are really members of a single entity." Although there is no complete agreement among geneticists as to these remarkable new and dramatic findings, there appears to be a greater consensus among geneticists as to their genetic data than there is among paleontologists as to their skeletal findings.

---

14. *Newsweek*, Jan. 11, 1989.

And so, there continues among evolutionist professionals an ongoing process of refinements and reinterpretations, some drastic, of Darwin's original postulates in the *Origin*. In the centennial year of Darwin's death, 1982, a Gallup poll was taken on evolution. It showed that fewer than ten percent of Americans (among the respondents, twenty-five percent were college graduates) accept the basic Darwinian theories of human origins. So in some ways, the tensions and strong feelings over evolution emanate not only from conflicting scientific views but also from disparate philosophic and religious viewpoints held by people with different backgrounds and upbringing. It is also most unlikely that scientific evidence can bring about a resolution of the complex issues involving evolutionary theory which divide proponents and opponents. At the heart of the impasse is the "larger question": Assuming that natural laws and the evolutionary processes may explain many phenomena, these explanations do not resolve the issue of whether or not such laws and processes are the creation of a Supreme Being Who put them into place to activate and direct the unfolding of overall creation. In a word, was not the evolutionary principle itself created by God?

There are some scientists who pose the following question in respect of the debate as to whether the universe originated through design or randomness: When created, was the universe in a state of order or disorder? If it was in an ordered state, this would strongly suggest the presence of a Designer at the time of creation. Now, these scientists point out, it is unlikely that the universe began within a condition known as "negative entropy" (entropy is defined as a disordered state) because otherwise no order at all could have been created. Most scientists believe that the probability of an accidental or random state eventually leading to orderliness is extremely unlikely in the presence of negative entropy. Roger Penrose, professor of mathematics at Oxford, evaluating the issue of what state the universe was in at its creation, has computed that the odds *against* the universe appearing by accident is in the range of one possibility out of the number 1 followed by eighty-seven zeros!

Yet another view is taken by Stephen Hawking, who collaborated with Penrose in 1970 in work which indicated that the universe began with the "Big Bang" and had a beginning in time. Subsequently, however, Hawking changed his mind, and in his bestselling *Brief History of Time*, theorized that there was "no beginning, no moment of creation, no commencement of time." The universe, he now postulates, may be viewed as completely self-contained, and there was therefore no choice or selection of the initial conditions which led to its creation. Hawking emphasizes, however, that this is "just a proposal; it cannot be deduced from some other principle."

So the scientific-philosophic-religious debate continues as it has for centuries over whether chance or design lies behind the origin and function of the universe and man. But since "objective science can never reconstruct non-observed events from the past,"[15] Jews remain at ease over (and generally apart from) the "chance-versus-creationism" debate. Moreover, we are not particularly troubled by the ascendancy of evolution in modern thought, for we do not regard evolution as an especially religious issue or an open-and-shut one. Most Jews take the position that our religious faith is grounded upon Judaism's spiritual insights; to gain understanding, we concentrate far more upon those insights than upon material ones such as a description of the mechanics of the growth of life.

In a word, Judaism is more occupied with why, not how, man was created.

Psychology

As to psychology, the "science of the mind," it, too, has undergone considerable revision as a consequence of the quantum revolution's devaluation of the Principle of Determinism. Freud's innovative writings on dreams, sexuality and the unconscious founded modern psychiatry. Even today they are regarded as among psychology's most original and brilliant insights into the workings of the human mind and personality. But his theory that our inner instincts are the key to what we think and do was drawn in large measure from his deterministic, mechanistic world-view that our "unconscious" drives and our instincts are the "cause," and our personalities and behaviors are the "result."

As early as the 1930's it became evident to a number of Freud's original students and followers, such as Jung and Rank, that while man is partially determined by his past and his instincts, he still

15. Branover, Herman, *Basic Principles in the Discussion of Torah and Science, Encounter*, ed. H. C. Schimmel and A. Carmel, Feldheim Publishers, Ltd., Jerusalem/New York, 1989.

possesses the freedom and uniqueness to develop and grow through his independent acts and decisions. They also faulted Freud for his unchanging belief that religion and its hope of immortality are escapism and directed towards children and the ignorant. Jung differed strongly, offering a counter-view on religion when he said that in over thirty years of treating hundreds of people from every civilized country, none who was over thirty-five became healed without re-acquiring a "lost religious outlook on life."

Rank likewise made it clear in his work that to achieve meaningful development, man must recognize his own puniness and direct himself to the beyond, to the Ultimate Power. Becker wrote that Rank firmly held that no amount of psychiatry alone will enable one to learn who or why he is on this planet.[16] To achieve fulfillment man must replace within himself the belief in immortality and cosmic divinity which the Enlightenment had taken from him.[17]

Astronomy

Findings over the past fifty years have convinced the astronomer that it is impossible to look directly backward to the remote past for original clues which could explain the beginning of the universe. It is now commonly accepted that the 100 million, million, million, million, million, million-degree centigrade intensity of the inferno which occurred at the moment of the "Big Bang" obliterated all such clues and foreclosed further direct investigation into why or how it took place.

Scientists are left, then, with such approaches as the intensive telescopic observations by Dr. Allan Sandage of the expansion rate of the universe and the indirect investigative route through what is known as a particle accelerator. There are medium-sized accelerator installations in Illinois, California and Switzerland. A giant one was scheduled to be built in Texas, but it was phased out because federal funding was withdrawn. The goal of science in this program is to cause protons to collide against each other at an intensity

16. Becker, Ernest, *The Denial of Death*, New York: Free Press, 1973, p. 193.

17. In respect of recent revisions of long-held scientific views, it is interesting to note that in astronomy and psychiatry we see the master figure's stance toward religion proven wrong by his own disciple: Albert Einstein by Friedmann as to a created universe, and Sigmund Freud by Jung, Rank and Frankl as to man's deep need for religious belief.

estimated to approach that of the "Big Bang" explosion, thereby hopefully gaining clues as to how creation unfolded. Some accelerator results to date have tended to add support to the "Big Bang" Theory, for the particles produced have appeared to be of a nature which astronomers predict would have been created by the "fireball."

Additionally, outer-space data collection by satellite-born instruments over the past decade has been especially revealing. Recently, Hubble's sophisticated High Resolution Spectrograph has been sending back most welcome confirmation of Hubble's ability to provide data previously beyond the capacity of earthbound instrumentation.

Thus, before Hubble was launched, the element of boron was found in younger but never in older stars. A short time ago, however, Hubble's Spectrograph discovered boron in an old star, one that is judged to be almost as old as the universe itself. This find has been interpreted by some astronomers as supporting the view (in contrast to the "Big Bang" traditional theory that in its beginning and early periods the universe was of smooth and uniform consistency, like a "custard pudding") that just a few minutes after the "fireball" explosion, the consistency of the universe began to condense in some areas, causing lumps like "raisins" to form in the homogeneous "pudding." These lumps, it is theorized, evolved over time into the stars, planets and galaxies which comprise the structure of the universe.

Recently, this structure has become more clearly visible through maps made by another remarkable new device, the Infrared Astronomical Satellite. Critics of the "smooth" universe theory take the position that the huge "chains" of galaxies shown on these maps would not yet have had sufficient time to form under the "Big Bang uniform universe" version.

These critics agree with the "Big Bang" view that the first elements to become formed were light ones — e.g., hydrogen — followed by heavier ones — e.g., boron. But, they maintain, these heavier elements came into being in some areas within minutes after creation, not after considerable time, as "Big Bang" postulates. This new timetable, they assert, is borne out by the newly detected presence of boron in a very old star. Nevertheless, they concede that the boron-in-old-stars discovery needs further confirmation, which ,even if achieved, will not prove that the "Big Bang" Theory is wrong, but rather that it is incomplete and needs revision.[18]

The "raisin-in-the-pudding" mystery was seen from quite a different perspective in a possibly landmark scientific announcement made on April 23, 1992. It received international media coverage and a prompt, wide range of reactions from leading astronomers and physicists. These most important findings were the result of the joint efforts of an investigative team headed by Dr. George F. Smoot of the Lawrence Berkely Laboratory.

In a twenty-year-long search, which in its earlier period employed aircraft, balloons and microwave detectors, even at the South Pole, Smoot and his associates sought to uncover the existence of any type of unevenness in the early universe which could account for the formation of "lumps" of galaxies in a universe whose background radiation measurements indicated that its consistency at creation was smooth and homogeneous. Conceding that time alone was insufficient to cause the formation of the gigantic structures (called the "great wall") recently mapped, the Smoot team turned for answers to data furnished by COBE (Cosmic Background Explorer), an instrument-packed satellite launched by the National Aeronautics and Space Administration in November 1989.

In early results, COBE's instruments had indicated that the strength of the background radiation in the universe fairly well matches that which the "Big Bang" Theory had predicted. Further, its infrared detectors showed that the early universe was composed of elements which could be anticipated to follow the "Big Bang" inferno.

But it was in the very recent, spectacular measurements of temperature variations in separate regions of the sky that the Smoot team struck pay dirt in its search for answers about how the stars and galaxies formed. Without such clarification, the validity of the overall "Big Bang" Theory would have been in serious difficulty; indeed, as Professor Steven Weinberg, one of today's leading cosmologists, put it, "There's no theory that would have survived."

What the Smoot team discovered from COBE's seventy million annual measurements of the entire sky is that there are temperature irregularities (COBE can measure as fine as a hundred-thousandth of a degree) in various regions of the heavens. These temperature

18. *Johns Hopkins Magazine*, ed. Melissa Hendricks and Lisa Hooker, interviewing astronomer Doug Duncan, April 1992, p. 34.

fluctuations presumably indicate the presence of density variation in cosmic matter. Thus, where the temperature registered in a given region was warmer, there was a greater density of matter, forming the conditions believed to lead to the growth of stars. Where the temperature was cooler and the area less dense, voids of empty space remain, since matter was not likely to gather there.[19]

This evidence of the existence in the early phase of the universe of unevenness in the cosmic background radiation was warmly welcomed by "Big Bang" adherents as a supportive and plausible explanation of how the structure of the universe came about.

Still, competitive theories are being advanced also, based on COBE's data, as to how our structure evolved. One such theory is the "inflationary universe" theory. Its principal proponent, Dr. Alan H. Guth of the University of Chicago, holds that COBE's radiation and density measurements tend to confirm his theory of inflation.[20] Another well-regarded physicist, Dr. James E. Peebles, believes that COBE's results neither prove nor disprove the inflation theory, while Boston University Professor Kenneth Brecker comments that in the absence of further astronomical findings which can support it, the theory will remain a "pipe dream."[21]

Perhaps the most settling overview of the divergent opinions which followed the Smoot announcement was that of Dr. Weinberg, who commented that as to any particular theory, "people shouldn't make dogmatic statements about it."[22, 23]

---

19. A year later, in April 1993, Dr. Smoot announced that his continuing analysis of COBE's data indicates that cosmic "gravity waves" which originated at the beginning of creation may have been a significant cause of the temperature irregularities he discovered in April 1992.

20. "Despite New Data, Mysteries of Creation Persist," *New York Times,* May 12, 1992, p. C9.

21. "The Phantino Universe," *Newsweek,* Dr. Kenneth Brecher, May 25, 1992, p. 52.

22. "Despite New Data, Mysteries of Creation Persist," *New York Times,* May 12, 1992, p. C10.

23. As discussed in Chapter II, the analysis sixty years ago by Edwin Hubble and Milton Humason of the red-shift phenomenon led to the publication of Hubble's Law, quite possibly astronomy's greatest discovery. It stated that the universe, following the enormous "Big Bang" inferno, began and continues to expand in all directions and from every point in the heavens. Yet, in a May 13, 1992 *New York Times* op-ed letter (following the Smoot announcement of cosmic background radiation fluctuations), Irving E. Segal, mathematics professor at M.I.T., characterized Hubble's Law as "irredeemably false" and the "Big Bang" Theory as "seriously flawed."

Lively, differing exchanges are also currently being published as to the validity even of Newtonian mechanics, a system once considered to be unassailable.

Notwithstanding such dissenting opinions, however, Newtonian mechanics, Hubble's Law and the "Big Bang" basic theory continue to be supported by mainstream cosmologists. As this book goes to press, astronomers report that the Keck

How does one begin to sort out this mélange of scientific opinions and both strident and muted dissents? It would seem that we are left once again with Max Born's wise observation, "The deeper we penetrate, the more restless becomes the universe and the vaguer and cloudier."[24]

Some years back, I visited the ancient Mayan City of Chichén Itźa in Mexico's Yucatan Peninsula. Among the accomplishments of this intelligent civilization (3rd-16th centuries C.E.) were advances in mathematics (they discovered the zero) and astronomy. The archeological remains of the Chichén Itźa observatory indicate an igloo-shaped structure with vents in the roof for sighting the movements of stars and planets. Based on the data gathered in a number of such observatories, the Mayans were able to calculate the precise duration of the solar year, calculations on which they based their famous calendar. And the Dresden Codex of Mayan hieroglyphics sets out highly exact Venusian and lunar tables and a method of predicting eclipses.

Yet, while during the next ten centuries Western man continued to study the heavens with newer observational devices, ranging from Galileo's improved 1609 telescope through the recent spectacular array of scientific tools such as highly powerful earthbound telescopes, a space telescope, the Magellan spacecraft and the COBE satellite, we still remain confronted in 1992 by the frank evaluation of Dr. Edward Harris of the University of Massachusetts.

Some years back, Dr. Harris had proposed the theoretical spectrum theory as an explanation of the origin of the structure of the universe, a theory which, some hold, is also consistent with COBE's newly released data. Yet, when interviewed shortly after Dr. Smoot's announcement, Harris did not claim that such consistency with his theory established any firm proof, observing, "I suspend all belief [about cosmology], because every ten years the ideas change. It's ridiculous to say you believe in any of them when things are always in such a state of flux with cosmology, and indeed, with science in general." [25]

Telescope, the world's largest, has detected additional evidence in support of "Big Bang." One astrophysicist reports that the Keck observations left scientists "dancing in the dark corridors" of observatories.

24. Born, Max, *The Restless Universe,* New York: Dover Books, 1981.

25. "Despite New Data, Mysteries of Creation Persist," *New York Times,* May 12, 1992, p. C10.

Why, then, aren't we able to attain more fixed beliefs in cosmology, as well as in science generally?

In Chapter IX, University of Sussex astronomer John D. Barrow's recent volume *Theories of Everything* is discussed at some length. Peeking ahead, let's examine some observations in his book which may give us more insight into our question, "Why don't we know more for certain?" Perhaps, Barrow explains, it is because we know almost nothing of the initial conditions that led to the beginning of the universe. Therefore, we may never know how the universe began. Nor will we ever be able to observe the *entire* universe, only its visible part. Barrow adds to these reasons the fact that at root, the world's function is best described mathematically; yet, mathematical reasoning has limitations which, in turn, limit our understanding of the world. Mathematical theory is unable to encompass, Barrow further points out, qualitative elements which contain great meaning for the individual, elements such as truth and beauty. These elements are *qualitative* attributes of reality that cannot find a place within mathematics' *quantitative* approach toward knowing more "for sure."

Lastly, I would submit that perhaps it is because most scientists still believe that only science is able to yield up answers to the great mysteries that continue to elude us, eschewing a "beyond-the-physical-domain" approach as lacking in objectivity and incapable of being demonstrated or proved. George Smoot, however, appears to be one of those modern scientists who recognizes that "beyond science" insights can augment the results of scientific investigation. For when he reported his COBE findings, he observed that the discovery of temperature variations within the cosmos was "really like finding the driving mechanism[26] for the universe, and isn't that what God is?"[27] While Smoot maintains that "what matters is the science," he still recognizes that his discovery can be seen as having religious overtones ("if you're religious, [the discovery is] like looking at God").[28] From the COBE findings,

---

26. Writing in *Physics and Philosophy*, Sir James Jeans expressed a similar observation when he pictured "a substrata below space and time in which the *springs of events* are concealed. . ." (emphasis added) (p. 215).

27. "In the Glow of Cosmic Discovery: A Physicist Ponders God and Fame," *New York Times*, May 5, 1992, p. C1 and p. C9.

28. At the June 1992 meeting of the American Astronomical Society, one of the most startling photos displayed was that taken by the Hubble Space Telescope of a spiral galaxy called M51. The computer-enhanced photo revealed a distinct black "X" which

he stated, he could feel "something of the *bigger meaning*."[29]

Astronaut Edgar Mitchell of the Apollo 14 moon mission (who had a ringside seat at the "Greatest Show of Earth") tells of his reaction when Apollo 14 rounded the dark side of the moon and he saw planet Earth suspended in the deep blackness of space. The sight he beheld of a universe of billions of stars and galaxies in "magnificent array" evoked an apprehension within him that he was gazing at an "intelligent system." It was not, he stated, the random product of random collisions of energy, as science teaches. There is, he concluded, "a coherence . . .an intelligence palpable in the universe."

How does Judaism view the cosmological developments of the last half-century? On the one hand, Judaism warmly welcomes the position of Nobel laureate Arno Penzias,[30] which is described by a *New York Times* reporter (in an interview with Penzias after the Smoot announcement) as follows: "The evidence of astronomy seems to him [Penzias] consonant with general biblical precepts. . . "[31]

On the other hand, Judaism is not particularly upset by the recent chorus of divergent views voiced by astronomers as to the "Big Bang" Theory. To the believing Jew, the Bible's account of creation is not dependent upon supporting astronomical findings. Still, science and Torah are steadily being recognized as exhibiting increasing harmony, and in the light of the variability of scientific speculation, it is quite rational for Jews to subscribe wholeheartedly to *Genesis.* Indeed, recent developments have led both the scientist and the non-scientist to recognize that the "bigger meaning" and the higher content of all things and all events may be seen, paradoxically, in what we cannot see.

Dr. Holland C. Ford of NASA's Space Telescope Science Institute stated appears to mark the position of a black hole, which he believes powers M51's intense radiation. "God has shown us exactly where the black hole is," said Dr. Ford, a comment which is reminiscent of Dr. Smoot's observations about God two months earlier.

29. "In the Glow of Cosmic Discovery: A Physicist Ponders God and Fame," *New York Times,* May 5, 1992, p.C1, C9.

30. As noted in Chapter II, in 1965, Penzias, together with Robert Wilson, discovered the faint microwave background radiation in the universe, an effect attributed to the explosion of the "Big Bang" fireball. This important discovery earned them a Nobel Prize.

31. "Despite New Data, Mysteries of Creation Persist," *New York Times,* May 12, 1992, p. C10.

Professor Jastrow, a self-styled "agnostic" in religious matters, closes his *God and the Astronomers* with a parable that conveys the discomforting impact upon the scientist of new findings and thinking in science. The parable, which I have taken the liberty of revising somewhat, follows: Scientists, the men of reason, labor at their blackboards and in sophisticated laboratories to advance the frontiers of their profession. Pursuing understanding, they grope their way up the sheer granite mountain of investigation, inch by inch. Finally, as their fingers are able to grasp the ledge of the summit and their eyes are able to peer over it, they are astonished to see a group of theologians already comfortably settled on the mountaintop!

Judaism maintains that Jewish theologians were the first to occupy such high ground. In the following three chapters, I develop how, centuries before modern science, Jewish theologians had dealt with and contributed to the fulfillment of man's yearning to discover basic truths and life's meaning.

7

The Enlightenment and the Jews

". . .that there must be a God could come to anyone who thoughtfully contemplates nature and the heavens . . . [however] . . . by merely looking at the heavens and earth, man will never discover the Divine law which governs his task in this world."

— Rabbi S. R. Hirsch, commentary to *Psalms* 19[1]

1. Hirsch, Samson Raphael, *The Psalms*, New York: Feldheim Publishers, Ltd., 1960, p. 34.

Despite the lofty spiritual mission with which Judaism is entrusted, it looks admiringly, not condescendingly, upon the scientific establishment and its startling accomplishments. Nor does it take satisfaction in noting certain impassable limits which science has recently encountered; Judaism simply views these as signposts irecting man to turn to the non-physical ld in the search for significance and purpose.

Judaism always has encouraged man to "pursue wisdom, to deduce one matter from another," taking care to distinguish conjecture from truth. Science is highly appreciated as a branch of the intellect which has contributed significantly to the welfare and knowledge of humanity. The science of the stars, Maimonides once wrote, "is an exceedingly glorious science,"[2] and again, that the "natural sciences" of physics, botany and zoology, as well as logic, are invaluable for those who wish to "study and know the truth."[3]

Like Maimonides, a number of other outstanding medieval rabbinical figures were physicians as well as philosophers. And Torah

2. Twersky, Isadore, *A Maimonides Reader*, New York: Behrman House Inc., 1972, p. 466.

3. Maimon, Moshe ben, *Guide for the Perplexed*, New York: Dover Publications, 1:34.

luminaries Bachya Ibn Pakuda, Ibn Ezra, Hisdai Crescas and Don Isaac Abarbanel wrote extensively on the elevated levels of knowledge and faith attainable through investigation and reason. By no means does Judaism ask that we close off the human mind from scientific inquiry.

Still, Judaism points out that the study of the physical world alone gives us knowledge *about* God, but not *of* God. Rabbi Joseph B. Soloveitchik, one of the highly regarded scholars of recent times, defined the difference: Study of the cosmic order provides secular knowledge, while the study of Torah Judaism's sacred texts and their interpretations provides divine wisdom. Together, science and Torah enable us to approach knowledge of God Himself.[4]

Despite Judaism's towering spiritual strength, however, it was discouragingly affected by the growth in eighteenth- and nineteenth-century Europe of discrimination, the sciences, secular humanism and the thirst for political freedom and social acceptance. As described in Chapter I, the Emancipation philosophers called for the dethroning of God and the replacement of religion with rational thought. Judaism, caught in the currents of the new philosophy and overt persecution, soon found its integrity and fundamental beliefs being eroded, with many of its adherents relinquishing their attachment to traditional Judaism.

In the late eighteenth century, there arose in Germany a new form of Judaism, called Reform. It was intended by its founders to replace the three-millennia-old creed of their fathers. This replacement did not succeed, but for half a century historical Judaism was enfeebled in its influence and growth by the powerful surge of the Reform movement in Germany, and later in the United States.[5]

Many Jews of that day reasoned that their failure to obtain social and political acceptance, with all their enticing benefits, stemmed from the differences in form, content and ritual between Judaism and Christianity. They felt that if these differences could be eliminated, modified or at least blurred, Jews would gain much wider acceptance by the gentile world.

At the outset, the leaders of Reform initiated changes which

---

4. Besdin, Abraham R., *Reflections of the Rav* (adapted from lectures of Joseph B. Soloveitchik), Jerusalem: World Zionist Org., 1981, pp. 71-72.

5. As Henry Steele Commanger commented in his *Empire of Reason*, Europe devised, but America realized, the Age of Enlightenment.

were limited to ritual and prayer, to make them more in keeping with the customs of their neighbors and with the liberal, rational views that were sweeping Europe. Later, in the 1820's and '30's, family laws respecting marriage and conversion, obligations such as the donning of phylacteries and head coverings, Sabbath observance, the prohibition of intermarriage, and kosher food all were considered outmoded and no longer requiring adherence.

Man alone, declared Reform, had the right and duty, within his honest convictions and intelligent selection, to retain Torah standards that were worthwhile and to discard those not in keeping with new experience and contemporary good sense. The Principle of Determinism, already entrenched in science, influenced European Jews to believe only in what was "certain," provable and rational in religion. More significant than any single rejection of the basic principles of historical Judaism was the rejection by Reform of the beliefs in revelation and in the divinity of the Torah. The Torah, it was asserted, was written not by God but by "inspired" men *about* God.

Jewish history has demonstrated that whenever Judaism became seriously threatened, special personalities of the time skillfully met the crises and strengthened their coreligionists as to Judaism's historic mission and chosenness under the Covenant of Sinai. Two such extraordinary men arose in the twelfth century, and with their classic writings succeeded in fortifying their fellow Jews: Judah Halevi by way of his great *Kuzari*, a time when Jewish imitation of Spanish culture dangerously undermined Jewish tradition and observance, and Moses Maimonides through his famous *Epistle to Yemen*, at a time when persecution of Jews raged in Yemen. So too, in the mid-nineteenth century, when Western European Jewry lay in great disarray as a result of Reform's offensive, there came onto the scene the resolute and fearless German rabbinical figure, Samson Raphael Hirsch. His strength stemmed from brilliant essays and orations which deflected and disproved the reasoning of those Enlightenment spokesmen who derided the teachings of Torah and enticed German Jews to break with the beliefs and traditions of centuries past. His eloquent and prolific writings called for the preservation of what he termed the "historical Judaism" of Sinai.

Samson Raphael Hirsch was born in 1808. By the time the Reform fire-storm reached its zenith, he had already achieved a distinguished career in various prominent pulpits and as a famous author of outstanding religious works. In 1846 he was elected a member of the Moravian (Austrian) Senate. A few years later it was he who, before the Emperor Franz Josef, conveyed the appreciation of the Jewish community of Austria-Hungary for the granting of civil liberties to the Jewish citizenry of the empire. He was selected also by the Jewish leaders of the day to become the official author of a written defense of Jews and Judaism, prepared for submission to the Czarist government in an attempt to ameliorate its virulently anti-Semitic policies.

Yet, in 1848, over the very strong protestations of his famed Moravian synagogue, Hirsch unhesitatingly relinquished all of his influential posts in order to accept the relatively obscure position of rabbi in the beleaguered community of Frankfurt-am-Main. At that time there were but 150 Torah-observant Jewish families in the city. Yet, upon Hirsch's death in 1888 some forty years later, Frankfurt and a number of neighboring cities could boast of an astonishing increase in the number of observant Jews living in these communities, as well as in the growth of many Jewish activities, institutions and schools which flourished during his tenure.

Hirsch stressed over and over again his thesis that if we are to achieve contact with God we must do so through *both* the natural world and The Torah.

Hirsch pointed out that just as the natural world is the sole source of natural laws which order our physical lives, the Torah is the sole source of the moral law and legal provisions which govern our spiritual and ethical lives. Well-versed in experimental physics and the natural sciences from his studies at the University of Bonn, Hirsch explained that the laws of the natural world are discerned by man solely through his [sense] "impressions." In his illuminating commentary to *Numbers* 18:5, he made it clear that since these impressions are limited, we can detect and understand only so much; the truth they reveal is only a fraction of the whole truth. Ultimate knowledge can be discerned only through a combination of scientific investigation *and* the truths revealed by the Torah. Unless scientists take into account these truths and the deep knowledge which they convey, he asserted, scientists have "no guarantee that they are not deducing a dream from a dream."

Hirsch held that there is another critical difference between nature and Torah. In nature, he pointed out, we see grandiose evidence of God's presence in starry heavens, majestic mountains, and vast oceans. But from this physical evidence we cannot learn what God expects of us, what is His *will*. This will is revealed only through the Torah's commandments. Newton also had been firm in the belief that the universe demonstrated not only God's work but also His will, while almost all post-Newton scientists were convinced, in Einstein's words, that the only "reliable source of truth [lies] . . . in mathematical simplicity." Hirsch vehemently refuted such rationalism, asserting that such truths, standing alone, are incomplete and therefore unreliable.

The authentic source of truth and morality was the issue over which was fought the battle between Hirsch and the Reform and humanist advocates of Emancipation philosophy. The latter built much of their case upon the writings of Kant, who held that man's sole moral compass is his conscience. They held that morality must come from the free exercise of one's inner feelings, not from any other source, not even from God Himself. Kant condensed this view in one famous observation: "Two things fill the mind with ever-new and increasing wonder and awe. . .: the starry heaven above me and the moral law within me."[6]

Hirsch never questioned, he even championed, the idea that a Jew will incline towards what is upright and noble. But no human, he went on to explain, can define with precision what is upright and noble without divine parameters. Only God can specify the standards of moral values. History has often and lamentably disproved the value of reliance upon man's conscience as the final determinant of morality. Not too distant from Hirsch's own Frankfurt are the five thousand square miles which comprise the district of Alsace-Lorraine. For over three hundred years the soil of this district has been soaked with the blood of tens of thousands of casualties resulting from wars fought there, in which each side, in each battle, was convinced of its moral rectitude.

Over and over again, Hirsch exhorted his fellow Jews to return to the revelation at Sinai as the original source of Jewish law, morality and mission. In writing after writing, he reiterated that the Torah which was revealed at Sinai is the keystone of the Jewish nation, its moral foundation, its legal constitution and the final arbiter in all

---

6. Kant, Immanuel, *Critique of Practical Reason*, Chicago: University of Chicago Press, 1949, conclusion.

things. The Torah is the *sine qua non* of Judaic belief and destiny, he emphasized, and through the Torah we became the possessors and disseminators of mankind's finest value system.

Still, one wonders how this conviction can be transmitted to those many thousands of Jewish men and women in America who are not affiliated with any Jewish institution, or who have drifted far away from Judaism, or who may regard themselves as agnostics or secularists.

Is Sinai a fable, a legend, a symbol, as many Jews believe today, or did it actually take place?

8

Man Encounters God

"For ask now . . . since the day that God created man upon the earth . . . whether there has been any such thing as this great thing . . . Did a people ever hear the voice of God speaking out in the midst of the fire, as thou has heard, and lived?"

— *Deuteronomy* 4:32-5

"All of Jewish history only makes sense in terms of the validity of this Covenant [with God . . . at Mt. Sinai over 3,000 years ago]."

— Rabbi J. B. Soloveitchik[1]

1. Besdin, Abraham R., *Reflections of the Rav* (adapted from lectures of Joseph B. Soloveitchik), Jerusalem: World Zionist Org., 1981, p. 170.

Several times in earlier chapters I have emphasized what is a principal thrust of this book, namely that at Mt. Sinai the Jewish nation witnessed a supernatural phenomenon in the form of a divine Revelation which endowed Judaism with a uniqueness through which its adherents may gain revealing insights into life's significance. Thus, it becomes most necessary to consider whether this Revelation at Sinai took place. If it did not, a basic premise of this book falls away. And in a much wider sense, the divine origin and authenticity of Judaism would be compromised. Our religion then would be anchored much like all differing religions, either in imitation of still other religions, or in a set of beliefs designed by man rather than God.

If Sinai *did* take place, however, it was surely the most important single event in the history of mankind. It marked the moment of the appearance of the *mysterium tremendum*, which filled the early morning skies with celestial fire and thunder. Never before or since had God's voice been heard or had His Majesty descended to earth to seal a covenant with a people. There, on the flaming summit of the mountain, the Ten Commandments were proclaimed, easily the most significant 172 words in history. There, the element of meaning to our Jewish lives took root.

But does this not strain one's credulity? Most Jews who espouse the rational philosophy of the Emancipation assert that Sinai is merely a metaphorical account of inspired but mortal authorship. We support the moral teachings of the Ten Commandments, they maintain, but it is childish to accept literally the account of an unearthly Revelation by God. Judaism replies that such views do not grant sufficient credit to the spiritual and mental potential of the Jew to rise above his transient creaturehood and deal with the supermundane. After all, Judaism asserts, man is able to comprehend highly advanced abstractions and even to conceive of a "soul" and regions of the human spirit beyond our earthly moorings.

But there is a more formidable case for the authenticity of Sinai. In the late eleventh century, there was born in Catholic Spain Judaism's greatest poet, Judah Halevi. He was destined also to earn an equally significant place in Jewish history for his literary masterpiece, *The Kuzari*, subtitled "An Argument for the Faith of Israel."

The *Kuzari* was written against the backdrop of the contest between Christian and Moslem forces for the control of Spain. For over two centuries the Jewish population in Spain had been wedged precariously between the warring armies of the Crescent and the Cross. In his youth and early manhood, Judah Halevi identified with a Jewish "aristocracy" which had evolved from a social emancipation movement within Spain. But as he grew older, he came to recognize that the Jewish courtier's view of Judaism was shallow and unduly influenced by Spanish culture and morality, similar to the erosion of Judaism by the Reform Movement six hundred years later in Germany.

To counter this decline in adherence to the traditions and beliefs of Judaism, Halevi labored twenty years to produce his classic *Kuzari*. It presents one of Judaism's most convincing and eloquent presentations of the content and divine origin of the Faith of Israel.

Among the several basic themes of the *Kuzari*, and one of its most widely quoted, is that of the trustworthiness of the Revelation. Halevi's assessment of that awesome event is that its occurrence is "irrefutable." Why? Because, he responded, it unfolded within the sight and hearing of the entire congregation that left Egypt, some two and one-half million men, women and children. Never before (and in person, probably not since) had so many people collectively witnessed an occurrence within their immediate sight and hearing.

Halevi described the setting which surrounded Mt. Sinai: ". . .Overwhelming phenomena, lightning, thunder, earthquake, fire. . ." Out of these "grand and lofty spectacles [the people] heard the Ten Commandments, the source and foundation of the Law." The result, he wrote, was that everyone "became convinced that the matter proceeded directly from God. Thus the belief in the Law . . . was firmly established in the mind."[2]

A century after Judah Halevi, Maimonides, in his famous *Epistle to Yemen,* restated the certainty that the Sinai occurrence took place: "Remember, my coreligionists, that this great, incomparable and unique historical event is attested by the best of evidence. For never before or since has a whole nation witnessed a revelation from God or beheld His splendor."[3]

The Five Books of Moses record God's own explanation for His having spoken on Sinai "face to face" with Moses: "So that the people will hear when I speak with you . . . [and] . . . they will believe forever." This belief was based not on wonders and miracles but on vision and sound.

This experience became the authentic link through which the Jew could believe in and establish virtually direct contact with God and His Torah. But God said "forever." How can such belief continue for all *post*-Revelation generations? After all, they did not physically participate in the unique "encounter" between the finite and the Infinite at Sinai; they did not hear God speak to Moses or experience the celestial spectacle of thunder and lightning.

Rabbi Soloveitchik pointed out in one of his essays that Jewish men and women have a "dual connection with the Master of the Universe, both as individuals and as the descendants of our forefathers."[4] Each of these connections was derived from the Sinai experience. But this encounter took place over three millennia ago on a remote mountain in the Sinai Desert. How can a thinking person be certain today that it actually occurred?

Judaism replies, as noted previously, that the encounter was wit-

2. *Jewish Philosophers: Philo, Sadye Gaon and Judah Halevy*, Atheneum Publishers, 1972, pp. 44-45.

3. *A Maimonides Reader*, transl. by Twersky, Isadore, New York: Behrman House, Inc., 1972, p. 447.

4. Peli, Pinchas H., *Soloveitchik on Repentance,* Paulist Press, New York: 1982, p. 215.

nessed by over two million Jews who stood at the foot of Mt. Sinai on that memorable morning. But this generation passed away in the desert. What witnesses remained afterward? The answer is that our very survival, our very historical continuation, bear witness to the encounter. Hence, millions upon millions of Jews who have lived or who are alive today are the collective body of witnesses, if you will, to the reality of the encounter with God and to the trustworthiness of the encounter having taken place.

Indeed, *Deuteronomy* 29:13-14 emphasizes that God's covenant was made with all future generations of His people: "Neither with you only do I make this covenant and this oath; but . . .also with him that is not here with us this day." This concept has been acknowledged by Jews throughout the generations, to this very day.[5] Implicit in this is the recognition by Jews past and present that we are at once the inheritors and the continuators of the divine covenant forged by God with the Jewish nation at the giving of the Torah at Sinai.

In his excellent article "Fundamentalism Reconsidered,"[6] Rabbi Dr. Jonathan Sacks, Chief Rabbi of the British Empire, discusses how the words of the Torah become contemporary in utterance to each and every generation in Jewish history. This is so, Sacks points out, because the Torah is read differently by the Jewish people than by any other people (especially those of the higher criticism movement), for the Jews read it *covenantally,* whereas others read it *academically,* in accordance with the principle of historicism.

In our final chapter, I treat at some length the recent bestseller, *The Closing of the American Mind*, by the late Allan Bloom. In his book, Bloom singled out Cornell University history professor Carl Becker as having brought about in his famous work, *The Declaration of Independence*, the current version of historicism.

Historicism was defined by Bloom as the approach that ". . .all thought is essentially related to and cannot transcend its own times. . ." It views past, traditional ideas and values as without real

5. Such an acknowledgment was made recently by Shulamit Aloni, an Israeli political figure who is a confirmed humanist-secularist and who has consistently and vociferously fought against any governmental policies favoring traditional Jewish belief or observance. Nevertheless, despite this highly activist, anti-traditional and bitterly contested stance, upon the occasion of the opening of the 13th Israeli Knesset (1992), Aloni acceded that "we are all one Nation, weaned on the same 3,000-year-old tradition. *We were all at Mount Sinai*" (emphasis added).

6. Sacks, Jonathan, *Jewish Action*, Summer 5751/1991, p. 21.

connection to the present; historical writings are interpreted as to their meaning at the time of their origin and are usually seen as out of keeping with the emergent ideas and newer beliefs of contemporary times.

In distinct contrast to the academic approach, Sacks points out, is the *covenantal* approach towards the reading of the Torah by the Jewish people — "the community of the Covenant." The divine author of the Torah, Sacks stresses, intended for the words He spoke at Sinai to be read and adhered to by all future members of the Jewish nation who "are not here with us this day." To read the Torah covenantally, Sacks continues, is to link Sinai with the here-and-now, to cause the reader "to be lifted on the wings of the Divine presence" and to "enter into its words not as they were addressed to the wilderness generations, but to me, here, now."

In this context, Sacks emphasizes, we can see the frightening predictions of the Torah coming to pass in the awesome realities of the Crusades, the Inquisition, the pogroms, the Holocaust — as well as in the fulfillment of "the promise of the ingathering" realized in the emergence of the State of Israel.

In his article, Sacks quotes from a work by the Jewish philosopher Leo Strauss, who fled Nazi Germany and became a professor of political science at the University of Chicago (where, interestingly, he greatly influenced the thinking of Allan Bloom). Sacks writes that Strauss made the "very telling point" that in its attack upon religion, the Enlightenment did not directly confront the issue of Revelation. During this period, in Sacks' words, traditional belief in revelation remained "neither refuted nor refutable." Continuing, Sacks quotes Strauss: "For that reason, Orthodoxy, unchanged in its essence, was able to outlast the attack of the Enlightenment and all later attacks and retreats."[7]

Strauss' observation thus provides an additional clue as to why, despite three centuries of assault by Enlightenment philosophers, Jewish belief in the genuineness of Revelation remains intact and undiminished to this day.

There is still another clarifying element of the uninterrupted belief of the Jewish people in the authenticity of the Revelation. This element became realized through the consistent retelling by Jewish

7. Strauss, Leo, *Philosophy and Law*, Philadelphia: Jewish Publication Society, 1987, p. 11.

parents to Jewish children of the happening at Sinai. In hearing the account and passing it on to our own children, we freshly and vicariously relive the Sinai experience of our ancestors. This is accomplished not by any Far Eastern mysticism or self-hypnosis, but simply through the power of our trust in the truth of unbroken Judaic verbal transmission.

> *Oh God, with our ears we have heard*
> *Our fathers have told us of the work You did*
> *In their days, in the days of antiquity*
>
> (*Psalms* 44:21)

Our sages tell us that those who witnessed the splitting of the Red Sea were so elevated by it that even the maidservants experienced more spirituality than the prophet Ezekiel did in his famous vision. Fathers and mothers of such ethical standing can be relied upon not to have distorted or fabricated the very first verbal transmission of the momentous event they witnessed. It is most probable that had Sinai not occurred exactly as recorded in the Five Books of Moses, many among the two and one-half million witnesses would have refuted or corrected the first oral description of the event at its inception. Yet Jewish history, noted for its frank recounting even of the unfavorable, does not record a single, reliable factual contradiction of Sinai.

It is also noteworthy that no other religion has denied what took place at Sinai or has claimed for itself a supernatural experience even approaching Sinai's magnitude. To be sure, Mohammedanism recounts Mohammed's ascent to heaven on his steed, but who witnessed it? And Christianity's account of the "rising from the dead" was allegedly seen only by three people.

To this very day, we are all familiar with the Jewish tradition of verbal transmission, wherein the father recounts to his children the Exodus from Egypt at the Passover Seder table or describes the victories of the Maccabeans when the Chanuka candles are lit. It simply is not plausible to question the reliability of such accounts because it is not in the nature of parents to pass on to their children fabrications of events with such sacred content and historical value.

We know from historical sources that both the *Mishna* and *Gemara* [comprising the Talmud's many large-sized volumes] originally were transmitted orally. Indeed, much of what we know of the history of civilization has come down to us in the form of oral transmission. Very little ancient written historical material has survived destruction and disintegration. Many gaps in our knowledge of events as recent as four hundred years ago have been filled by historians solely through the word-of-mouth accounts passed on from generation to generation.

Thus, we know a great deal about the history-making voyages of Sir Martin Frobisher in the sixteenth century. Commissioned by Queen Elizabeth I to discover the fabled Northwest Passage, he probed much of Baffin Island and the waters lying northeast of Canada during his three voyages, attempting to forge through the Passage. No written journals had recorded Frobisher's first attempt, and most of what we know of that first voyage comes from the 1862 research of American historian Charles Frances Hall. Hall had but a single source: the native residents of Baffin Island, who had preserved the details of Frobisher's three visits to the island through verbal accounts from father to son, which, by 1862, had spanned 275 years.

In his book *The European Discovery of America*, Samuel Eliot Morison writes of Hall's two-year sojourn on Baffin to learn the native Eskimos' language and to record their oral history. Their transmission proved to match *almost perfectly* with the dates of Frobisher's sailings and the number and description of his ships as recorded in British Admiralty records. The previously unknown fate of five sailors whom Frobisher was compelled to abandon on the first voyage was disclosed by the natives' verbal account to Hall. In 1943, aerial photographs and on-site investigation also confirmed the accuracy of the natives' detailed description of the camp which the sailors had built while fruitlessly awaiting rescue. This matching compatibility of facts is rated by Morison as "an amazing example of the reliability of oral tradition."[8]

Similar verification of French exploration on the west coast of North America has come down to us through a number of word-of-mouth accounts by North American Indians such as the Tlingits, who lived, and still live, on the coast of present-day Alaska and Western Canada.

Several years back, a national magazine carried an article by a

8. Morison, Samuel Eliot, *The European Discovery of America: The Northern Voyages, 500-1600*, New York: Oxford University Press, 1971, p. 526.

man who, sixty years earlier, had interviewed a ninety-five-year-old Civil War veteran on Memorial Day. The veteran regaled the then-teen-age reporter with an account of having seen Abraham Lincoln at Gettysburg. As the youngster thanked the veteran for a fascinating story, the latter replied that he understood why the boy was thrilled. For, he explained, when he was eight years old, he was brought by his grandfather to a town meeting honoring a ninety-three-year-old veteran of the Revolutionary War, who thrilled the meeting with stories of having served at Valley Forge under General Washington. Here we see a chain of verbal history that stretches over two hundred years, the veracity of which few of us would have cause to doubt.

But how can we Jews reach back 3,300 years in time? The above verbal historical accounts of the Frobisher voyage and the Civil War veteran can serve as models to demonstrate how we can be chronologically transported from the past to the present. But there is still another avenue for such a return to the past, in the form of "on-the-ground" stimuli of recall. Thus, in the past few years, archaeological finds in the City of David have provided us with an abundance of striking artifacts and vivid coloration which make the reign of King David come very much alive and make it appear to be part of our recent, rather than our ancient, past. These finds have included the uncovering of the monumental stairway to David's palace, as well as a number of nearby residences of his contemporaries. Clay seals have also been found in the city's remains, bearing the names of men who are specifically mentioned in Scripture and who lived during the reign of King David's son, Solomon.

We recall King David's direct and close linkage with the Revelation, through his temporary custody three millennia ago of the Ark containing the Tablets given to the Jewish people at Mt. Sinai. Yet, extensive contemporary City of David explorations have brought to light such a vivid picture of David and his era that time appears to melt away, and one tends to view David more as a beloved, familiar figure of just-past history rather than of centuries ago. As a result, Jews who see David in this telescoped time frame ask: Can we not, then, span the gap between our generation and King David's (as well as the three- to four-century gap between David and Sinai) through our confidence in the trustworthiness of our ancestors' father-to-son accounts of Sinai's occurrence, just as we accept the accounts of the Baffin Island natives and that of the Civil War veteran?

Supplementing the feeling of having "been there," which oral testimony evokes in us, is the element of "memory." When we view what archaeologists have exposed to date in the City of David, graphic memories are evoked of King David's comings and goings and of the young Solomon descending the stairway to (today's still regularly flowing) Gihon Spring, there to be anointed as king upon his father David's death. We experience a near-actual present encounter with our ancient past. We stir the memories that have shaped our Jewish history and destiny.

In Israel especially, such recalls to memory proliferate; the country is a virtual time capsule of recalled and reenacted events. We experience such an event while witnessing the annual kindling of the Chanuka oil lamps by the Chief Rabbi at the Western Wall, the very site where, in 164 B.C.E., the victorious Maccabeans rekindled the Temple's menorah, which had been extinguished by the tyrannical legions of Antiochas IV. In that era, the third Hasmonean battle in the Valley of Ayalon (now a peaceful sunflower and cotton-growing site which one passes while driving from Jerusalem to Tel Aviv) was almost a reenactment of the battle Joshua fought in that valley one thousand years earlier, when the sun was held back. It was in that valley also, over three thousand years after Joshua, that the inexperienced Israeli Haganah troops fought the Jordanians for control of the strategic former British police station that stood on the crest of the valley.

Any tourist to Israel who stands on the summit of Masada can, without trying hard, see in his mind's eye the encampment of the Tenth Roman Legion spread out below, with its catapults and siege matériel menacingly placed on the famous ramp. Several years back, I had a "memory" experience while visiting a recently restored fourth- to fifth-century C. E. synagogue originally discovered in 1948 underneath an Arab home in Jericho, revealing an exquisite mosaic floor still in a near-pristine state. One member of our group suggested that we avail ourselves of the opportunity to pray the afternoon service since there was a *minyan* of ten men present. We did so, and I recall thinking that it may well have been the first time a service was held in that synagogue during the past sixteen centuries.

Step into a narrow doorway off the main square of the Jewish Quarter in Jerusalem and you find yourself, as the plaque on the wall correctly describes, "back two thousand years to the Upper City of Jerusalem in the Herodian period." View the reconstructed site, on a lower level, of a large urban expanse containing a number of splendid homes of the Jerusalem priestly nobility. Breathtaking remains are visible of spacious courtyards and salons, stone utensils, furniture, frescoes, and mosaic floors, most of it in excellent, some in mint, condition. Under a protective plastic dome is a charred timber left in place where it fell after the Romans set fire to the city in 71 C.E.

For an hour or so, you are transported back in time, and with just a bit of imagination you are living in the first century of the Common Era. You stand just paces from the site of the Temple Mount itself, where a newly excavated underground passageway brings you to a special point in the Western Wall, behind which was the very place where the Ark of the Covenant rested. This is the site from which, Judaic tradition tells us, God's presence has never departed.

Memories. History. It is said that Napoleon, riding through a Jewish quarter, noticed a group of Jews sitting on the floor of a synagogue on the eve of Tisha b'Av, the ninth day of the Jewish month of Av, mourning the destruction of the First and the Second Temples, both of which occurred on that identical day of the Jewish calendar. When the scene and its remembrance were explained to him, Napoleon is said to have remarked: "These people perform the impossible. They recreate history."

It is as if the Revelation on a mountaintop over 3,000 years ago left within the souls of Jews in all generations a glow of belief in God's existence and in the trustworthiness of revelation, comparable to the faint glow of radiation which Penzias and Wilson discovered had been left in the universe by the original fireball of the "Big-Bang."

And then, there is that rarest of encounters — the inexplicable sensation of having felt God's very Presence nearby, of having been touched by Him. Not in a fantasy or dream but in a real honest-to-goodness experience. Perhaps we do not share it with anyone for fear of being labeled a mystic or a dreamer. Still, in our hearts and minds, we *know* that it was real.

But whether through personal encounter, covenantal linkage or historical memory, the reverberations of Sinai remain forever, for every Jew to detect if he listens acutely — even when God seems silent and hidden.

9

The Case for Judaism

"In spite of Bolingbroke and Voltaire, I will insist that the Hebrews have done more to civilize men . . . [and] . . . have influenced the affairs of mankind more and more happily than any other Nation."

— John Adams, second President of the United States[1]

"Man was thus given the power to influence the world and its creatures in any manner his free will desires."

— Rabbi Moshe Chaim Luzzatto (1707-1746)[2]

"[Freedom of the human will] . . . is a question which each one must dwell upon for himself if he thinks seriously on what the meaning of life may be."

— Max Planck, physicist (1858-1947)[3]

---

1. Letter to F. A. Van der Kemp, 1808, Pennsylvania Historical Society.

2. Luzzatto, Moshe Chaim, *The Way of God*, trans. by Aryeh Kaplan, Jerusalem: Feldheim Publications Ltd., 1977, p. 79.

3. Planck, Max, *The New Science*, New York: Meridian Books, 1959, p. 64.

Judaism maintains, it was noted at the end of Chapter VI, that in the universal race to discover reality, Jewish theologians have held the high ground over the proponents of science, secularism and humanitarianism. What support is there for this somewhat grandiose claim?

Considerable support comes from scientists themselves. In recent decades, outstanding scientists have asserted publicly that through reason and our five senses alone, without spiritual attachment, we are unable to comprehend fully the world in which we live. In an important speech delivered in 1937, Max Planck pointed out that when the scientist, through sense impressions, measurements and inductive reasoning, tries to "approach . . . to God and to the order which He has established in the universe," he finds that this approach is an "unattainable goal," because, Planck stressed, "reason cannot apprehend God." However, he goes on, to "the religious man," God is apprehended "immediately and primarily."[4]

Still, if one grants that fuller understanding of the order of the world is achievable only through a non-physical "approach to God," upon what grounds do I base a principal theme of this book, that among other thought systems and other religions Judaism appears most able to part, albeit to a limited degree, the curtain

4. Planck, Max, *The New Science,* New York: Random Books, 1959. p. 72, Also see Barth, Aron, *The Perennial Quest,* Jerusalem: World Zionist Org., 1984, Appendix A.

which separates man from the mysteries of life?

The "case" for Judaism's distinction in dealing with this mysterious realm rests upon the remarkable elements which constitute the foundation of the Jewish religion. Among the most important of these are the concept of one God, the Revelation at Mt. Sinai, the continuation of divine guidance through the Prophets, the confirmations of the authenticity of Jewish history and writings, Judaism's enlightened code of laws, the against-the-odds survival of the Jewish people, man's freedom of choice and man's partnership with God as a "co-creator."

To best understand why and how these various elements invest Judaism with the ability to penetrate the baffling questions pertaining to our existence, we should view Judaism "in the round," that is, from a *composite* of its past, present and future.

A helpful illustration of such panoramic viewing can be found off the coast of Alaska. In the icy Bering Strait between Siberia and Alaska lie two islands which straddle the International Date Line. To the west of the Line lies Big Diomede Island, under Russian sovereignty. To the east of the Line lies Little Diomede Island, state of Alaska. Only two miles of water separate the two islands, which belong to different continents, Asia and North America.

In recent years, Russia transferred all of Big Diomede Island residents to the Siberian mainland. Until then, the inhabitants of both islands, part of an extended family, would meet at the International Date Line to celebrate holidays or family events and to barter Marlboro cigarettes for Russian vodka. If, at such a gathering, one of the natives sat in his skin boat and anchored exactly on the Date Line, facing directly towards the North Pole, he was in the time frame of "today." If he turned his head ninety degrees to the right, towards Little Diomede, he was looking into "yesterday." If he turned his head ninety degrees to the left, towards Big Diomede, he was peering into "tomorrow."

In viewing Judaism "in the round" we see that to the "yesterday" of Jewish history belong the Revelation at Sinai and its proclamation of a single God, the authenticity of Jewish history and writings, the Age of Prophecy and civilization's earliest democratic and humanitarian codes. To both yesterday and "today" belong the unfolding of the miracle of Jewish survival and man's legacy of freedom of choice. Within all three streams of time — yesterday, today and "tomorrow" — we find man's partnership with God as a "co-creator." (This element is treated separately and at length in the last chapter.)

Let us begin this panoramic "Case for Judaism" with those components of Judaism which emanate from the "yesterday" of our history:

Mount Sinai and the One and Only God

Foremost among the credentials of Judaism is the exclusive witnessing by the Jewish people of the most momentous event in the history of mankind, God's Revelation at Sinai. It was there established for all time that there *is* a God, that He is the only "real" Reality and that His Torah is the Jew's moral universe. It was at Sinai also that God entered into an eternal Covenant with our people. This compact established that the Jewish nation was to be God's treasured and protected people forever. Reciprocally, the people undertook to fulfill God's will, as expressed in His Torah, in order that it might develop into a "light unto the nations of the world."

Sinai was the second (the exodus from Egypt being the first) of the two most widely viewed encounters that have ever taken place between the finite and the Infinite. Notwithstanding some detractors, the veracity of the stirring events at Sinai has never been challenged by any of the great, differing religions which derive from Judaism. Nor has the continuum of the verbal verification of Sinai ever been broken during the past three millennia, even by such powerful forces as widespread Jewish dispersion, persecution or the many enticing ideologies which compete for the mind and heart of the Jew. Throughout the generations, Sinai has been the source of Jewish hope, strength and unity.

Judaism was also the first belief system to present to the world the concept of a God Who is at once the Sovereign of the fiery heavens as well as the God Who descended to earth at Sinai to give His Torah to His chosen people. He is both the God of Justice and also a caring, personal Friend who is the "Father of orphans."

He is neither the detached, unapproachable God of other religions nor the impersonal, mechanical "force" of the rational scientist. It is only the God of Israel to whom the Jew can turn "when my cares are many within me. . ." Though Master and Judge of the universe, He is at the same time the God of love and mercy Who has placed a consoling arm around past generations of Jews in distress.

Still, it is most important to recognize that the foregoing divergent qualities, stern justice and compassionate mercy, in no way are regarded by Judaism as demonstrating the existence of a duality in God. On the contrary, He is perceived in Judaism as a limitless and transcendent Unity, best described in the declaration familiar to Jews everywhere: "Hear O Israel, the Lord is our God, the Lord is One!"

This affirmation proclaims that God is truly unique, that there is but one God Who is both near and far and Who encompasses the universe but is not encompassed by it.

In this last decade of the twentieth century, many young, bright scientists have devoted their efforts to the search for a single scientific law that will unite all the laws of the physical universe. Among the most outstanding of the contemporary researchers is 1979 Nobel Prize winner Steven Weinberg, who aptly described the elevated nature of this search when he observed, in his book *The First Three Minutes*, that "the effort to understand the universe is one of the very few things that lifts human life a little above the level of farce. . ."[5] In Weinberg's view, today's scientists are gaining steadily on the elusive goal of universal understanding.

Yet, in the recently published *Theories of Everything*, University of Sussex astronomer John D. Barrow questions whether that goal can ever be achieved. This intriguing, informative book presents and analyzes eight "essential ingredients"[6] which the author feels need to be fully explored and understood in the search for a scientific formulation which could combine "all the laws of Nature."

One of Barrow's eight "essential ingredients" is that of the initial conditions which existed at the beginning of the universe and which influenced the course of its development. These conditions, he writes, are the "most uncertain aspect of our knowledge." They "remain always partially within the realm of philosophy and theology."

In the light of the "metaphysical consequences" of cosmic initial conditions, Barrow finds himself asking, "If there are special initial

---

5. Weinberg, Steven, *The First Three Minutes*, London: Fontana Paperbacks, 1984, p. 149.

6. This and all other direct quotations or paraphrasings of John D. Barrow which follow are taken from the pages of Johen D. Barrow, *Theories of Everything: The Quest for Ultimate Explanation*, New York: Oxford Univ. Press, 1991.

conditions which start the Universe upon the course that leads to the present, what is it that selects those rather than any other starting conditions?"

With this question, Barrow highlights the sticking point inherent not only in the theory of how the universe evolved but also in Darwin's Theory of Evolution: Namely, what force originated and powers all evolutionary processes?

In view of this and other apparently unreachable explanations, Barrow concludes with the observation that "no Theory of Everything can ever provide total insight." Judaism concurs in this conclusion, for Judaism holds that only in God can total knowledge of everything be found.

The Authenticity of Jewish History and Writings

The believing Jew is fully confident of the Bible's veracity because its contents are confirmed by the historically uncontradicted testimony of those who witnessed the Revelation at Sinai, a witnessing that has been transmitted through all subsequent generations down to the present. Thus, the committed Jew never questions that the Bible, consisting of the "Five Books of Moses," was given over to Moses directly by God and that these five Books are identical with those we possess today. The Jewish-Roman historian Flavius Josephus, in *Contra Apion*, records: ". . .how firmly we . . . [Jews] . . . have given credit to . . . [the Five Books of Moses] . . . is evident by what we do . . For we do not have an innumerable multitude of books disagreeing with one another as the Greeks have . . . For during so many ages as have already passed, no one has been so bold either to add to them or take anything from them or to make any changes in them; and if the occasion arises, willingly to die for them." [7]

But the validity of the Bible has not always been accepted in other times and by other peoples. In the "modern" era, the Enlightenment has exerted a strong, rationalistic influence upon the study and interpretation of the Bible. Baruch Spinoza (d. 1677) was among the leaders of this new approach. In his writings, he

7. Josephus, Flavius, *Contra Apion*, Book I, 5,6,7.

espoused radical criticism of the Bible, maintaining that it was of very questionable authorship and origin and that it contained multiple and significant differences and variations in style, language and chronology. Other prominent forerunners of biblical criticism were Hugo Grotius (17th century), Jean Astruc and Johann Eichhorn (18th century).

Out of the thinking of these early personalities there arose what came to be known as "higher" biblical criticism, a system which analyzed the text, source, dating, historicity and authenticity of biblical literature, particularly the Five Books of Moses (the "Pentateuch"). Astruc was the first to propose that *Genesis* actually was composed of two parallel "documents," a concept which was built upon and elaborated early in the nineteenth century by de Wette and Vatke.

In the mid-nineteenth century, K. H. Graf further refined the de Wette-Vatke "documentary" hypothesis, and out of his work grew what came to be known as the "documentary theory." Instead of two documents, it listed four (thereafter designated as documents "J," "E," "P" and "D") and claimed these as the primary sources of the Bible's narrative. Initially, most English and German scholars (among them Schrader and Riehm) opposed Graf's thesis, but mainly on technical grounds relating to the order and dating of the documents.

It was at this point that the most influential figure in higher criticism made his entry. He was Julius Wellhausen (1844-1918), German professor of Oriental studies at Halle, Marburg and, from 1892 on, at Göttingen. With Graf's thesis as his beginning thrust, Wellhausen proceeded to rise to the leadership of the higher criticism movement, mainly through the influence of his famous *Prolegomena to the History of Ancient Israel* (1878).

The *Prolegomena* catalogued earlier baseless views of the claimed falsification of the Bible and added many new ones. These claims, in essence, asserted that the Bible's content is the pure invention of priests and scribes who lived in the fifth century B.C.E., the era of the Prophet Ezra. These men were held to have falsely and cunningly described imaginary people and events and then "back-entered" them into the text in order to make them appear genuine.

The book launched powerful attacks on respected past and present authorities whose views differed from Wellhausen's. It set out numerous iconoclastic interpretations of the Bible, couched in unabashed irreverence. It was his daring use of every possible device to establish his inventive, *a priori* conclusions that brought the *Prolegomena* its notoriety and, paradoxically, induced even many of the most intelligent and investigative biblical scholars to swallow its contents and sing its praises for the next three-quarters of a century.

The first and primary subject of investigation which Wellhausen treated was his hypothesis of "centralized worship." It is important to note that Wellhausen wrote in the *Prolegomena* (p. 368) that he rested his *entire* case of higher criticism on this hypothesis. In brief, it flatly denied divine revelation as the source and force of the religion of the Israelites and claimed that Judaic "worship and religiosness" (p. 255) did not arise until shortly before the Babylonian exile in 586 B.C.E. The laws of the Judaic religion, he maintained, were first written after the exile, in the form of the "P" (Priestly Code) document and Chronicles.

This Wellhausen reconstruction of biblical history revolved about the famous incident of the discovery in 621 B.C.E. of "the book of the Law," found in the course of the restoration of the Temple during the reign of King Josiah (637-608 B.C.E.). Josiah was the grandson of King Mannaseh, who reigned for fifty-five years, longer than any other Jewish monarch. This reign encompassed the darkest and most idolatrous period in Israelite history. Under the influence of the despotic and cruel Mannaseh, nearly every previous Judaic religious practice was obliterated.

Small wonder, then, that by the time Mannaseh's grandson Josiah ascended the throne, the holy writings and teachings of the Jewish faith had become nearly forgotten or disregarded. However, the fortuitous discovery of a hidden copy of an authentic scroll of the Torah served to greatly enhance the already-instituted efforts of Josiah to rid the nation of heathenistic places and practices (*Chronicles II* 34). He was convinced that the scroll was genuine and identical with the original book which set forth the beliefs of his forefathers.

Upon the proclamation of the Prophetess Huldah that only a return of the people to the practices of its ancestors could avert widespread punishment, a quiet revolution occurred. Josiah assembled the people in one place, and in the sight and hearing of the entire population, the "book of the Law" was read. The king undertook that henceforth he and the people would observe the neglected laws and commandments. Full service was restored in the Temple and religious practice was resumed as in previous generations (*Chronicles II* 35)

The *Prolegomena* rendered this account in Chronicles into an entirely different scenario. Until Josiah's time, Wellhausen dogmatized, the people worshipped at cultlike shrines and all religious observance was individualized and decentralized. It was upon this boldly unauthentic scenario that he erected what was to become, in addition to the documentary theory, the second principal foundation of higher criticism, namely, the "reconstruction of the history of Israel's religion." This theory viewed Israelite history as "evolutionary," i.e., as developing from a primitive cult-form to gradually higher levels of religious and social order.

Before long, this spurious theory of "evolution" and the documentary hypothesis dominated the higher criticism movement and received the support of almost the entire body of U.S. and European Bible scholars. But with the advent in the 1930's of independent archaeological written evidence substantially corroborating the Bible's account of early Israelite religion, together with more accurate textual interpretation over the last fifty years, Wellhausen's evolutionary theory has come unglued and virtually has ceased being one of higher criticism's principal foundations.

Wellhausen alleged that the ancient Hebrew society bore no resemblance to the pre-exile culture described in the Bible. Moreover, he wrote, the Bible could not have been set down in the ancient period because writing was unknown to the Hebrews in that era. (This assertion was later proved to be false, writing having existed as early as the Patriarchal period, centuries before Moses.)

In particular, the *Prolegomena* claimed that the Tabernacle never existed and even that the Temple (whose existence had not been questioned in previous ages) was "unhistorical." Israelite central worship, it was asserted, originated only after the discovery of the lost scroll and the eradication by Josiah of the many places of private worship. At that point in history, Wellhausen hypothesized, there first came into being the idea of a Hebrew "church," based on a "book" containing its laws. Thereafter, he continued, centralized worship was first instituted; until then the religion was formless, polytheistic and private, without a coherent theology and simply imitative of Canaanite and Philistine beliefs. Any picture to the contrary was challenged as the work of deceiving and misleading scribes and priests.

In truth, the picture drawn in the *Prolegomena* was itself extremely misleading and based on a serious and willful misreading of history. For centralized worship had existed as early as the time of the forty-year Israelite journey in the desert, a journey accompanied by the Tabernacle containing the Tablets handed down at Mt. Sinai. It is correct that during the fourteen-year-long conquest of the Land of Israel, private "high-places" (*bamoth*) were permitted (for only optional, personal, non-required offerings), but following this period, *bamoth* were prohibited because thereafter the Ark was housed in a stone, central Sanctuary at Shiloh (*Joshua* 18:1) for 369 years. During this long period, the Sanctuary at Shiloh was revered by the people as the centerpiece of Israelite religion.

Following the destruction of Shiloh by the Philistines, the Ark was moved to Nob and, later, Gibeon. In this fifty-seven-year period, it rested not in a Sanctuary of stone but in a structure fashioned of the boards and curtains which remained of the Tabernacle. Until such a stone Sanctuary was subsequently erected in Jerusalem, *bamoth* were again permitted. The Pentateuch makes it clear, however, that here again the only offerings which were permitted to be brought on such *bamoth* were "free-will" offerings. These were occasional *voluntary* offerings of thankfulness not required by law. All Torah-decreed offerings, such as Passover, first fruits and sin offerings, could *only* be brought at the *central* place of worship.

Following the Ark's stay at Gibeon, it was brought to Jerusalem by King David. After David's death, his son Solomon proceeded to construct the Temple in Jerusalem in the mid-tenth century B.C.E. At this point *bamoth* were barred for all time. With the completion of the Temple, its site in Jerusalem became and has remained ever since, even after its destruction, the singular symbol of Jewish worship and the epicenter of the faith of Israel.[8]

---

8. It is true that there had been periods in which scattered, idolatrous "high places" were built even when prohibited by law. These were erected through the influence of heretical priests and idolater figures such as Mannaseh who favored foreign religions, especially that of the Assyrians. Eventually, however, such "high places" were mainly stamped out by the reformations of King Hezekiah and later, King Josiah, to prevent the erosion of centrality of worship in the Temple, the divinely sanctified place which "Your God shall choose to rest His name there. . ." [*Deuteronomy* 12:11).

Jewish scholars had entered the higher criticism movement as early as the start of the nineteenth century. Among them were Geiger, who held *Leviticus* to be earlier than *Deuteronomy* but who also supported the belief that textual additions had been entered after the exile. Zunz, a student of de Wette, placed the Pentateuch's dating three centuries later than King Josiah's reign. Both Geiger and Zunz fully supported a documentary hypothesis even before it was refined by Graf. Within a year after the publication of the *Prolegomena*, however, the well-respected scholar Hoffman, writing in the German publication *Journal of Judaic Scholarship*, mounted a strong and skillful attack upon the book's theory regarding central worship. Hoffman relied on the interpretations of the Jewish Sages in shaping this rebuttal. (In this position, he was supported by a number of Christian scholars, among them Robertson and Sayce, and in later generations by Löhr and Staerk, the latter commenting that the long influence of Wellhausen's theory had "been fatal to the proper understanding of Israel's religion.") Overall, Hoffman espoused a "conservative" critical view.

Jewish scholars who followed, such as S. D. Luzzatto and I. M. Wise, were also basically conservative in their approach. They argued that the authorship of the Pentateuch was of divine origin, although Wise conceded some of the then-current chronology and dating positions of the critical movement. Leading Jewish critics of the early twentieth century were Margolis and Jastrow, both of whom were "moderates," and Jampel, who fought to prove the accuracy of the biblical account and who came down hard on Wellhausen and Graf and, to a lesser extent, upon Margolis and Jastrow. An important Jewish historian of the period, who represented a "conservative" rather than a "moderate" or "liberal" view, was S. Rubaschow, who was later to take the name Zalman Shazar and go on to become the third President of the State of Israel.

Another twentieth-century important figure was Moses David (Umberto) Cassuto, principally a foremost researcher of Italian-Jewish history, who also developed a strong interest in higher criticism. In his writings, he opposed Graf and Wellhausen and based his approach to the documentary theory on Jewish oral tradition. In the 1960's, Harry M. Orlinsky, a leading expert in the critical specialty of the Hebrew language, contributed respected writings on the discipline of textual criticism, publishing his views in such organs as the

Journal of Biblical Literature. His contributions stressed that biblical investigation was deteriorating in quality and quantity because there were fewer scholars being trained with adequate knowledge of the Hebrew, Aramaic and Greek languages. (This viewpoint has been supported by recent writers, including Professor G. W. Anderson of the University of Edinburgh, who in 1979 edited *Tradition and Interpretation*, the updating, successor volume to H. H. Rowley's well-known *Old Testament and Modern Study*.)

Modern archaeology has not obtained the degree of endorsement it expected from the higher criticism establishment of archaeology's exceptional discoveries over the past fifty years. Nor has archaeology achieved a high degree of consensus among archaeologists themselves as to the interpretations of those findings. Of course, archaeology does not carry the conclusiveness of such modern techniques as the video cassette or the live interview on tape. Still, it must be acknowledged that archaeology has proven to be of exceptional help in bringing to light the backgrounds of ancient civilizations.

Possibly the most significant early finds in terms of impact upon biblical investigation were the Tel El-Armarna letters, unearthed in 1887. These confirmed that a relatively rich culture of trade, science, language and social life existed in what is now called the Middle East, even in the period preceding the exodus of the Jewish people from Egypt.

The Tel El-Armarna find was followed by numerous breakthrough archaeological discoveries in the modern period of the 1920's (a development that coincided in point of time with the many new findings in the physical sciences discussed in earlier chapters). Such recent archaeological and topographical discoveries relating to the ancient beginnings of the Jewish nation have established that writing already existed in Hammurabi's time, four centuries before Moses, and also provided strong support for the authenticity of the Bible's account of Jewish beginnings, personalities, events and beliefs. These findings exposed the unscientific approach and methods employed by all too many Bible critics, even in the modern era.

Archaeological findings in the 1940-1960 period by archaeologist-scholars, such as Glueck, Aharoni, Ben Dor, Mazar and Amira, pointed out that even as late as the 1920-1950 period, Bible critics relied upon guesswork and reckless hypotheses which had very little validity. Common and even rampant[9] emendations in biblical text were later recognized to be unreliable and inventive. New digs corrected misimpressions, such as the conclusion of numerous Bible scholars to the effect that "biblical history was of doubtful trustworthiness in many places"[10] and that Abraham lived as late as in the fourteenth century B.C.E. (six centuries later than British excavations at Ur indicated).

One particular result was the discreditation of Wellhausen's theory of the development of the history of the religion of Israel. The combined discovery, deciphering and publication of the Tel El-Armarna letters, the Mari tablets, the Laschish Ostraca letters, the Elba findings, the historical data yielded by many newly recovered and reliable pre-Byzantine papyri, stelae, sarcophagi and especially the famous Ugaritic tablets, led William Albright, one of the century's most prominent archaeologists, to comment as to the "impossibility of the views of Wellhausen in the evolution of Israelite religious culture. . ."[11]

This era of archaeological activity came to be known as the "biblical archaeology" period, and its value must be recognized because no amount of text analysis, dating, hypotheses or other "tools" of higher criticism can in themselves provide the independent, supporting evidence of ancient documents which archaeology can supply. Thus, in 1956, a British Museum Babylonian chronicle was published which is the only non-biblical report we have of the fall and capture of Jerusalem by Nebuchadnezzar II, even supplying its exact date! The discovery of the Gezer Calendar (a schoolboy's exercise book listing the segments of the agricultural year) provided us with invaluable clues regarding the history of Hebrew writing and spelling and established the state of the art of writing during the age of Solomon. This "writing tablet," belonging to a long-ago child, gave us proof of the existence of writing among the early Hebrews and rendered as pure fiction the long-held hypothesis of numerous biblical "experts" to the contrary.[12]

---

9. Rowley, H. H., *The Old Testament and Modern Study*, Cambridge: Oxford Press, 1951, p. xv.

10. Thompson, J. A., *The Bible and Archaeology* (3d ed.), Wm. B. Eerdmans Publishing Co., 1982, p. 4.

11. Albright, W. F., "The Bible After Twenty Years of Archaology (1932-1952)," *Religion in Life*, Volume XXI, Nov. 4, 1952, p. 544.

And the science of archaeology continues to unearth a veritable harvest of significant artifacts and writings. The most important manuscript of recent times, the Dead Sea Scrolls, contains every book of the Bible (except the *Book of Esther*), either complete or in fragments. Thus, the Scrolls establish the authenticity and integrity, as far back as the first century of the Common Era, of the very Bible which we Jews read in this last decade of the Common Era's twentieth century. Moreover, the Scrolls provide historians with rich detail of the Jewish presence in Palestine more than two thousand years ago, further verifying Jewish historical and political claims to the Holy Land.

In 1987, a silver amulet dating from the late seventh-early sixth century B.C.E. was found in Jerusalem, engraved with the biblical threefold priestly benediction that is set out in the *Book of Numbers.* This amulet is the earliest known fragment of a biblical text, predating the Dead Sea Scrolls by three hundred years. And the discovery a short time ago of a late eighth-century B.C.E. ivory pomegranate provides us with the only known surviving object of the First Temple, which was built by King Solomon on a site selected by his father, King David.

Nevertheless, since 1950 there has been a reaction against the "biblical archaeology" school in some circles, especially as to the strong support positions taken by the school in respect of the Bible's accounts of the Patriarchs and the development of monotheism. These positions are judged to be "insufficient" because, critics claimed, the sources of the correlation and the "filling-in" details were "non-biblical."

These critics (mainly the Alt-Noth school) argued that "non-biblical" (i.e., archaeological) sources are not as convincing in reconstructing history as are the procedures of higher criticism, namely tradition, source and form criticism. This school stresses the elements of "memory" and oral tradition as the most valuable adjuncts to textual analysis. The "biblical archaeology" school countered that archaeological data is unique, for it bears empirical, independent

---

12. A minor but pointed finding was that of the existence among Northwestern Semites in the eighteenth and fourteenth centuries B.C.E. of the names Shiphra and Puah, the authenticity of which Bible scholars had frequently denied. From this evidence we have a strong indication that the Bible's account of the Jewish midwives in Moses' time is indeed ancient.

witness to historical fact, which is more reliable and objective than literary interpretation of sources.

Several other points are advanced as to the weakness of the Alt-Noth position. One is that the volume of biblical accounts has remained static for a considerable time, and another is that the school has not established any new approaches to existing accounts. Moreover, it is argued, the school's procedures of analysis are negative in that they have a greater tendency to devalue and a diminished tendency to upgrade the reliability of texts.

What was the status of the Bible criticism movement as of 1960? How did scholarship circles then view the two principal foundations of criticism, the Wellhausen theory of Israel's religious history evolution and the documentary hypothesis? Dr. John Bright, in his well-regarded essay *Modern Study of Old Testament Literature,*[13] summarized how things stood in 1957: Generally, the field of Bible criticism, he wrote, is in a state of flux. Frequently, he observed, it appears to be moving in "mutually canceling directions." Recent discoveries have so enhanced our knowledge of the background to Israel's ancient history and language that, Bright went on, "Wellhausenism, in its classical form, has all but ceased to exist."[14] Bright commented that "critical theories of yesterday" need "so drastic [a] revision as to amount to virtual abandonment." And the documentary hypothesis, while still widely adhered to, with exceptions, must be "placed in a new light." Bright also made the point that the "critical approach has become outmoded, without as yet having been replaced by any new one."

By the 1960's, a number of scholars strongly opposed the critical method. Gunkel's work on the importance of oral tradition was the starting point of the twentieth century reaction against conventional criticism, with the question being raised, "Could we all along have done without Graf, Wellhausen and the rest?"[15] Building on Gunkel, the Uppsala school under I. Engnell launched a sweeping

---

13. *The Bible and the Ancient Near East*, ed. Wright, G.E., Garden City, NY: Doubleday and Company, 1961, Ch. I "Modern Study of Old Testament Literature."

14. Today, it might similarly be said of Wellhausen's *Prolegomena* what Edmund Burke said of Viscount Bolingbroke's religious (among other) views: "Who ever read him through? Ask all the booksellers of London what is become of all these lights of the world." Herman Wouk has written that he may be the last man to have read through the five hundred pages and five thousand references of the *Prolegomena*.

15. Thompson, R. J., *Moses and the Law in a Century of Criticism since Graf*, E. J. Brill, London, 1970, Epilogue.

attack on conventional approaches, not only rejecting Wellhausen's interpretation of the evolution of Israel's religion, but also announcing a virtual parting of the ways with the documentary theory, as well by giving oral tradition a major emphasis in the establishment of biblical material.[16]

Although other scholars felt that Uppsala had given "too exclusive a role" to oral tradition, the Scandinavians (Pedersen in Denmark and later, Engnell in Sweden) demonstrated that chronology can far more accurately determine matters through the conditions found in historical narrative than can documentary analysis. As a result, Dr. Bright has noted that such analyses are of diminished value in future Bible studies, even for those who still accept the documentary theory.[17]

In the late 1960's, conflicting opinions between the Alt-Noth and "biblical archaeology" schools took a complex turn. For challenges arose to each school from within the school as well as from the opposing school. Thus, recent studies of Noth's "tradition-historical" analyses have been contested by even more recent analyses. And newer archaeological evidence as to dating have been used to argue against the chronology of the "biblical archaeology" school. The latest trend appears to see archaeology less from a biblical viewpoint than from a scientific, academic one.[18]

One of the more discernible trends of today is that of growing attention to the study of philology and linguistics, especially Hebrew. One writer feels that there may be a "shift from the historical to linguistics."[19] And Jewish researchers are said to be making a contribution to "international inquiry."[20] Meanwhile, archaeology is expanding in the number of digs and in the search for a new emphasis,

---

16. *The Bible and the Ancient Near East*, ed. Wright, G.E., Garden City, NY: Doubleday and Company, 1961, p. 21.

17. Ibid., p. 20.

18. Archaeological excavations in the 1960's used modern equipment such as mine-detectors, a proton magnetometer (which detects not only metal but burnt buildings as well), together with improved radioactivity measurement (which can establish dates of wood, leather and linen within a two-hundred-year margin of error).

In the 1970's and 1980's, other devices appeared, such as the Hewlett-Packard laser-beam transit, photogrametry and photo-mechanical drawing devices. Such modern equipment has greatly advanced the ability of archaeology to furnish accurate data in the scientific investigation of the Bible's contents.

19. *The Hebrew Bible and Its Modern Interpreters*, ed. by D. A. Knight and G. M. Tucker, Chico, CA: Scholar's Press, 1985, p. xvi.

20. Ibid., p. xiv.

"sociological evidence." Yet, it is difficult to delineate any major, new trends in the biblical study discipline. The contemporary situation appears to be in fairly the same "state of flux" that Dr. Bright described at the end of the decade of the 1950's.[21]

Dr. Bright's further notation of the recent, frank admission by Bible critics that inventiveness and conjecture were employed by a large number of past scholars and that the hypothesis of "priestly fraud" has in the main been rejected reflects refreshing changes in the field of higher criticism. Hopefully, we will in the future see no more of the unfounded hypotheses which so influenced the thinking of past scholars. Rudof Kittel, a prominent scholar and compiler of two generations ago, highlighted this misleading danger when he wrote concerning the rejection of the deception-by-the-priests charge that it was that type of hypothesis which is repeated so often that, finally, everyone believes it to be correct. Then, he observed, "One seems ultra-conservative and unscientific not to believe it. Who, nowadays would take upon himself the odium of being behind the times?" Hopefully, such cautionary advice will be carefully noted by present and future biblical scholars.

In an overall review of biblical criticism one also detects somewhat more than a faint whiff of anti-Jewish bias. Jewish belief has never recognized the classifications of the "Old" and the "New" Testaments. To Judaism, there is only one Bible, the Pentateuch; but it is seen in many different lights by Christian theologians. To some, it contains a message of divine revelation, and while it cannot be "read as a Christian book, yet it is part of the Christian Bible."[22] To other Christians, like Wellhausen (and twentieth-century Harry Emerson Fosdick), the Bible is a literary instrument of evolutionary nature, providing theology with the many primitive, childlike ideas that eventually culminated to final maturity in the Christian gospels.[23]

Strongly dissenting interpreters see Judaism not as an evolutionary product but as a revolutionary, intuitive departure from the

21. Anderson, G. W., *Tradition and Interpretation*, Cambridge: Oxford Press, 1979, p. 72.

22. Rowley, H. H., *The Old Testament and Modern Study*, Cambridge: Oxford Press, 1951, p. xxx.

23. Wright, G. E., *The Old Testament Against Its Environment*, London: SCM Press, 1966, pp. 9-10.

polytheism that prevailed in the pre-Mosaic era. To theologians like George E. Wright, past professor of Old Testament history and thought at Harvard, the Bible's account depicts not an evolution but a religion which is *sui generis*, a *mutation* which is unique in the history of religious belief and practice.[24]

Yet Wright's view is not the most prevalent in Christian theological circles. More frequently there is a clear tendency to downgrade the Bible as the creation of a backward culture; hence, the Bible must be "systematized," that is, it must be organized in its contents by experts, so as to give it value as a "witness for the modern Church." and to promote the "revival of evangelical theology."[25] Despite the Bible's looked-upon potential in the Church's "mission," Professor Wright reported that after World War I, the study of the Bible was considered by many Church authorities as "an exercise of futility" and not to be taken "seriously."[26]

How much of this mind-set is simply bias and how much is genuine anti-Judaism is difficult to evaluate. Regrettably, there is still much unwarranted critical doubt among researchers as to the veracity of the contents of the Bible, although it is to be hoped that new developments over the past fifty years will motivate the new generation of Bible scholars to approach biblical criticism with far greater objectivity, to abandon the falsehoods and distortions of the past, to properly value new scientific discoveries and to finally recognize that a new day is long overdue as to the attitudes and practices of higher biblical criticism. Until then, it would seem prudent to judge with skepticism and especial caution any claimed impartiality and objective scholarship of past and future conclusions of the higher criticism school regarding the accuracy and validity of the Bible. A most realistic assessment of the higher criticism movement's efforts to date was made by Meir Steinberg in his volume *The Poetics of Biblical Narrative*: ". . .rarely have such grandiose theories of origination been built . . . on the evidence equivalent to the head of a pin; rarely have so many worked so long and hard with so little to show for their trouble.[27]

---

24. Ibid., pp. 7-15.
25. Wright, G. E., *God Who Acts*, London: SCM Press, 1950, pp. 11-12.
26. Ibid., p. 15.
27. Steinberg, Meir, *The Poetics of Biblical Narrative,* Bloomington: Indiana University Press, 1985, p. 13.

The discipline of biblical research is not, however, the exclusive domain of those in the field of higher criticism. Other researchers have made creditable progress in this area, relying not on criticism but on the tools of historical corroboration, logic and reason in their search for truth as it relates to the content of the Bible.

Experts start with the unchallenged fact that the Bible, as we know it, was in existence and well known as early as 250 B.C.E., because the Bible was rendered into Greek (the "Septuagint") under the patronage of Ptolemy II Philadelphus (285-246 B.C.E.). And evidence remains that Demetrius, in the reign of Ptolemy IV, wrote in Greek, quoting the books of *Genesis* and *Exodus.*

But what of the period proceeding the Septuagint? Here, researchers point out history's subsequent confirmations of pre-Septuagint events which were described in *Deuteronomy* 28 and *Leviticus* 26 and which predicted the Jewish nation's future defeats, exiles and returns, all of which predictions ultimately came about. A new book by Dr. Benzion Allswang, *The Final Resolution,*[28] is one of several recent publications which carefully analyze the documents and facts underlying the uncannily close fulfillment of these prophecies, as well as other predictions in the writings of the Prophets Ezekiel, Amos and Isaiah. Among these accurately fulfilled prophesies are the destruction of the first Temple by the Babylonians, the destruction of the second Temple by the Romans, the exiles and dispersions of the Jewish people, and the survival and ingathering of the Jewish people.

Some scholars consider predictions in the Five Books of Moses as to the ingathering and return of the Jewish nation to have been confirmed by the founding of the State of Israel, the return from Yemen of Jews "on the wings of eagles," and the emigration from Russia in the post-Soviet Union period.

During the Gulf War, millions of Israeli citizens, to protect themselves against the danger of chemical poisoning, were forced at the siren's alert to enter into what were called "sealed rooms," rooms whose doors and windows were taped to prevent the entry of Scud-delivered poison gas. The Israelis fled into these sealed rooms thirty-nine times as Iraq fired missiles at Israeli targets, with miraculously only a singly fatality recorded. In those tumultuous days, one

---

28. Allswang, Benzion, *The Final Resolution*, Jerusalem: Feldheim Publishers Ltd., 1989.

could not help but recall the 2,500-year-old message of the Prophet Isaiah (26:20):

> *Come, my people, enter thou*
> *Into thy chambers,*
> *And shut thy doors about thee.*
> *Hide thyself for a little moment,*
> *Until the indignation be overpast*

In addition to the approach of historical confirmation of prophecy, researchers have utilized the tools of logic and reason. Thus, it was asked by modern Bible scholars, why would forgers of later generations write an historical account of their ancestors which in many segments is highly unflattering and even self-demeaning? No other chronicles of ancient states have been found which describe the internal rebellion of their people, their national defeats or the weaknesses of their leaders. Written Egyptian discoveries consistently boast of their present and past victories and prominence. Even the most significant happening of the conquest of Egypt by the Hysksos is omitted from Egyptian records written in subsequent times.

Yet the Bible's narrative openly records unfavorable historical details such as the intrigues of King David's court and the backsliding of the people in the desert just days after the exodus from Egypt, matters which deal frankly with human failings. Even Moses' own punishment for having struck the rock is mentioned, demonstrating that the Torah holds its greater personalities to a higher level of conduct and a more exacting form of punishment than ordinary people. *Numbers* 14 freely speaks of the overwhelming defeat of the Jewish people at Hormah by the Amalekites and Canaanites, a defeat as grave as any in Jewish history. The unconcealed nature of this important happening gives strong credence to the Bible's other historical accounts. All of these accounts are set out in a candor not found in the chronicles of other nations. Nor is such frankness often seen in the history books of many modern nations in segments dealing with their military history and policies in past wars.

Moreover, the Bible records that the ancestors of the Hebrew people did not originate in the land of Canaan but were nomads who came from Ur Kasdim in Mesopotamia. This is a clear written indication of truthfulness, for such origin hardly strengthens the Jewish people's claim of right and title to its national homeland.

It is also asked, for example, how forgers in Ezra's time, however clever, could have been able to invent facts about events and persons unknown to them at the time and not uncovered by researchers until modern times. Thus, while the Tel El-Armarna letters paint a picture of a relatively high culture existing in the Patriarchal period, this written picture simply was not accessible to those who lived a thousand years later in the era of Ezra. Moreover, why would forgers set up a system of laws previously unknown to their generation and which imposed strange and burdensome obligations, contrary to the social mores of the region and the interests of the rich and influential? What chance of acceptance could be expected for such unique and demanding codes?

Nor would it make sense to attempt to dupe an entire people into accepting the belief that it witnessed and participated in past events which never took place. There is only a bare possibility that a forger could convince his generation that it once had outstanding leaders, great victories and bitter defeats if these leaders, victories and defeats were inventions. Such a scheme to defraud would appear on its face as too transparent and contrary to generational memory to have any reasonable chance of adoption by millions of people.

Judaic experts remain confident that archaeological and historical corroboration will continue to emerge and thereby provide, for those who may still question, further and enhanced validity of the Bible's contents as well as those of other Jewish sacred writings.

The Prophets

Jewish tradition teaches us that after the Revelation at Sinai, only the Prophets of Israel were privileged to have communication with God. "He revealed His counsel to His servants, the Prophets" (*Amos, 3*:7). The chain of communication between the Prophets and God is nothing less than a continuation of the Revelation at Sinai, for it is an authentic further disclosure of God's messages to the people of Israel.

The Age of Prophecy which began with Abraham and ended with Malachai bequeathed to humanity a body of terse but majestic, divinely inspired literature. It faithfully reveals God's will and records Judaism's past spiritual encounters, triumphs, failures and memories.

Referring to the Age of Prophecy, Professor Albright wrote in his *Archaeology and the Religion of Israel*: "Thanks to archaeology we see more clearly that the Prophets of Israel were neither pagan ecstatics nor religious innovators. In them we see the first great exponents of . . . direct communion with God."[29]

The Prophets of Israel personified the apex of human ethics, morality and self-sacrifice. To contest that they spoke in the words of God Himself is tantamount to asserting that truth and integrity have never existed in human history.

Judaism's Democratic and Humanitarian Codes

Three thousand years ago, Judaism introduced into civilization man's earliest democratic and humanitarian legislation and institutions. Many hundreds of years later, the Greek and Roman Empires also enacted codes of laws, but they almost exclusively pertained to the rights of property owners. Precious few of their laws related to the protection of the individual's human rights.

Throughout the reigns of these greatest of the ancient empires, the dominant morality toward the masses was that of the gladiator's arena and the cruel, life-threatening treatment of the debtor. Indeed, until a century and a half ago, debtor prisons continued to exist in England. And even today, in Iran, Libya, Pakistan, Saudi Arabia, Singapore and Bangladesh, laws exist which permit such inhumane punishments as caning and amputation of the hands of convicted thieves.

Judaism's social and legal traditions, however, have always been endowed with the qualities of humaneness and enlightenment, as evidenced by these "world's earliest" examples: a system of philanthropy to the poor; fair and democratic labor relations; human-rights standards opposing the oppression of citizen and stranger alike; debtor protection laws; an enlightened system of criminal and civil

29. Albright, William Foxwell, *Archaeology and the Religion of Israel*, Baltimore: Johns Hopkins Press, 1968, p. 178.

justice; the prohibition of usury; and the prohibition of the sale of land in perpetuity. All these and more make Israel a "light unto the nations." And, where permitted by secular law, Jewish courts enforce many of these remarkably just codes to this very day.

These codes were remarkably just because they were endowed with exceptional humaneness, being derived from a divine source, the Torah. Unlike other codes of law, from that of Hammurabi to the Uniform Codes of present day U.S. jurisdictions, the Torah's codes are not the creations of political bodies. Judaic law is always based on the divine imperative that the dual purposes of all the statutes of the Torah are to observe the commandments and to uphold the universal sanctity of man. Thus, justice, equality and ethics are defined by divine standards rather than those of a legislature, a law revision commission or individual judges.

The cornerstone of Jewish law, the basis of the Judaic *corpus juris*, is the Revelation at Sinai, during which the first two commandments of the Ten Commandments were heard by the Jewish nation. The balance of the Five Books of Moses (the Pentateuch) were dictated by God directly to and recorded by Moses. These five books constitute what is known as the "written law." At the same time, God transmitted to Moses what is called the "oral law," a supplement to the written law, which interprets, explains and details the written law.

In time, the oral law was written down, first in an abbreviated form called the *Mishna*. Later, the general principles set out in the *Mishna* became the framework for the great, multi-volume work known as the *Gemara*, which at length sets out the legal analyses, interpretations and opinions of the most outstanding post-*Mishna* sages, judges and commentators. Later generations of sages supplemented the rulings and interpretations of the written law, oral law, *Mishna* and *Gemara* by way of codifications, commentaries and rulings. Such commentaries and opinions (responsa) on newly presented issues continue to be expounded and published to this day.

But always, rabbinical interpretations were formulated within the "thirteen hermeneutical rules" originally set forth by the oral law. Being of divine origin, these thirteen rules of interpretation cannot be modified or supplanted by man-made rules or constructions. True, there are frequent differences of opinion within Jewish law and among Jewish judges, but they are differences which derive from *within* divine interpretive rules and parameters, not from human innovation. New approaches to Jewish law are not new ideas but new *discoveries* of ideas that have always been imbedded in our ancient law.

This is not to say that decisions of Jewish law are unaffected by social considerations, economic conditions or political events. Since common-law decisions are also affected by similar factors, however, one could well ask, what distinguishes Jewish law from common law? The answer is that in the development of Jewish legal rulings, political, social and economic factors are not determinant but always *subordinate* to the fundamental purposes and goals set out in the Torah. Though the interpretive rules and standards of justice of Jewish law are flexible and provide for adaptation to new situations that may arise, the system of hermeneutical rules guards against law being made through the subjective outlook and personal views of individual judges.

This is not always the case in other legal systems. Thus, while the U.S. judicial system is held in the highest regard in this and other countries of the Western World, the history of the U.S. Supreme Court demonstrates the significant influence which the personal and social leanings of its judges have had upon its legal outlook and decisions. The early phase of the Court, from its beginning until the Civil War, was one in which, especially under Chief Justice John Marshall, it established the sovereignty of the federal government and the Court's overriding power to interpret the Constitution. From the Civil War to the Franklin D. Roosevelt administration, the Court's judicial trend was to blunt the effectiveness of legislation which aimed to curb the increasing power and influence of U.S. industry.

In the early 1930's, the Court's conservative philosophy began to shift, with the additional appointment of more liberal-minded judges such as Justices Holmes, Brandeis and later, Cardozo. Until then, social legislation designed to further human rights, typified by wage and hour laws (which were enforced in Jewish society for thirty previous centuries), were frequently struck down as unconstitutional interferences with free enterprise. Slowly, however, the new liberally oriented appointees were able to bring about the Court's approval of a series of statutes in various states regulating commerce and industry.

But within a decade, the composition of the Court again was changed to a conservative one. Laws protecting the rights of the individual found little support in the post-Brandeis-Cardozo period until after the early 1950's, when the Warren Court became more evenly balanced. Since then, once more the trend has been towards a conservative Court, as more Republican than Democratic presidential appointments have been made to the Court.

This brief review of the judicial history of the U.S. Supreme Court demonstrates that our prevailing law is very much a product of what the sitting majority of the Court believes is the law. For sixty years, the Court justified the "separate but equal" rule which established segregation in the nation. Yet in 1954, in *Brown v. the Board of Education,* that rule was declared unconstitutional. As one legal expert has put it, "The [common] law under which men are ruled is unavoidably a law written by men."[30] In some "swing vote" decisions, it becomes law written by one man.

Yet Torah law, based on the Divine Rule of Law, is often regrettably characterized by critics as concerned mainly with hair-splitting and non-relevant discussions typified by out-of-date situations, such as what the monetary consequences are if one ox gores another ox.

That this view of Torah law is both narrow and uninformed is evident from even the earliest pages of the tractate of the *Gemara* which deals with the subject of oxen which gore. The student soon discovers that the references to oxen serve mainly to introduce one to the fundamental laws of damages, laws which are basic to any civilized code of jurisprudence. In these early pages of the *Gemara* we come across a curious dictum of the Sages: "He who wishes to be pious must absorb the teachings of the Torah's laws on damages." What is the connection? The Sages understood that the key to a system of ethics lies in not causing damage to your fellow man. An ordered, moral society is attained when harm is not inflicted upon others through slander, the human hand, economic means, fraud, theft, or a weapon of violence such as a dangerous ox, the ancient counterpart of today's automobile. The tort-feasant ox is no more than the Torah's useful symbol that the purpose of law is to preserve or redress the rights of the individual, for he was "created in the image of God." It is this principle which has left a marked influence

30. Professor Milton R. Konvitz, "The Original Intent of the Framers: What the Establishment Clause Means," *Midstream*, December 1989, p.13.

upon human thought and legislation down through the centuries since it was first enunciated by the Torah.

In the application of the Torah's statutes, any form of conduct which threatens or undermines the well-being, health, livelihood, safety or freedom of the individual is prohibited. Such acts of unlawful conduct range from the possession of false weights and measures to the extreme act of the taking of a life other than in self-defense.

In the mid 1960's, on quiet Austin Street in Kew Gardens, New York, in the early evening and in front of a multi-storied apartment house, a young woman named Katherine Genovese was cruelly attacked and then murdered. What made the case so notorious and so widely reported throughout the Western world is that the entire course of the grisly episode was witnessed by thirty-eight law-abiding apartment dwellers looking down from their open windows upon the struggling, screaming woman and her assailant, who stalked and stabbed her in three separate attacks that took place over a thirty-minute period, while not a single person came to her defense or rescue.

Yet, the onlookers could not have been held to have violated any statute by withholding assistance to the victim. Indeed, more often than not the prevalent, contemporary attitude is "not to get involved." Under Jewish law, however, the deliberate avoidance of an act which could rescue another from distress or peril was denounced as a biblical transgression and codified as such by rabbinic authority:

> He who sees his neighbor drowning or being attacked by robbers or by wild animals and is able to save him himself or to hire others to do so and did not do so . . . or even one who was able to comfort his fellow man for his agony or sorrow and does not do so with words — whoever does all these or similar things is guilty of transgressing the biblical commandment "You shall not stand upon thy brother's blood" (*Leviticus* 19:16).[31]

31. *Shulchan Aruch, Chosen Mishpat, Hilchos Shmiras Hanefesh* 426:1 (quoted by Meir Tamari in *With All Your Possessions*, New York: The Free Press, 1987, p. 300). See also Rabbeinu Yonah of Gerona, *The Gates of Repentance*, trans. by Silverstein, Schraga, Jerusalem: Feldheim Publishers, 1971, 3d Gate, LXX, pp. 189-191.

Similarly, kidnapping a human being is one of the Torah's capital offenses (*Exodus* 31:16), although it did not become so under U.S. law until the Lindbergh kidnapping in the 1930's. Nonetheless, execution for a capital crime was a rare occurrence in Jewish life, and a court which found for execution once every seventy years was considered "destructive" (*Mishna Maakos* 1:10). Trial procedure required proof that the accused had been warned not to commit the crime. Circumstantial evidence, however convincing, was not admissible in capital cases, and an act of murder needed to be attested by two or more actual witnesses. A majority of at least two judges was required to convict where the death penalty might be involved. More remarkably, judicial ruling required that a unanimous verdict in a murder trial was considered an acquittal (*Tractate Sanhedrin* 17A) because the court may have failed to note an extenuating item of evidence.

Yet, in recent years, the U.S. Supreme Court has made it increasingly difficult to obtain the traditionally protective "writ of habeas corpus," which requires review of death sentence convictions. Thus, in a 1991 ruling, the Court held that a convicted murderer awaiting execution had forfeited a re-hearing of his case on constitutional grounds simply because his attorney had overlooked filing the petition for appeal on time. And in the *Herrera v. Collins* 1993 decision, the Court refused to reverse a conviction in a capital case partly on the ground that evidence pointing to the defendant's innocence came to light several years before it was brought to the Court's attention; hence, the Court ruled, the evidence was to be disregarded because too much time had elapsed between the discovery of the evidence and its subsequent submission to the Court.

From the famous injunction of *Leviticus* 19:18, "You shall love your neighbor as yourself," and from the exhortations of the Prophets there came many laws and traditions extending justice, kindness and generosity to others. Even kings had no greater rights or privileges than commoners in the matter of justice under the law. Every fifty years, patrimonial fields were returned to descendants to prevent the land falling into the possession of the few. Every seven years, debts were to be wiped clean so that the debtor could gain a new lease on his economic life. Gracious hospitality to the traveler and the displaced[32] could be found in every city and village, and

32. Most Jews in this generation are descended from parents or grandparents who were likely to have been beneficiaries of the aid, comfort and hospitality extended by indi-

comfort to the sick and infirm was made mandatory by rabbinical decree. These were ancient traditions of Jewish life, stemming from the divine command to "love the stranger," a sentiment stated thirty-six times in the Five Books of Moses.

Similarly, the concept of charity to the poor was a time-honored institution, stressed in the Five Books of Moses, *Psalms* and the writings of the Prophets. Such charitable acts included gratis and unimpeded gleaning in the fields, interest-free loans to overcome economic emergencies and the gift of money[33] where neither the donee knew the donor, nor vice versa.[34] Even the destitute, who themselves subsist on alms, are required to help those who are in even more distress. For the gift of charity *belongs* to the poor as a legal property right. It is not simply a voluntary, optional act of generosity on the part of the donor.

From the universal nature of the Torah's laws, there emerged a large body of laws governing society which could be classified as a Code of Social Law. A detailed account of the various branches of this code is better suited for another time and place. But it is appropriate at this point to discuss those aspects of Judaism's social laws which relate to a few of the most significant and controversial issues of our time.

Ecology

Judaism maintains that the world was created to enable man to enhance his physical and spiritual growth. All men have rights in common to use of the planet on which we live. But to accomplish the earth's purposes, we are commanded not to destroy anything

viduals or organizations (e.g., HIAS) to Jews who emigrated to the United States from Europe in the fifty-year period 1890-1940. See also the Babylonian Talmud (*Tractate Shevuoth* 39A) on the principle that all Jews are responsible for one another.

33. From Maimonides' codification of Jewish law, we learn that it was a ruling of the Sages that Jews should support the poor and visit the sick, *even those of idolaters*, a ruling derived from the verse "God is good to all and His mercy is on all His work," a verse from Psalm 145 which Jews traditionally recite three times daily.

34. The tradition to give charity to bereaved persons "sitting *shiva*" (a mourning period) and unable to attend to their livelihood was carried out in some communities by bringing a covered silver urn filled with an uncounted sum of cash to the home and requesting one of the bereaved to carry the urn into a private room, take whatever sum he wished out of the urn, replace the cover and return the urn to the community charity representative.

without reason or to perform an act which may endanger society's health. In the early pages of the Pentateuch, we find that the needless spoilage of fruit trees and the unhygienic disposal of waste material were prohibited, to safeguard the welfare, health and safety of the population.

As early as the Mishnaic period, pollution of the air by smoke, odors or dust was already being regulated by rabbinic decrees (*Mishna Bava Basra* 2:8-9). These decrees were followed by other enactments in later periods, the effect of which was to guard the ecological balance and to preserve the individual's and society's right to an undisturbed, non-deleterious environment. (The persistent, costly undertaking of the Jewish National Fund to reforest the Holy Land is viewed as one of the most energetic and productive ecology projects undertaken by any country in the last century.)

Yet it was not until the first United Nations Environmental Conference in Stockholm in 1972 that protection of the environment was officially declared to be the policy of most developed nations. The purpose of the 1992 Rio Earth Summit was to commit the world community to a planetary environmental cleanup, global reforestation and the curbing of harmful greenhouse gases.

Whether these optimistic goals will be achieved before permanent and disastrous planetary environmental damage occurs is problematic because the 120 nations at the Summit were divided into roughly two divisions: the rich, developed "north," principally interested in protecting its industrial complex and economic growth, and the poor, undeveloped "south," mainly concerned with its day-to-day survival, which depends largely on intense cultivation, unregulated tree cutting and uninterrupted overgrazing. And even where there are areas of policy agreement between the north and the south, the sides are divided over who is to pay for the implementation and enforcement of an improved world environment.

At the conclusion of the Summit, President Bush commented that what is important in the future "is the road *from* Rio." While the U.S. opposed strict environmental controls at Rio and refused to sign the important "biodiversity" treaty aimed at protecting genetic resources, President Bush did sponsor an agreement protecting forests. But meanwhile, the ancient prohibition of *Deuteronomy* 20:19-20 not to "wield an axe against" the fruit tree still remains unheeded; one acre of precious tropical forest is still being erased every second.

The Right to Live (and Die)

The issue of abortion has become one of the most politically explosive and strongly fought issues of these times. Like the parallel "right-to-die" proposition, the issue of abortion revolves around the controversial question: Does one "own" his or her life, be it a living embryo in its mother's womb or a terminally-ill octogenarian on a life-support machine?

Torah adherents respond to this question in accord with the principle of Judaism that life is given by the Creator, belongs to Him and can only be taken by Him. Life is ours as a loan, not as a possession. Thus, the Torah does not permit one to place his own life at life-threatening risk even to save another, because we do not have title to our lives as we do to property. For this reason, when a pregnant mother's life becomes in jeopardy because the fetus threatens the mother's right to continued life, Jewish law permits an abortion. However, by the same principle of the sanctity of life, Jewish law does not sanction abortion "at will" in any other instance.

There is a great deal of public support throughout the United States for the *Roe v. Wade* Supreme Court ruling upholding abortion "on demand" under certain conditions. Torah adherents recognize that underlying such support in most cases is an understandable compassion for women whose lives are highly complicated by unwanted pregnancies, many of which result from vulnerability, hasty marriages, ignorance and rape. It is also clear that such pregnancies can bring about despair, severe hardship and bewilderment. Moreover, some segments of the anti-*Roe v. Wade* movement have resorted to militancy and extreme pressure tactics not in keeping with the Torah's standards of approach to social problems.

Still, the root question remains: Does a woman have the right to extricate herself from her burdensome situation by taking the life of another who is innocent and defenseless? The Torah says "no," but must not the answer be the same even from a non-religious and purely human-rights standpoint? Is the issue of "freedom of choice," upon which the pro-choice movement mainly rests its justification of over two million abortions annually in the U.S., being asserted to achieve retroactive birth control, thereby causing the fetus to pay the price of the mother's original actions? Is this "freedom of choice" a fundamental right under the protection of the Constitution? Torah authorities argue that it is not. If so, how do we reconcile the earlier statement that under Jewish law, abortion on demand is prohibited, but in a case where the mother's life is seriously threatened by the fetus, abortion is permitted?

The answer is twofold: First, in the latter case, a human life is at great risk; in the "on-demand" case, it is not. Secondly, the "right" of a mother to an abortion where her life's continuation is in great jeopardy is a right grounded upon religious belief. As such, it is a fundamental, religious liberty protected by the U.S. Constitution. However, it is argued in a brief submitted to the Supreme Court by Torah adherents, the act of obtaining an abortion on demand is *not* such a fundamental right. These experts in constitutional law point out that religious rights are "deeply rooted in the nation's history and tradition," whereas the right to an abortion on demand is not.

Similar questions may be raised as to the slowly growing acceptance of euthanasia, in either its passive or active form. What at one time was widely considered a horrendous act is now the subject of calm, rational consideration. In some states, legislation authorizes the enforcement of the so-called "living will," which directs that life-prolongation measures are to be withheld from a dying testator under specified circumstances.

This issue is one on which there is fairly uniform agreement among all Jews that the so-called "right-to-die" position should be opposed. In the main, the U.S. Jewish community has stood firm behind the Torah principle that only the Creator has the right to terminate a life, however heartrending and hopeless continuation of that life may appear.

This Torah stand was echoed in a related matter which received nationwide public attention in early 1992. It involved a child who was born with only a brain stem but no brain cortex (the largest part of the brain), a condition which could only result shortly in the child's death. Her parents petitioned the Court to have the child declared "brain dead" in order that some of her organs might be taken to donate for transplant into other children. However, under the Florida law, where the family lived, death cannot be established until all brain activity ceases, including that of the brain stem. The judge who ruled in the case rejected the petition of the parents, holding that "I can't authorize someone to take your baby's life, however short, however unsatisfactory, to save another child . . . Death is a fact, not an opinion." The Appellate Court confirmed and the Florida Supreme Court declined to intervene.

Judaism does maintain that heroic measures to prolong life briefly are not required in the instance of a medical determination that a patient cannot survive and that the process of death has already begun. But at any earlier point, the abandonment of life-saving or extension measures is not permitted. Does this position appear unrealistic? Judaism answers that, on the contrary, it is realistic, for it is a position which is consistently on guard against the changing cultural mores of society which in some periods may condone what in other periods may be regarded as abhorrent and gruesome. Thus, in Canaanite culture, an overt, cruel form of euthanasia, that of killing aged parents, was common. (One instance of such an act was witnessed by the great Jewish figure Rabbi Akiva.) In the later eras of the Greeks and the Romans, the custom of exposing to certain death children who were weak, handicapped or retarded was frequently practiced.

Judaism recognizes that if the concept of "mercy" as defined by contemporary libertarianism succeeds in weakening the once-unassailable belief in the sanctity of human life, we can expect a process of erosion (called "the slippery slope") of that belief to set in which will gather more and more momentum. The tragic results of this erosion process are already being evidenced in some societies where various degrees of euthanasia have been given legal sanction. Therefore, it remains the Torah's unchanging principle that the continuation of every moment of your life and mine is inviolate and of infinite worth. Compassion or the personal grief of others cannot overcome the supreme value of human existence.

Business Ethics

Jewish law does not frown upon the acquisition of property and the pursuit of economic advancement. The earning of money to provide for the needs of one's family is recognized as a laudable social obligation of man. The pursuit of wealth is wrong only when one pursues nothing else or when it is not acquired in accordance with the Torah's business value system. A corollary to the principle that life is a gift from God is the Judaic principle that one's possessions are similarly a gift from the Creator.

To this end, there are numerous rabbinic decrees and decisions which underlie and shape Judaism's ethical and economic standards. The use of money as a weapon of power over others is denounced by rabbinic authority, as is the concentration of wealth and property in the hands of the few. Equally condemned are the exaction of interest, the use of financial devices to deprive another of his rightful property, the retention of identifiable lost property ("finders are not necessarily keepers" under the Torah) and dealing in products which can cause damage to another, such as weapons in ancient times (and silicon implants in our own times).

Beyond these fairly obvious practices are those which are more difficult to detect, but which nevertheless harm or deceive the unsuspecting by stealth, subtlety and indirection. Thus, to eliminate profiteering, the rabbinical authorities provided inspectors who checked markets to enforce the Torah rule that retailers were limited to a profit no more than one-sixth of the total purchase price of essential foods. "Price fixing" was outlawed centuries before U.S. anti-trust laws were enacted in the early twentieth century. The existence of a conflict of interest is considered illegal, as is the act of concealing defects in products which one sells ("caveat emptor," buyer beware, is a Roman principle, not a Jewish one). Tax evasion is decried as a breach of secular law and also as stealing under Torah law, since it is likely to result in higher taxes being levied upon complying, honest individuals, as well as in depriving the needy of social services which are supplied by tax funds.

Until the middle of the nineteenth century in the United States, the corporation was conceived as a public trust, chartered by the state for the interests of society. In later decades, the social responsibility of the corporation was supplanted when it became used principally for private, commercial benefit. It became a legal vehicle for monetary gain, a device in which the individual was insulated against personal liability and ethical responsibility. In recent years, however, the courts have more widely applied the principle of "piercing the corporate veil" to uphold causes of action against the officers and principals of corporations for such violations as bribery, personal siphoning of assets and failure to disclose. Yet Jewish law has always held to the proposition that the members of a corporation-like vehicle are to be held to the same standards of morality and ethics as those demanded of the individual.

One of the crowning aspects of the system of Jewish law is its quality of looking beyond the letter of the law, to temper a harsh result that an otherwise legal enforcement of rights may cause. This quality is called in Hebrew *lefinim m'shurat ha'din,* an equitable standard that has come down to us by way of courts and individuals through twenty centuries of Jewish life. It is a remedy that is a blend of justice with mercy. It is a yielding up of legal rights when a technically correct decision is found wanting in the element of fairness.

As a young lawyer, I once attended a lecture which dramatically demonstrated why, in special circumstances, the equitable concept of going beyond the letter of the law became and has remained embedded in Jewish character for centuries.

The lecture was given by Federal Judge Harold R. Medina, who had presided over the famous 1949 trial of the eleven leaders of the U.S. Communist Party charged with advocating the overthrow of the United States by force and violence. A Columbia University law professor for thirty years and known as a "lawyer's lawyer," Judge Medina spoke about the serious responsibility which the lawyer owes to his client, even in cases which involve what appear to be small stakes. He recollected that as a starting lawyer in a large firm he was assigned one of the firm's minor cases involving a motion for repossession by a finance company of his client's automobile because the monthly payments were in arrears.

Judge Medina related that he prepared for the case to the best of his ability but was opposed by an attorney highly experienced in repossession cases. The court almost summarily found for the plaintiff and authorized the car to be repossessed immediately. As Medina was gathering his papers together, a shot rang out in the corridor and he, along with most of those present, ran out to discover that the client had shot himself. Apparently, without the use of his car he would have been unable to earn a livelihood for his family.

Clearly, the finance company's contractual rights entitled it to repossess the car. Millions of cars in the United States are financed today under similar contracts, most of which entitle the finance company in case of payment default to repossess the auto wherever it can be found and without prior notification to the defaulting party. Last year, one million automobiles (and even gravestones) were repossessed under such contracts by "bounty hunters" employed by the finance companies.

But it is to the credit of the remarkable evenhandedness and ethical balance of Jewish law that while it decries the failure to pay a debt, it also denounces the summary action of repossession against the economically weak. Humane consideration must be shown so that a defenseless person shall not be deprivation of his food, shelter or the tools needed to provide a livelihood. For such deprivation can become equivalent to depriving him of his basic dignity, his protection and even his life. While other assets may be subject and applied to repayment, *Deuteronomy* 24:6 admonishes, "One shall take the mill an upper or lower millstone as a pledge, for he would be taking life as a pledge." All to the end that, as also is said in *Deuteronomy* 6:18, one should do what is "upright and good in the eyes of God."

The remarkable ethos of Jews in going beyond the letter of the law is not confined to repossession, nor was it only an ancient practice. My former synagogue recently relinquished its valuable property rights to a house occupied by a widow in difficulty, closely resembling the action taken four hundred years earlier by the Council of the Jews of Padua, Italy (Rabbi M. C. Luzzatto's home city, in his early years):

> "It has been decided to release the widow of Abraham Safarty from all her debts to the community arising out of the rental of the house in which she lives at present. Furthermore, this house will be available to her as an act of mercy so that she may dwell therein for free until such time as the community will decide otherwise."[35]

Jewish men and women can view with justifiable pride such admirable goals of our Torah. On the one hand, the Torah is the source from which Thomas Jefferson drew the democratic centerpiece of the Declaration of Independence: "All men are . . . endowed by their Creator with certain unalienable Rights. . ." At the same time Jewish law brought to the world a code of societal morality which

35. *Va'ad Kehila Kedosha Padua,* ed. D. Karfi, Jerusalem, 1973 (quoted by Meir Tamari in *With All Your Possessions*, New York: The Free Press, 1987).

became and remains the ideal of civilized men and nations and encourages us to "walk in the ways of good men" (*Proverbs* 11:20).

It is this dual message which the Jewish people have been "chosen" to carry to the world and why we are called the "Chosen People" ("You shall be unto Me a Kingdom of Priests and a Holy Nation" — *Exodus* 19:5-6).

But the word "chosen" must be defined, lest its meaning be mistaken. Is it a quality of snobbery or superiority? Certainly not. Rather than a designation of privilege, it is one of heavy responsibility. For in the Torah's context, Jews are bidden to excel in all conduct and to serve as examples of the heights to which man can aspire and rise. Jews are selected or "chosen" to assure that God's laws will be heeded and not neglected or forgotten. Rabbi Ovadia Sforno, Judaism's eminent sixteenth-century sage, clarifies this selection in his interpretation of the foregoing words of *Exodus* 19:5-6: ". . . although the whole of the human race is precious to Me . . . nevertheless you shall be My own treasure . . . giving understanding and teaching to the whole of mankind. . ."

We now continue our panoramic review of those two elements of the "case for Judaism" which belong to both the time periods of "yesterday" and "today": the survival of the Jewish people and man's freedom to choose.

The Survival of the Jewish People

The historical fact that the tiny, persecuted Jewish nation has stood at both the cradle and the grave of the world's greatest empires — those of Egypt, Babylonia, Persia, Greece, Rome, Hitler's Third Reich — points up more than historical chronology. It establishes that Judaism's survival is a phenomenon of such magnitude that it is a near-unassailable validation of God's intent to guarantee the continuing ability of the Jewish nation to fulfill its unique role as a "light unto the nations" in the unfolding of world history.

No other deduction seems logical in the light of the survival of a people dispersed throughout the world, always a minority within dozens of differing countries and cultures. Some of the host countries were friendly, but most were either indifferent or overtly hostile. Since the destruction of the Second Temple in the year 70 C.E., hardly a generation has passed which did not see a systematic attempt to destroy a portion of the Jewish people. How, then, do we explain its survival?

Mark Twain once wrote: "All things are mortal but the Jew; all other forces pass, but he remains. What is the secret of his immortality?"[36] A plausible explanation to Twain's query lies in the previous observation that the Covenant between God and the Jewish nation extended God's protective grace over the nation forever, to ensure that it would be able to discharge its historical mission.

If one wishes to apply the scientific method to the subject of Jewish survival, one might recall the standards set by Thomas Huxley two generations ago. Huxley was the spokesman for the methods of modern science. He explained that the "strongest possible foundation" of a scientific law results if it is subject to every possible proof and is still verified by the "universal experience of mankind." For over three thousand years, the Jewish nation has been subjected to just such proof and has successfully defied all attempts to destroy or abort its continuity. Endurance in the face of such harsh testing can only be attributed logically to a cosmic "strongest possible foundation."

In the Israeli Galilee there is a small village called Peki'in, in which Jews have lived continuously despite the exile of the Jews by the Romans nineteen centuries ago. It was in a Peki'in cave that R' Simeon ben Yochai, to whom is attributed the authorship of the *Zohar* (Judaism's ancient volume of mysticism), hid for thirteen years to escape Roman persecution and to continue the writing of his monumental work, subtitled *The Book of Splendor*.

Today, only one Jewish person continues to live in the village of Peki'in, but continuity is assured by the presence of a recent Jewish settlement, Kibbutz Peki'in, which adjoins the village. This extraordinary survival of Jews in Peki'in, through two thousand years of openly hostile Roman, Byzantine, Arab, Crusader, Mamalouk, Turkish and British rules, presents to skeptics among us an example and a proof of Jewish continuity and historical authenticity which cannot easily be controverted or dismissed.

---

36. Twain, Mark, *The Man That Completed Hadleyburg*, London: Chatto & Windus.

Freedom of Will

The thunder and trumpet sounds of Sinai are no longer, but the legacy of free will, gifted there to the Jewish people, remains. Man's freedom to choose is that remarkable tool with which man can attain exceptional personal elevation and also influence the spiritual growth of others.

As mentioned earlier, for three centuries past, many leading thinkers of the world — scientists, philosophers and social reformers — overlooked the ancient recognition of the significance of free will. They rested their beliefs upon the unsound foundation that everything, even man and his behavior to a recognizable degree, is virtually predetermined. However, as we have seen, this deterministic view has been significantly eroded over the past fifty years by the quantum revolution.

Chapter VI discussed at length Heisenberg's Principle of Uncertainty and the stimulus it provided in bringing scientists to view freedom of choice as a property not only of the natural world but of man as well. Man's ability to alter physical events was recognized as indicating that his influence over the physical world is more penetrating and creative than previously understood.

It gradually became evident that this exceptional quality in man had curious but persistent overtones of mind and spirit — non-material concepts that had long been excluded from the traditional view of the rationalist scientist.[37]

---

37. It should be noted, however, that not all recent scientists subscribed fully to the implications of the Principle of Uncertainty. As indicated in Chapter V, the most noteworthy demurral was that of Albert Einstein. He conceded only that determinism had been placed "in doubt" and held that uncertainty's approach was but a "temporary expedient." His most consistent supporter, Cornelius Lanczo, has written that Einstein always hoped that the "strict causality of all natural events would be restored."

Even today there are some scientists who express the same hope. Others accept the validity of quantum's denial of determinism and causality in the atomic realm; but, as to the concept of free will, they view as an "overstatement" any claim that it was reinstated in the world by the Uncertainty Principle. (Quantum's position on this issue was expressed early on by Sir James Jeans, who observed in his *New World of Physics* (p. 29) that modern physics' contribution is that it presents "a picture [of the universe which] contains *more room* [for elements such as free will] to exist within the picture itself. . ." [emphasis added]).

The prevailing view as to determinism vs. uncertainty continues to be that set forth by the Bohr-Eddington-Jeans-Heisenberg school. Challenges to the Uncertainty Principle and its implications, e.g., free will — like challenges to the "Big Bang" Theory, discussed previously — are not unusual or unexpected when dedicated, objective scientists investigate what Dr. Allan Sandage has called the "frontier" of science.

Thousands of years earlier, however, these post-quantum scientific observations already were part of Jewish belief. At Sinai, the Torah invested the "inherent and inescapable" attribute of free choice in man through God's ringing call:

> *I have set before you life and good*
> *and death and evil. . .*
> *Therefore, choose life that you may live,*
> *you and your seed.*
>
> (*Deuteronomy* 30:10)

This statement of the doctrine of free will, Maimonides wrote, is the "pillar of the Law. . ." He clarified that man is not predetermined, as Freud mistakenly believed to be the case to a great degree. In Maimonides' words:

> We know beyond doubt that a human being's activities are in his own hands and the Almighty . . . [does not decree] . . . that he should act thus or not act thus. It is not religious tradition alone by which this is known. It is also supported by clear proofs *furnished by science*.[38]

The option is clear. Man is given the unconditional ability to select among all the ethical and social alternatives of good and evil, to elevate or to debase himself. Although he is entreated to strive for good, there is no coercion. Man is the actor, the initiator. He is, comments Maimonides, privileged to take whichever moral path he elects. Although he is constrained by the physical laws designed by the Creator for the operation of the universe, no limits are placed upon the human capabilities that have been vested in man. In his insightful essay entitled "The Uncertainty Principle and the Wisdom of the Creator," physicist Leo Levy observed, "how, perhaps, the Creator in His wisdom has devised a principle [Uncertainty] capable of resolving the contradiction" between two divergent concepts found in the Torah: (1) the necessary constraints of nature's physical laws upon man and (2) the independence which free will grants to man.

This divergence, Levy writes, may be seen as reconciled by the Uncertainty Principle because it is confined to the microcosm, the hidden world of the ultra-miniature. And while the principle allows

---

38. Maimonides, *Mishneh Torah* (Laws of Repentance), ed. by Moses Hyamson, Jerusalem: Feldheim Publishers, Ltd. ,1971, Ch. 5: XIII, p. 87b.

man to influence that world through his free will, at the same time the principle leaves intact and undisturbed nature's much-needed physical laws. Thus, Levy feels, we may regard the principle as helping us to "appreciate the essential unity of God's natural world."[39]

Rabbi Soloveitchik made the interesting point that the divergence between universal laws and human free choice has significant theological and psychological implications. He stressed that while man functions within laws of cause and effect, "it does lie within his power to act in opposition to his natural inclinations. . ." Man can even develop "in advance" his responses to events, so that ". . . his reactions become natural, a part of his psychological makeup. . ."[40]

In one of his discourses, Rabbi Soloveitchik gave us a clarifying insight into the nature of the human will. He explained that in the *Zohar*, we are told that at Sinai the Jewish people received two wills: a Higher Will and a Lower Will.[41]

He distinguished between the two Wills: our Higher Will is not an instrument of greater intelligence, but rather a loftier perception "which transcends man's intellect." Higher Will is intuitive, spontaneous and deals with decisions and concepts that can change our lives, such as the selection of a mate or a lifelong profession. Lower Will, he continued, is cautious and practical, directed towards materialism, social success, reasoning. It deals with lower level, utilitarian decisions, such as the choice of a new home or a second car.[42]

Unaided though he may be by his five senses, by resolute stretching of his mental ability beyond his utilitarian self, the Jew can activate his Higher Will to grasp ideas which our limited intellect may find difficult to comprehend. Thus, through Higher Will he can

39. *Challenge*, ed. by Aryeh Carmel and Cyril Domb, Jerusalem: Feldheim Publishers, Ltd., 1978, p. 296.

40. *Soloveitchik On Repentance*, transl. by Peli, Pinchas H., New York: Paulist Press, pp. 172-173.

41. *Reflections of the Rav* Besdin, Abraham R., (translated or adapted from lectures of Joseph B. Soloveitchik), Jerusalem: World Zionist Org., 1981, p. 89 et seq.

42. Modern investigators have confirmed the existence of a concept similar to the Higher Will. Max Planck in *The New Science* called it "one of the most precious gifts that man possesses, this power of lifting himself in thought into the realm of light. . ." Albert Einstein described it as a "higher plane of knowledge." Otto Rank called it by the name of "creative will," which, he held, can help us to attain a bond with the spiritual realm.

intuitively perceive such fundamentals of Jewish faith as the Revelation at Sinai, the authenticity of Jewish verbal transmission and man's partnership with God in the completion of creation.

Why didn't God save everyone a lot of effort and bother by creating a perfect human being and a perfect world in the first place, eliminating man's need to choose between good and evil? Because, Judaism's sages respond, what would have been the purpose of creating perfection, leaving no goal for which man could strive? What would a perfect, static man do in a perfect, static world ruled by a divine Master Puppeteer and inhabited by other perfect men who were programmed moral robots, with no freedom to select between self-gratification and self-elevation?

Instead, we fortunately were endowed at Sinai with the gift of free will, which grants to us choice, individuality and creativity. It is in the wise, moral exercise of this free will that we become able to partake in the process of perfecting ourselves and to experience the unique loftiness to which a human being can ascend.

10

The Wellsprings of Judaism

"But where shall wisdom be found?
And where is the place of understanding?"

— (Job 28:12)

To Jews, the completion and perfection of creation represent the *pinnacle* of history. In two widely read but controversial articles and a recent book (*The End of History and the Last Man*), Francis Fukayama, formerly of the U.S. State Department's Planning Staff (and currently a consultant with the Rand Corporation), proposed that the collapse of the Marxist-Leninist political structure in Eastern Europe marked the *end* of history. He does not use the word "history" in its usual sense, such as a "history" book, but rather as the conflict between and the unfolding of political ideas. In his writings, which created a considerable stir among intellectuals in the U.S. and Europe, Fukayama observes that recent events in Europe signal the end of all anti-democratic political forms. After centuries of conflict over the ideal form of society, the world has now reached the belief that "liberal democracy is that ideal"; we are at history's end, he writes, because we are left with only "universalization of Western liberal democracy" and "consumerist Western culture." Instead of the struggles of political idealism, from now on, he predicts, we will simply experience universal boredom and meaninglessness.

Many contemporary intellectuals disagree with Fukayama.

George Will and others (including Allan Bloom, who was Fukayama's teacher) contend that history is not at an end and that future non-democratic political doctrines and striving for nationalism will keep it ongoing. Confirmation of this view can be seen in the right-wing nationalism and anti-Semitism, reminiscent of the Nazi era, which have recently surfaced in newly "democratized" Russia, Germany and a number of Eastern European countries. This ominous emergence and the brazen invasion of Kuwait by Iraq cast doubt on Fukayama's thesis that we are seeing the end of anti-democracy. Moreover, brutal, ideological and religious civil wars over non-democratic ideologies continue unabated at the moment in Yugoslavia, India, Pakistan, the Philippines, Morocco, the Sudan, Peru, Angola, and Algeria.[1]

Still, despite disagreement over Fukayama's end-of-history thesis, there is little dissent that in the decades ahead we are likely to witness Fukayama's predictions of an astonishing increase in crime and drugs, mounting terrorism, greater ecological and nuclear threats, major droughts and spreading AIDS, as well as plain meaninglessness.

From these scary but realistic forecasts, we are compelled to expect that in the future man will have an ever-growing need for an underpinning of sense and direction. Yet we can also expect that most people will continue to be entrapped either by their hedonism or their fascination with power, consumerism and money. More than likely, men will continue as before to slight or overlook the supportive and vital role which religion can play in their lives.[2]

Ernest Becker concluded in *Denial of Death* that one of the major faults in our society is the failure of man to recognize that religion offers the hope of understanding life, of comprehending the "fantas-

---

1. Fukayama's essays were followed by the writings of others on the "end of science" and the "end of nature." Science, it is argued, is no longer objective and idealistic but rather heavily influenced by social and political considerations, as well as profiteering. Nature, we are told, is at an end because of man's greed and technology, which have robbed nature of its once-virgin state.

2. Carl Jung once pictured how dark society would be without man as the "second creator": "Man is indispensable for the completion of creation; [he] is the second creator of the world who alone has given to the world its objective existence, without which, unheard, unseen, silently eating, giving birth, dying, heads nodding . . . it would have gone on in the profoundest night of non-being down to its unknown end." (Jung, Carl G., *Memories, Dreams and Reflections*, New York: Pantheon Books, 1961, pp. 255-256.)

tic mystery of creation" and of gaining an inkling of the "beyond." These insights, he said, can make a "mockery of earthly logic," the logic upon which all too many of us still rely.

Much of our "earthly logic" is shallow and limited because it is based on ideas which, in recent years, have been drastically altered. In the introduction, I made the point that we must recognize the impact of the quantum revolution if we are to appreciate some of the new vistas of life and reality which quantum physics has opened for us. In *Microcosm*, an exceptionally fine book by George Gilder, we are presented with a brilliant overview of how drastically quantum has changed the world industrially, politically, scientifically and even philosophically in the relatively short period between the Bohr-Heisenberg era and today's age of the computer, the mighty child of the Quantum Theory. Quantum has enabled us to achieve nuclear power, the laser, the superconductor, the electron microscope and remarkable insights into the sciences of chemistry and biology.

Microcosm points out that when, in the early twentieth century, quantum pioneers exposed the inner workings of the invisible world of the atom, man's comprehension of the universe expanded dramatically. The material world no longer could be relied upon as totally predetermined or the source of all understanding.

Gilder emphasizes that the primary achievement of the quantum revolution was "the overthrow of matter,"[3] causing a far-reaching shift in world power from natural resources, capital and territory to human thought, mind and imagination.[4] He cites Japan as an illustration of a bleak island, without sizeable population, raw materials or extensive territory, which nevertheless has gained a primary position among the world's economic powers through intellectual achievement and innovation.

The "central test of reality," Gilder asserts, is no longer that of our five senses. In shifting from dependence upon our sense impres-

3. This and all direct quotations or paraphrasings of George Gilder which follow are taken from the pages of Mr. Gilder's *Microcosm, The Quantum Revolution in Economics and Technology*, New York: Simon & Schuster, 1989.

4. It is interesting to compare this conclusion with an observation made 250 years earlier by Rabbi Moshe Chaim Luzzatto: "The only way [man] can overcome the physical is by growing in wisdom. . ." (Luzzatto, Moshe Chaim, *The Way of God*, trans. by Aryeh Kaplan, Jerusalem: Feldheim Publishers, Ltd., 1977, p. 61). His phrase "overcome the physical" clearly resembles Gilder's "overthrow of matter." In both statements, materialism is dethroned by the intellect.

sions to reliance upon the power of the mind, we become able to gain *"access to a higher power and truth"* (emphasis added).

In previous chapters, it was noted that distinguished physicists such as Planck, Bohr, Eddington and Heisenberg advanced the then-startling proposition that the search for scientific truth must be directed towards the non-material, spiritual sphere as well as the physical world. Like Isaac Newton before them, these exceptional men made clear that experience and logic alone give us less than a complete picture of truth, just as Otto Rank made clear that psychiatry must consider not only the "self" but also man's "soul" and his search towards the beyond if it is to deal effectively with man's unhappiness and aimlessness.[5]

It is becoming increasingly clear to us that only through the power of our intellect can we come to fully comprehend observations such as that of Ernest Becker, who pointed out that, "one's existence has meaning in some ultimate sense because it exists within an eternal and infinite scheme of things brought about . . . by some creative force."[6] Through the mind alone, not the senses, can we recognize that the cosmic approach is the only way we can hope to penetrate the mystery of life's purpose and to gain a taste of immortality.[7]

Judaism, which I described in the introduction as the nonpareil "religion of the mind," has traditionally stressed the importance of the intellect and the workings of the mind. Thus, R' Moshe Chaim Luzzatto spells out Jewish belief in the clearest of terms: "The elements of perfection through which man can perfect himself are his intellectual powers. Material matters . . . on the other hand, are the elements of deficiency."[8]

---

5 Becker, Ernest, *The Denial of Death*, New York: Free Press, 1973, p. 191.

6. Ibid., p. 90.

7. *Microcosm* also makes reference to the subject of immortality. In describing the elements of mind and consciousness, the author reports the revealing findings of neurosurgeon Wilder Penfield, who, over a thirty-year period, performed surgical probes of the brains of more than one thousand epileptic patients. Penfield concluded at the end that he could find no evidence of the mind within the material brain; presumably, the mind has an existence detached from that of the brain.

Gilder reports further that Penfield also concluded that the mind does not decline or deteriorate as do the body, memory and brain. And he was never able to isolate human consciousness. A devoted medical practitioner and researcher, this lifelong scientist felt these results might state a case for the immortality of man.

8. Luzzatto, M. C., *The Way of God*, trans. by Aryeh Kaplan, Jerusalem: Feldheim Publishers Ltd., 1977, p. 43.

Two hundred and fifty years ago, Luzzatto wrote of concepts of the mind and uncertainty which were first advanced only recently by quantum mechanics. Judaism holds, he explained, that, "the world therefore contains two opposite general influences. The first is that of natural determinism, while the second is indeterministic."[9] Again, he wrote of Judaism's belief that man can, through free will, affect events not only through his "deeds but even [through his] speech and *thoughts*" (emphasis added).[10] And centuries before quantum mechanics established the extensive impact of probability upon science, Maimonides set out his theories of probability and of statistical reasoning in his *Guide of the Perplexed*. His observations subsequently impressed Leibnitz, one of the greatest of the early scientists.[11, 12]

Consequently, a number of modern science's perplexing and challenging principles, such as uncertainty, probability and free will, are neither unacceptable nor unfamiliar to Jewish belief. Thus, Judaism has no quarrel with the apparent contradictions between free will and predetermination or between free will and the physical laws of nature. Nor does Judaism find incompatibility between the symmetry and regularity of such physical laws, which enable the clocklike, precision functioning of the universe, and the slight deviations of symmetry in the universe which make it possible for the universe to exist and have structure.[13]

The existence of inherent uncertainty within the unseen microcosmic realm and the recently detected presence of disorder within even our macrocosmic, visible world are at odds with society's conventional conception of a Deity Who is viewed as having created a perfectly designed and neatly ordered world. The Jewish conception of the Creator, however, is broader than the conventional one. To the Jew, uncertainty and disorder may be seen as special conditions

9. Ibid., p. 81.

10. Ibid., p. 81.

11. Rabinovitch, Nachom L., *Rambam as Scientist (Encounter)*, Jerusalem: Feldheim Publications Ltd., 1989, p. 244.

12. It is also worth noting that the theory of "many universes" which is current among some of today's cosmologists and quantum physicists was foreseen some sixteen centuries ago in the Talmud's discussion of the possibility of "18,000 worlds." (See Wilkinson, Denys, Sir, *Our Universes*, New York: Columbia University Press, 1991, and also the Babylonian Talmud, *Tractate Avoda Zora* 3b.)

13. See discussion at the end of Chapter VI relating to the announcement by Dr. George Smoot in April 1992 of one such deviation (that of temperature), which appears to explain how the universe's stars and galaxies formed.

which God created to convey to man that only He shall always possess the keys of understanding to some humanly unfathomable properties of the universe, thereby establishing one of the many indicia of His absolute sovereignty over both nature and man.

While there is considerable movement in contemporary society towards greater emphasis on the intellect, nevertheless, as Gilder observes in *Microcosm*, many people still "worship things they can see and feel." They continue to idolize "gold and jewels, land and labor" and to believe that "mechanical and mindless interactions of . . . matter are the ultimate foundations of reality." Thus, they continue to disregard quantum's crucial lesson that materialism has been replaced by intellectualism.

It is true that in the decade of the seventies, many Americans began to downgrade the role of materialism in their lives, but not because they embraced quantum's outlook of "mind over matter." Rather, the seventies saw conventional, materialistic thinking powerfully impacted by a societal surge far removed from quantum's philosophy. It came in the form of an intense drive to achieve "self-fulfillment."

In his popular, well-received book, *New Rules: Searching for Fulfillment in a World Turned Upside Down*, Daniel Yankelovich writes that the sociological studies of his prominent research firm indicated that by the late seventies, "the rage for self-fulfillment had now spread to virtually the entire U.S. population."[14] He explains that in the 1950's and 1960's, the average American had dealt mainly with such issues as success, raising a happy family and earning a good living. In the decade of the 1970's, however, a high percentage of Americans became less concerned with success and material considerations[15] and far more interested in their inner growth and development, leisure and personal freedom. They wanted to jettison the "self-denial" of their parents and to replace that ethic of past generations with a life of their own — a life of greater choices, more enjoyment and fewer restraints.

The Yankelovich studies also demonstrated clearly that by the

14. This and all direct quotations or paraphrasings of Daniel Yankelovich which follow are taken from the pages of his *New Rules: Searching for Self-Fulfillment in a World Turned Upside Down*, New York: Random House, 1981.

15. In the eighties, however, this concern markedly returned, Yankelovich comments, because of the erosion of personal income caused by rising inflationary forces.

1980's, the self-centered philosophy of the previous decade was seen to have been seriously flawed. Instead of fulfillment, it brought its adherents anxiety and destructive results. Moreover, Yankelovich observes, the "I-come-first" conviction proved that it releases only "merely selfish or hedonistic" qualities and promotes neither the individual's nor society's best interests.

From its inception, the "me-first" advocates had become strongly attracted to the theories of the existentialist movement (whose development was traced briefly in Chapter IV). Existential psychology, like the philosophy of the Enlightenment, stressed the sovereignty of man rather than of God. It opposed self-denial and encouraged self-freedom. It theorized that one should search for successively higher goals but held that this process should occur *within* the self, since the individual is meant to be the true repository of all ideals.

As Chapter IV notes, however, twenty-five years before existentialism was established in the U.S., psychiatrist Otto Rank wisely counseled that one must reach *beyond* the self for higher levels if one is to attain mature growth. This view can make all the difference in the world in achieving man's quest for fuller realization of his potential. Yankelovich makes clear that "one is a *real* self only to the extent that caring and reaching *beyond* the self continue."

When our "reaching" is beyond ourselves, we demonstrate a fundamental truth of the human condition, namely, that we are not isolated or detached from all other beings or from our heritage. To discover who we are, we need to understand that we are intimately connected with the world about us and are an intrinsic part of its past and future.

Four years after Yankelovich's *New Rules* appeared, a five-year-long sociological study by five collaborating sociologists was published under the title *Habits of the Heart*. It is a skillfully researched and insightful book, drawn from interviews of over two hundred white, middle-class men and women. The book, which became a surprising best seller, updates a thesis of Alexis de Tocqueville's famous commentary of the 1830's, *Democracy in America*, which cautioned that the American penchant for individualism was fraught with danger. "Individualism," de Tocqueville wrote, is one's desire "to draw apart from his family and friends. He willingly leaves society to itself. . ."

Habits of the Heart reevaluates de Tocqueville's apprehension and deals with a number of societal phenomena similar to those investigated by Yankelovich, in particular the widespread desire for fewer restraints and less conformance with life styles of the past.

One special line of inquiry pursued by the *Habits* team was whether we can, through the realization of personal autonomy alone, achieve happiness, without attachment to and the support of family, our historical "community," our traditions. In the end, the researchers are quite firm in their conclusion that there is a pressing need in today's society to regain the wisdom and meaningfulness given to past generations by their "biblical and republican traditions."[16] "Biblical" traditions are defined as those which stem from the biblical religions of our forbearers; "republican" traditions are those which are derived from ancient and American democratic beliefs, history and institutions.

The book emphasizes that our passion for personal freedom can trap us within a mainly isolated world that leaves us with feelings of loneliness and emptiness. More often than not, we cannot draw enough strength from peers with outlooks similar to our own to meet our need for support. Frequently, we jettison our religion because it is seen as too restrictive, too many do's and don't's, but left without attachment to our past religious institutions, we find ourselves unable, *Habits* points out, to clearly devise an ethical code to pass on to our children.

Almost all those who were interviewed by the *Habits* team confirmed that while there is value in independence and personal freedom, adherence to our culture and institutions is requisite to discovering the moral values and happiness we seek so ardently. In detaching ourselves from our traditions, we seriously risk losing the "good life" and finding out who we are. The study makes clear that acquisitions, independence and being a "somebody" have not been able to reward us with true satisfaction. Many of the interviewees spoke of their longing for what *Habits of the Heart* calls the "small town," with its strong biblical and religious traditions, its coherence, simplicity, moral sense, structure and belief in working for the common good.

---

16. This and all direct quotations or paraphrasings of the sociological viewpoints of Robert N. Bellah and associates which follow are taken from the pages of *Habits of the Heart*, ed. Robert N. Bellah, Los Angeles: University of California Press, 1985.

A great deal of what the *Habits* study found has close relevance to an outlook prevalent among large numbers of modern American Jews who have alienated themselves in various degrees from their religion because, among other reasons, Judaism is seen as incompatible with their striving for individualism. Still, as *Habits of the Heart* observes, people who have separated themselves from their religion can frequently be more strengthened than they realize by "their communities of origin." This strengthening is especially realizable as we recall the picture of the "small town" of the Jewish past, where charity and decency flourished, where each person felt responsible for his fellow, where the sanctity of the individual was upheld and where simple faith prevailed. It is a picture which can, at least in some measure, restore to our lives the coherence and richness which have become so diminished by separation from our traditions and generational memories.

A damaging result of such distancing, the *Habits of the Heart* authors caution, is that many have gone too far, discarding a history "we cannot abandon." Why must we not "abandon" our history? Because, they stress, to "find oneself" one must find the "narrative" in terms of which one's life makes sense. This narrative is more than a collection of facts. It is our "history." It "identifies us," provides us with "meaning and coherence" and links "the life of the individual to the life of society and the meaning of the cosmos." For its heightened meaning, the authors observe, the narrative (the "life course") "must be set in a larger, generational, historical and probably, *religious* context" (emphasis added).

Because Judaism's narrative can furnish the identification and connectedness so many Jewish men and women seek, I have devoted much of this book to a recounting of the numerous wellsprings that make up our Judaic narrative, more specifically, the unique wellsprings of our traditions, history, law, beliefs, ideals, survival, mission and memory. Together, these sources coalesce into what can be said to be the richest and most inspiring of all narratives and a fount of deep meaning for the Jewish people.

Towards the end of *Habits of the Heart*, the authors point out that we "seldom consciously think" of our "biblical and republican traditions," and they ask whether the eventual disappearance of these traditions may not divest us of meaning "altogether."

Why, then, do so many Jews in this generation "seldom consciously think" of their Judaic traditions? One partial answer may be that this generation is still influenced by the Enlightenment's deep suspicion of and opposition towards all religion, even though most of that suspicion and opposition can be traced mainly to the Church's long and sad history of medievalism, bigotry and hypocrisy. Another partial answer may lie, as discussed in the introduction, in our past, misplaced reliance on psychiatry, science, socialism and materialism for answers to the purpose of existence. Still another reason may be that offered by Walter Lippmann, the articulate and wise past dean of American journalism: "We reject the religious heritage because . . . we are afraid to face . . . the deep, disconcerting issues of the nature of the Universe and of man's place in it and of its destiny."[17]

The most important reason may be that many Jews were no less than the remaining population caught up in the new currents of the last three decades, especially the upheaval of the 1970's, with its aggressive belief that the individual should separate from his previous traditions in order to lead a fuller, happier life. It has been recognized, however, that this belief was myopic and defeated the hope of discovering the worthwhile goals in life, for these goals are mainly to be detected within the very generational linkage which the 1970's tried to negate.

An insightful sentence from *Habits of the Heart* drives home the exceptional contribution which past tradition can make: "Our lives make sense in a *thousand* ways . . . because of traditions that are *centuries, if not millennia, old*" (emphasis added). I feel that this opinion of objective, professional sociologists furnishes strong support for my conviction that the primary source of a Jewish person's life-meaning can be found in "millennia-old" Judaism, which originated 3,300 years ago at Sinai and remains with us to this day.

In the past several decades, thousands of Jewish men and women have returned to their ancient Jewish source of meaning. Most of them had sensed that something is drastically wrong with today's world. They saw the widening of an abyss between their contemporary culture and the values and inner satisfaction they

17. Lippmann, Walter, *Education for a World Adrift*, R. W. Livingston, 1943, p. 111.

were trying to capture. Too many social trends were heading in wrong directions: unprecedented permissiveness, erosion of family cohesiveness, exaggerated material acquisitiveness, strange new moralities.

The investigation of Judaism by these Jewish men and women revealed, as some scientific disciplines have discovered during the past fifty years, that there really *is* "something out there." They found that Judaism's value system makes a great deal more sense than they believed possible. Discarding many earlier, indiscriminate acceptances of conventional wisdom, these once-skeptical men and women have discovered that while Judaism may regulate our lives, it can also elevate them. Although religious practices may moderate our freedom to do entirely as we please, such practices can also supply the structure and underpinning we need and miss. A life lived without structure can be compared, in Robert Frost's phrase about free verse, to "playing tennis with the net down." Undertaking a kosher home is described by an Atlanta Jewish therapist interviewed in *Habits of the Heart* as achieving for her a measure of order in our "chaotic universe." And no matter what the previous six days have brought, spending a Sabbath with a Sabbath-observant family can affirm the possibility of bringing a new dimension of tranquility, purpose and joy into private lives lived within our turbulent environment.

In these and in dozens of other ways, the Torah's content can bring added value to every phase of our lives, to our business, social and family relationships and to our ethical views of what is right and wrong, fair and unfair, ideal and ordinary. It is this ability of the Torah to touch each of us in numerous ways that endows Judaism with its unique value and attraction to so many previously alienated Jewish men and women.

Yet, in all this, the Torah-observant Jew need not withdraw from the world about him or her, for our religion encourages that we live fully. Indeed, the Torah looks with disfavor upon self-denial of any of life's Torah-permissible enjoyments and accomplishments.

In a renewal of commitment to Judaism, one comes to detect the special distinction of our religion, which, as we noted previously, rests on two basic foundations: the equality of man and the sanctity of the individual. In the former, we see the ancient source of what *Habits of the Heart* calls our republican traditions. In the latter foundation, we see what *Habits of the Heart* calls our biblical traditions. These traditions blend together in Judaism, enabling a Jewish person who returns to his religion to benefit simultaneously from both of these recognized keys to a more satisfying and meaningful life.

In the preface to *Habits*, the researchers note that the "fundamental question" they asked those interviewed, and which many of those interviewed frequently asked the researchers, was "how to preserve or create a morally coherent life." Probing for guidance toward this frequently elusive goal, the authors turned to de Tocqueville's writings for his insights.

To de Tocqueville, the individualistic, personal pursuit of economic gain spawned unworthy attitudes in early American society because that pursuit tended to erode man's civic spirit. To develop as a good citizen, he held, we must "occasionally look at something other than ourselves." Yet, while a strong drive toward acquisitiveness was present in early nineteeth-century America, it was often tempered by a traditional, sympathetic interest of many citizens in the needs and well-being of their neighbors. Such ethical considerations contributed a great deal to the nineteenth-century American outlook on "How might we live?"

In the closing pages of *Habits*, the researchers deal at length with these same issues but view them in the setting of the late twentieth century. They note that despite exceptional social advances over the past one hundred years, material accumulation and the striving for recognition have greatly accelerated and have come to personify the meaning of life, especially in the middle class.

The goals of economic and social prominence have become, for many, integral parts of the great American dream, and in the process have seriously undermined those older, traditional mores which in the past helped tie each of us to one another. As a result of this fragmentation, *Habits* points out, we are faced with a damaging "internal incoherence" of our society. In placing getting above giving, we have substantially compromised our chances of attaining our deep-down dream of "a morally coherent life." Our goal of living in a more ideal society becomes steadily more distant.

The *Habits* research team is hopeful, however, that things can still be turned around and that we will "reconsider the course" we are following. In the penultimate page of the book, the writers offer some penetrating observations directed toward the logic and desireability of such reconsideration.

In the tenor of those final *Habits* observations, I venture to submit the following reflections of my own, directed to those Jewish men and women who may yet "reconsider [their] course" and return to their ancient Judaic roots: Perhaps the building blocks of a "morally coherent life" can best be found in those unique Jewish values which helped forge such lives for our forebears. Perhaps ambition to serve may bring greater reward than ambition to succeed; there may be more twentieth century relevance than we realize in the advice which King Solomon gave us in *Ecclesiastes:* "The race is not to the swift, nor the battle to the strong." Even more so, it may be that we can discover our most worthwhile goal in the final words written in *Ecclesiastes* by that wisest of men: "The end of the matter, all having been considered: fear God and keep His commandments, for this is the whole duty of man."

And, as a final reflection, perhaps in the long, long run, a rediscovery of God is the most important triumph of all.

One would hope, then, that we Jews would "consciously think" of our Judaic narrative and withstand any conformance to popular life styles and beliefs which lack content, direction, sense or at times, even sanity. For there is no finer exercise of our free will than to resist being drawn into modern society's vortex of pro-self materialism, hedonism, and aimlessness.

But if we do not so resist, if we permit ourselves to become or remain part of the near-meaningless, half-mad whirl in which most of modern society is trapped, if we naively blind ourselves to the superiority of the intellect over possessions, if we discard our Judaic narrative and the self-identification and connectedness it provides, if we allow ourselves to scoff at the value of attachment to God and the mores of our grandfathers, then we throw away our only real hope of discovering that elusive "something more to life" and the moral coherence which lie at the heart of our search for a more meaningful existence.

There is a Chassidic tale about a faraway kingdom whose wheat crop became infected and would cause insanity if eaten. The king's advisors petitioned him for a solution to the dilemma: If the wheat was fed to his subjects, they would become deranged; if the wheat was destroyed, they would starve.

The king pondered the dilemma for a day and then issued his decision. To forestall starvation, he ruled, distribute the infected wheat to the entire population except for the king, his family and a few randomly selected subjects. To this latter group, distribute what little remains in the public granary of non-infected wheat left over from previous crops. "In this way," concluded the king, "there will be some of us left who will know that the rest of us are crazy."

While much of contemporary society spins and thrashes about in the grip of excessive consumerism, an infatuation with pleasure-seeking and a widespread reliance upon a virtually irrational "earthly logic," Judaism waits patiently in the wings, prepared to welcome every Jew who strives to learn what life is all about.

11

Reason vs. Revelation

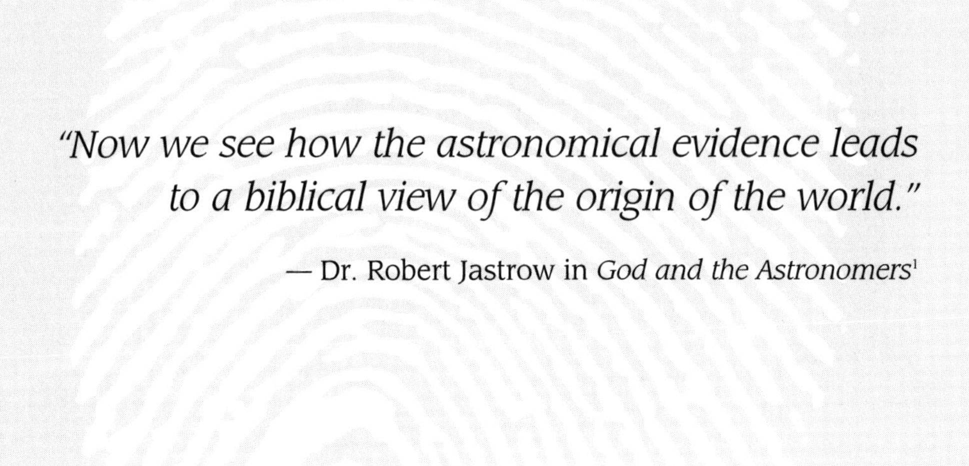

"Now we see how the astronomical evidence leads to a biblical view of the origin of the world."

— Dr. Robert Jastrow in *God and the Astronomers*[1]

---

1. Jastrow, Robert, *God and the Astronomers* New York: Warner Books, 1978, p. 3.

In the last chapter, we explored the goal of most of the two hundred men and women interviewed in the *Habits of the Heart* survey, that goal being to "preserve or create a morally coherent life." They sought answers to the grand question, "How might we live?" At the chapter's close, I ventured the observations that these crucial goals are approachable, even attainable, by "a rediscovery of God" and a reconnection with time-honored Jewish values.

How well founded are these observations? Some distanced-from-religion Jewish person may ask, for example, "Does Judaism enable Jews to achieve a morally coherent life? Does Judaism provide truly beneficial insight into how one might live?"

These questions may best be answered when first considered against the background of the Enlightenment and the Emancipation. Each of the ages that preceded the Enlightenment had its particular achievement. Thus, the Graeco-Roman period is associated with philosophy, architecture, literature and military conquest. The medieval period is seen as characterized by the ascendancy of the Church and its domineering hold on the mind and will of man, tempered somewhat by the intellect and scholarship of cloistered monks who collected and stored thousands of Greek and Roman manuscripts throughout Europe.

The Age of Enlightenment can be regarded as having begun one of its early stages with the discovery and editing of these manuscripts by a new class of intellectuals, the humanists. They had two parallel motivations: the translation and dissemination of the ancient classics and the elevation of man as the successor to the divine sovereignty of God.

It was the first of these twin motivations which helped bring about the rise of science as the new revolutionary force in the world. As early as the fourteenth century, the humanists occupied themselves with the translation of manuscripts on scientific subjects such as astronomy and mathematics, and the introduction of such texts into the universities of Europe. Greek works that had been hidden for over a thousand years found their way, translated into the vernacular, into the hands of a new class of knowledge-seeker, the student of science. Much of the credit for this important development belongs to the enthusiasm of the humanist for the classics of antiquity, such as Euclid's famous work on geometry, which greatly influenced Isaac Newton and, centuries later, Albert Einstein.

The growth of the scientific disciplines, however, was accelerated not only by the penchant of the humanists for scholarship but also by the printing press, gunpowder, the magnetic compass, the discovery of the New World, the circumnavigation of the earth, and in later centuries by the steam engine, the locomotive, the dynamo, the telegraph, the airplane, fibre optics and the powerful computer. These and dozens of other technological triumphs endowed science with an influence that was no less than revolutionary. In *My Views*, Max Born wrote that because of their superb technological successes, scientists established a "decisive position in society."

One way of evaluating the degree of science's influence upon society is to contrast what people believed before and after Isaac Newton, Charles Darwin, Albert Einstein and Werner Heisenberg. The resultant changes in man's thinking and philosophic outlook were drastic. When such recognized greats in science spoke, sooner or later their viewpoints were obediently accepted by significant numbers of people.

While few among us can accurately explain the findings of science,[2]

2. A recent survey of college students indicated that only a small percentage were able to explain the relatively well-known phenomena of why our days are shorter and colder in winter than in summer.

we rarely question or challenge scientific conclusions. Generally we remain content to accede to them, even in such important matters as our world-view towards not only the physical world, but at times toward the spiritual one as well. Little wonder that the word "revolutionary" is used so frequently to describe the powerful effect of science upon us and our culture. And it is because science has so broadly impinged upon our lives and outlooks that I have included science-related material here and there in this book, to trace the growth of the prominence which science has achieved in our culture.

The Enlightenment set out to liberate mankind from despotism, cruelty, darkness and want, but it can well be argued that it has fallen far short of its goals. At the end of the twentieth century, which witnessed the nadir of human morality in the bestiality and inhumanity of the Third Reich, we face a world of ideological fanaticism, ethnic wars, intertribal slaughter and oppressive regimes. Equally depressing is the specter of atomic weapons possessed by a number of former Soviet republics, which may in the future allow such non-conventional weapons to fall into the hands of terrorist states or terrorist cells, threatening the possible destruction of part or all of our world.

In the centuries that preceded the Emancipation, man's search for meaning centered upon his search for God. With the coming of the Emancipation, however, increasingly greater numbers of people focused upon a quest for reason, for rational analysis. As a result, since that era, the search for meaning has taken two divergent approaches, that of reason and that of religion.

The advocates of reason maintain that through our intellect alone we can apprehend "god," described as a cosmic power which undergirds the cosmos and is the source of the harmony and grandeur of nature. Contraposed is the position taken by the advocates of religion, who argue that reason by virtue of its human origin is too limited to attain truth or to access the spiritual mysteries of the universe; only through religious faith can man hope to learn about God or discover the true purpose of his life.

Still, the lines of this centuries-old debate were not always sharply drawn or clearly discernible. A number of our past, highly-regarded Jewish thinkers (Moses Maimonides being the most prominent) did not regard reason and religion (or "revelation," a term which I feel relates more accurately to Judaism in this context than the more generalized word "religion") as mutually exclusive in all ways, granting to reason an important role in man's quest to draw closer to his Creator. They cautioned, however, that reason is not to be employed unassisted, but only as an adjunct to Judaic tradition and prophecy.

The Reason-vs.-Revelation dichotomy continues to this very day, restating the classic arguments of its partisans. But in modern times, the scientist gradually has replaced the philosopher as the exemplar of the "rationalist." For the widespread influence of the social writings of such philosophers as Rousseau, Paine, Voltaire, Mendelssohn, Bentham and Locke began to wane after the mid-nineteenth century, and the persuasiveness of social philosophy was gradually eclipsed by the growing dominance of science upon the individual and upon society.

And although since the 1920's we have seen the intriguing emergence of a leaning by a number of distinguished scientific figures towards the recognition that there may be a "theological" aspect to the physical world, the majority view of today's scientists is substantially the same as that which science's hero-figure, Albert Einstein, had held. Hence, I have selected Einstein as a fitting spokesman for the modern-era rationalist's view towards reason and towards religion.

As we have seen earlier in this book, Einstein's contributions to science, especially his two Theories of Relativity, revised our conception of the physical universe to such a degree that we no longer can accept such ideas as absolute time or absolute space. Rather than confining himself to the long-accepted scientific goal of describing the material world, Einstein considered it his ultimate goal to understand it. He followed a course of intuitive reasoning, abstract theory and what has been described as "pure imagination," bypassing conventional truisms. He directed his brilliance towards exploring the ancient mysteries, viewing nature more through the eyes of a philosopher than those of a physicist.

When Einstein wrote about god, he did not have in mind "God." Instead, he meant a god of nature, describing this concept as "the harmony of natural law which reveals an intelligence of such superiority that, compared with it, all systematic thinking and acting of human beings is an utterly insignificant reflection."

In his early years, Einstein was enrolled in a Catholic elementary school because the Jewish school was too distant and the tuition too high. At the age of ten, he entered the Luitpold gymnasium in Munich, where he received the Jewish education provided for Jewish students. Years later, he said that the Bible educaion he received there gave him the lasting impression that all Bible accounts were childish tales and need not be taken seriously. Nonetheless, he was attracted to the Bible's "historical value." Although raised in a house where a freethinking father was often heard to make disparaging remarks about religion, the young Einstein keenly felt and wrote about "god's majesty." But it was a god he identified only with the physical world, and as the influence upon him of his study of the natural sciences grew, he gradually rejected all religious affiliation.

Einstein's approach to the issues of Reason vs. Revelation was that of the classic man of reason. He defined his view as a "cosmic religious feeling" engendered in him by the "grandeur of reason incarnate in existence." This, he wrote, is the highest form of religion, for it enables us to free ourselves from the "shackles of personal hope and desires."

To Einstein, the idea of a personal God was totally inconsistent with the thinking of a rational man. Instead, he adopted a Spinoza-inspired pantheism in which god becomes all events and all things, and all things and all events become manifestations of god, such things and events spanning the entire range from the natural to the supernatural, the exceptional to the commonplace, the good to the evil.

Einstein conceded that a personal God can provide guidance, comfort and assistance to man. He asserted, however, that to the man of reason, a belief in a personal God is spiritually immature and anthropomorphic[3] in nature since men "appeal to the Divine Being in prayer and plead the fulfillment of their wishes." As Einstein put it, the flaw in the concept of a personal God is that we are told that

3. Partisans of rationalism frequently charge Judaism with anthropomorphism, the ascribing of human attributes or forms to god. These usages are metaphorical, employed as an attempt to overcome the limitations of human language and perception. This is the import of the Talmudic dictum that "the Torah speaks in the language of men."

The rationalist-scientist's criticism of Judaic anthropomorphism is rendered ironic, however, by the scientific tradition (referred to in earlier chapters) of speaking not in the language of men but in the esoteric jargon of science, a linguistic method which Nobel laureate Erwin Schrödinger correctly described as "colourless, cold, mute."

God punishes and rewards man for his deeds; yet if all man's deeds are also God's, how can we hold man responsible for what are also God's actions?[4]

It is a source of wonder that Einstein could have overlooked seeing the error in this logic. Had he, like his great hero Isaac Newton, "on whose shoulders he stood," but familiarized himself with the writings of Moses Maimonides, Einstein would have recognized the speciousness of his reasoning. For Maimonides wrote extensively on the concept of man's freedom of will,[5] a principle which he termed "the pillar of the law." In his famous *Mishna Torah*, he makes clear that "a human being's activities are his own and the Almighty . . . [does not decree] . . . that he should act thus or not act thus." Man's deeds are not also God's deeds but solely man's own doings and responsibility. It is interesting to speculate[6] what Einstein's philosophic outlook might have been had he been exposed to Maimonides' writings on the free will principle; perhaps then he would have accepted both the existence of human free will as well as the concept of a personal God Who also can act freely and independently of all else. Instead, Einstein, like many realists of the past and present, remained with the implausible pantheistic belief which Spinoza held, that god is an impersonal being who acts only out of necessity.

In espousing the theory of necessity, Einstein raised one of the basic disputes in the Reason-vs.-Revelation controversy: What brings about existence, the causality of the laws of nature or divine purpose? Judaism's belief is precisely set out by Rabbi Moshe Chaim Luzzatto in *The Way of God*: "[God can] act and direct things as He wills. . . There is absolutely nothing He must *necessarily* do."[7] The

4. Einstein, Albert, *Out of My Later Years*, London: Thames & Hudson 1950, p. 27.

5. See Chapter IX for a more complete discussion of free will.

6. There was a parallel episode in Einstein's life, related in Chapter II, which demonstrated the occasional tendency of Einstein to succumb to oversight. It will be recalled that Newton firmly believed in creation-in-time, while Einstein did not, claiming for a long period that it did not appeal to his scientific instinct. As a consequence, he stubbornly resisted the entreaties of the Russian mathematician Alexandre Friedmann that Einstein's own General Theory of Relativity supported the creation-in-time theory. He pointed out that this critical finding was embedded in Einstein's theory but was concealed by a simple error in algebra which Einstein had made in his mathematical calculations. Finally, after a series of letters from Friedmann, Einstein publicly acknowledged his miscalculation, commenting later that his opposition to the expanding universe principle (which led to a creation-split-second theory) was the greatest mistake he ever made.

7. Luzzatto, Moshe Chaim, *The Way of God*, trans. by Aryeh Kaplan, Jerusalem: Feldheim Publishers, Ltd., 1977, p. 167.

necessity concept, however, denies that will or purpose underlie and direct the unfolding of the order of nature; instead it holds that all events and all things occur simply out of a necessity caused by the eternally existing, unalterable physical laws of the universe. It is in this clash of two fundamental postulates that there arises one of man's oldest and most troubling perplexities.

The spokesman I have selected to present the case for revelation in the Reason-vs.-Revelation controversy is Moses Maimonides (1135-1204). A towering figure in Jewish history, considered the foremost Jewish thinker of the Middle Ages, a master interpreter and codifier of Jewish law, an outstanding physician of his times, the author of classic volumes which grace the desks of scholars and laymen to this very day, a fearless seeker of truth and "knowledge of God," a saintly, humble, selfless leader of the Jewish people — this is but a partial thumbnail sketch of this exceptional man.

Raised in an atmosphere of Jewish scholarship and intellectualism, followed by his years of study and introspection, Maimonides concluded that to best bring about a more complete understanding of God, one should "combine Torah and reason and in this way reduce everything as much as possible to natural principles."[8] "Human" wisdom and "divine" wisdom are not opposed but complementary to each other, he wrote, and both stem from a heavenly source.

In these views, Maimonides was supported by a number of his contemporaries as well as sages who lived later, but his position was not without its detractors, some of whom bitterly opposed him and his usage of an Aristotelian framework. Today, as well, there are outstanding Jewish personalities who feel that the principles of our faith are and should be independent of pure logic, reason and intellectualism.

Maimonides upheld the merit of such restraining views as being in keeping with the cautions in *Psalms* 131:4-7 ("I did not involve myself with things too great and too wonderful for me.") and that of our Sages that human intellect is limited in its scope and that if one does not remain within those limitations, intellectual and theologi-

---

8. Direct quotations and some general reference material in this chapter related to Maimonides were taken from the pages of Isadore Twersky's *A Maimonides Reader*, New York: Behrman House Inc., 1972.

cal damage may result. He held, however, that *within* such limiting constraints, reason and even speculation may be employed to accomplish man's primary goal, that of achieving "knowledge of God." Specifically, reason can assist man to comprehend and appreciate the wisdom of divine law.

Nonetheless, he insisted upon a critical *third element* in his construct of Jewish belief: the authentic and final authority of *tradition* and *prophecy*. In his famous *Letter on Astrology*, he explained that one should not believe anything which is not established by one of these three elements: rational proof, as in mathematical science; the perception of the senses; or Judaic tradition and prophecy.

As to element one, the famous Mishnaic tractate *Ethics of our Fathers* teaches that "astronomy and geometry are the auxiliaries of wisdom." The great Torah authority of the eighteenth century, the Vilna Gaon, thus encouraged the study of astronomy and mathematics, in keeping with that Mishnaic dictum. As to element two, we find many references in the writings of our Sages that the knowledge gained through our five senses enables man to recognize his puniness compared with God's awesome creations, thereby leading him to the humility ("I am but dust and ashes," said Abraham the Patriarch) he must attain if he is to truly accept upon himself the sovereignty of God and His laws.

It is the third element, however, which is the crux of the controversy between purely rationalistic Jews who believe unaided reason to be the source of the highest wisdom and Jews who believe that the ultimate source of true wisdom is to be found in revelation, Judaic tradition and prophecy.

The importance of revelation in the formulation of Jewish belief and thought was stressed as one of the key points in Judah Halevi's classic, *The Kuzari*, written during the decade in which Maimonides was born (1130-1140). In this work, Halevi, who was also the poet laureate of the Jewish people, brilliantly presented Judaism's position vis-à-vis Reason vs. Revelation. Logic, he wrote, can indicate the concept of a god of nature, but only our historical experience (of God's manifestation in historical events, such as Sinai) is trustworthy and free of doubt. Reason may point us toward knowledge about God, but only revelation and tradition can clarify ultimate issues, resolve questions and draw us closer to an attachment with our Creator.

Halevi clearly spelled out this distinction between revelation and reason, through the observation of the king of the Khazars: "Now I understand the difference between . . . the God of Abraham and the god of Aristotle." Sinai, Halevi penned, was the most authentic event in the history of religion. It was there, in the clear, undisputed view of nearly three million of our people, that God revealed our chosenness and our role in human destiny. The God of Revelation, Halevi continued, unlike the god of nature, is a personal God Who came down from the heavens to embrace man. The god of reason can only be apprehended through logic, whereas nearness to the God of Revelation may be achieved through love and *imitatio Dei*, man's imitation of God's actions.

Although Maimonides went beyond Halevi in supporting the view that rational thinking can aid in the search for wisdom, he drew a firm line of resistance against any philosophic denial of the existence of a personal God or limitation of God's freedom to act independently, to create or even to interfere in the functioning of the universe. He totally rejected the Aristotelian (and Spinozist) approach which held that all events come about through "necessity," a position which he asserted was beyond possible proof.

Maimonides stoutly defended the Torah's teaching that the universe came into being simply through the will and design of God. He rejected all other scientific or philosophic explanations, including that of an eternally existing universe. To reinforce this position, Maimonides wrote at length in the *Guide* about what he called the "creation-in-time" theory, emphasizing that the universe was created in a single, split-second moment sometime in the remote past. "Everything is bound up with this problem," he wrote.

Why "everything"? Because, Maimonides stressed, belief in creation-in-time confirms the critical and fundamental Judaic beliefs that *there is a God* and that all that happens in the world is not due to chance but to *His design and purpose*. These principles have always been bedrocks in Judaic belief, and in the *Guide*, Maimonides emphasized them in his rebuttal to Aristotle's "eternal universe" theory. With a "belief in the creation of the world in time," he pointed out, "all the miracles become possible . . . and all questions that may be asked on this subject vanish," questions such as: Why did God establish the Law? Why was the Law given to the Jewish people and not to another nation? Why did He not program us to automatically perform its commandments and observe its prohibitions?

Maimonides' response to such questions was simply that God, in His wisdom, decreed that everything unfold in the way it has. It was His will alone that determined in what form and at what moment the universe was to be created, and it is not within our power to know either the mysteries underlying creation or His purpose and will in other things. Maimonides concludes, quoting Isaiah 55:8: "For My thoughts are not your thoughts, neither are your ways My ways. . ."

Although, as I stress in past and forward pages, Jewish belief stands on its own, without need of scientific validation, the eventual vindication of Maimonides' conclusion regarding creation in a single, finite moment (described in Chapter II) stands as a remarkably persuasive case for the validity of the Torah's *Genesis* account. Some 850 years ago, he wrote (one can almost detect a sense of yearning in his words), "For if creation in time were demonstrated . . . all the overhasty claims [as to necessity] made to us on this point by the philosophers would become void." And we have seen, within the last fifty years, that science *has* substantially corroborated that the universe was created within a single instant of time; yet, as late as 1932, the brilliant scientific pathfinder Eddington opposed the probability of a "beginning" and Einstein still regarded the Expanding Universe Theory (upon which, to a large degree, the "Big Bang" Theory rests) as making no sense. Both of these preeminent physicists eventually conceded their significant mistakes.

Although it involves a number of collateral issues, the tug-of-war between the proponents of reason and revelation centered mainly upon our principle disputation: Was the universe created by the physical law of nature or by God?

We live in a time when mankind is still very much influenced by the Enlightenment's original devaluation of religious belief. Consequently, when man deals with the concept of God, more often than not he ponders whether God exists at all, and if He does, to what extent does He control events? Until half a century ago, the most prevalent view among scientists was that of causality, the deterministic principle that everything has a cause which in turn brings about an effect, and that everything that happens can be traced to this chain of events.

Until the mid-twentieth century, the concept of biblical creation as described in *Genesis* was an anathema to almost all cosmologists, and its endorsement was generally considered to be an act of scientific apostasy. The so-called "steady-state" theory (holding that the universe has always existed as it now appears) was embraced by a number of prominent scientists. Others were taken with the "oscillating" theory or model which, similar to "steady-state," neatly finessed the "In-the-beginning" account of *Genesis*. It was only shortly before his death in 1955 that Einstein stated in an interview that he finally accepted the idea of a "beginning."

But with the impact of the exceptional discoveries made by Edwin Hubble and Arno Penzias and Robert Wilson in the generation between 1935 and 1965, the science of cosmology was remarkably modified. Hubble's most important finding of an expanding, explosive universe led to the evolvement of the famous "Big Bang" Theory. In 1965, the work of Penzias and Wilson established the radiation traces left in the cosmos by the fireball of the "Big Bang," pretty much nailing down the validity of the "Big Bang" Theory.

These developments had curious overtones. Scientists dusted off the long-shelved biblical description of creation and took a hard look at the implications of the *Genesis* account because the steady-state and the oscillating theories had by then almost entirely been replaced by "Big Bang." It became quite clear that the cause-and-effect approach could no longer stand unrivaled as the sole, coherent explanation of creation. For while the details do not match precisely, the underlying components of the scientific and the biblical accounts appeared alike, namely a sudden beginning at a single moment in time, accompanied by a fiery explosion emitting an incredible force of energy and light. A similar viability or co-existence between scientific findings and such Judaic beliefs as creation *ex nihilo* [i.e., out-of-nothing, a belief also staunchly defended by Maimonides], free will, indeterminism, and the age of the universe also has been established in recent years.)[9]

As a result, mainstream cosmology has generally conceded that there was a "beginning," and *Genesis* has earned a parallel position

9. An excellent treatment of these and other highly interesting developments can be found in the recent publication of Professor Nathan Aviezer's fine book *In the Beginning: Creation and Science*.

Another recent book which ably presents the case for the compatibility of Jewish faith and science, especially as to the age of the universe, is Dr. Gerald Schroeder's *Genesis and the Big Bang*.

to causality in the presentation of what occurred when the universe came into being. Of course, *Genesis* introduces a factor which science has always declined to recognize, namely that God is the cause of creation. How (if?) science will otherwise treat this all-important element in the "new story" of creation is anybody's guess. Distinguished particle physicist Steven Weinberg, in his *The First Three Minutes,* has written a fine account detailing what he considers took place in the early moments of creation, but he makes it clear that the conditions which existed in the earliest fraction of a second of these three minutes are so obscured from scientific view that it was necessary for him to begin his account a fraction of a second after the very beginning. For the estimated 100 million, million, million, million, million-degree heat of the cosmic explosion had totally devastated any evidence of what had existed in the earliest of moments.

In effect, then, science appears to be left without any reasonable promise of reaching back to the past (as it has so often succeeded in doing by the approach of tracing a chain of cause-and-effect backward) to establish the "initial conditions" indispensable to the formulation of any scientific theory as to what, if anything, preceded creation.

At the same time, there continues on, without interruption or disproof, *Genesis'* inherent thirty-three-centuries-old proclamation of the God of Israel being the source of all creation. And as *Genesis's* description of creation takes on increased credibility in the environment of our time, so too does its proclamation, stated in the words, "God created heaven and earth," which immediately follow the opening phrase, "In the beginning." Interestingly, Robert Jastrow, in concluding his *Miami Herald* article (October 22, 1978) on the "new story of *Genesis,*" made the observation that this new story has offered "the reassuring message that modern man can reconcile science with his belief in God."

It is even more interesting to note the observation of one who co-discovered the evidence of the creation fireball, physicist-astronomer and Nobel Prize recipient Arno Penzias. One might expect that Dr. Penzias would hope that his work not be overturned and continue as a famous scientific landmark. Yet he made clear his consistent adherence to the constancy of our Sinai-derived law, even in the face of a possible disqualification of his findings, when he commented in an interview by a *New York Times* reporter regarding his personal Judaic beliefs, "If someone disproved the Big Bang Theory, I wouldn't start lying or cheating. My faith is not dependent on physics."[10]

For the committed Jew remains resolute in his faith with or without scientific confirmations, and even if scientific findings were to prove incompatible with Judaic belief.

10. *The New York Times*, May 12, 1993, p. C10. See fuller account in Chapter II of Dr. Penzias' famous co-discovery of background radiation.

12 Three Worlds

"The unified field theory is now finished . . . In spite of the vast amount of work put into it I am unable to verify it in any way. This situation will prevail for many years, all the more so as physicists do not accept logical or philosophical arguments."

— Albert Einstein (in Lettres á Maurice Solovine, Paris 1956)

". . . the chief aim of man should be to make himself, as far as possible, similar to God; that is to say, to make his acts similar to the acts of God. . ."

— Moses Maimonides, *Guide of the Perplexed*

". . . observe how great an honor the Creator has accorded the righteous by considering them partners with Him in the universe. . ."[1]

— Rabbi Moshe Chaim Luzzatto

"Therefore, I shall speak of Your glories. . ."

— "Song of Glory," attributed to R' Yehuda HaChassid, 12th century scholar and Kabbalist

1. Luzzatto, Moshe Chaim, *The Knowing Heart,* trans. by Schraga Silverstein, Jerusalem: Feldheim Publishers, Ltd., 1982, p. 279.

The previous chapter's discussion of the classic confrontation between reason and revelation furnishes a helpful background against which we can consider the important questions posed at the beginning of the previous chapter by a distanced-from-religion Jewish man or woman: Does Judaism enable a Jewish person to achieve a "morally coherent" life? Does Judaism contain truly beneficial insights into how one might live?

To provide authentic replies to these challenging questions, we should familiarize ourselves a bit more with the potential of Judaism to furnish a searching Jew with the spiritual resources needed to gain moral coherency and to arrive at an understanding of how one should live.

At the outset, it is important to note that swirling about such a searching Jew is a multitude of unsettling, competing issues and viewpoints: Was the universe divinely created? Is it governed by divine will and purpose, or is it abandoned to randomness, caprice and chance? Is truth absolute or simply relative? Is morality certain or as varied as fingerprints? Where and how are life's real meaning and happiness to be found? Why am I here in the first place?

In contemplating these issues, our questing Jew discerns three contrasting worlds found in twentieth-century society, any one of which he or she may enter: the world which Saul Bellow called the "world of the streets," the world of reason and the world of revelation. Let us explore each of these worlds in that order:

The World of the Streets

Bellow's phrase above was used in his foreward to one of the most surprising and unlikely of recent best sellers, Allan Bloom's *The Closing of the American Mind.*[2] Within weeks of its publication, this scholarly, not-so-easy-to-read book climbed to the top of the best-seller list, and by the end of the year placed second in nonfiction sales for 1987. It received a number of lauditory reviews, among them that of the *New York Times,* which rated it as a "genuinely profound book." *The Closing* is essentially a keen inquiry into what Bloom asserted was the failing mission of American universities to provide the time-honored traditions and thinking which are invaluable to a student in his search for answers to the questions of human existence, especially the question, "What is good?"[3] As a result, Bloom's subtitle reads in part, "How Higher Education Has . . . Impoverished the Souls of Today's Students."

Although Bloom's book occasionally overstates and at times evidences a bias toward stern conservatism, I found it to be, in the main, an illuminating account of a growing crisis within the precincts of American universities, and outside as well. It is Bloom's thesis that the crisis was spawned by the influence, upon popular belief, of "openness," a concept which declines to assess the worth or worthlessness of values and ideas; truth, beliefs and morality are merely relative.

"Openness," in Bloom's words, "is the great insight of our times." It has become a "moral virtue," the inalienable right of every man to

2. As with two other books to which I have paid special credit in previous pages, I wish to acknowledge my indebtedness to the late Professor Bloom for his penetrating commentary on our present culture. Much of what follows in the subsections "The World of the Streets" and "The World of Reason," as well as portions of "The World of Revelation," were derived from his analysis of today's society and the culture and traditions of the past.

3. This and all direct quotations or paraphrases of Allan Bloom which follow are taken from the pages of Allan Bloom's *The Closing of the American Mind,* New York: Simon and Schuster Inc., 1987.

practice any and all beliefs, ideas and values as he sees fit, without apology to or interference by others. In the name of openness, any "life style" becomes legitimized, as do many strange deviations from long-accepted models of social behavior. The result, Bloom warned, is a creeping undermining of a great number of intellectual and ethical standards of American society.

I have used the term "world of the streets" to describe that growing facet of society which has transformed a once-admirable and democratic "openness" into an alarming permissiveness, typified by the popular expression "Just do it!" And inside the university system, Bloom asserted, we have begun to see the implementation of an educational laxity which a generation ago would have been regarded as intellectually and culturally unacceptable. Such trends within a number of universities can be traced, at least in part, to the intimidation and pressures of groups of small but vocal activists seeking to impose their new theories of relativism and "openness" upon university authorities.

The early beginnings of educational unrest on the campuses were described by Bloom against the background of the 1969 take-over of Cornell University's Willard Straight Hall (the university "union") by a group of militant students (to this day, it is not precisely clear whether they went in armed or whether their arms were smuggled in later). As a professor in the university at that time, Bloom observed the crisis personally and dealt with several of the leading personalities involved. The book relates in detail his dismay and disappointment over the eventual capitulation of the administration's officials to the take-over group's demands, especially the demand that the university's core curriculum be revised to conform with current student tastes and inclinations.

There are instances in *The Closing* where Bloom's contentions are so strong — especially as to the weakness shown by administrators and other professors when subjected to the pressures of student activists — that one wonders if Bloom's outrage and sharp criticism were fully warranted. However, his concern that the administration's surrender of Cornell's autonomy boded badly for other universities in the future proved not to be exaggerated. Indeed, several recent capitulations by other universities have shown Bloom to have been quite prescient in his concerns.

Thus, in the highly publicized "behemoth" incident at the

University of Pennsylvania, a student named Eden Jacobowitz was threatened with dismissal for having cautioned a group of noisy co-eds to be quiet and for calling them "behemoth" (the Hebrew equivalent of "oxen") as they were passing beneath his dormitory window at two o'clock in the morning. He was brought before a board of inquiry for "violation of the Code of Conduct" and for "racial harassment." When he resisted the charges, the administration — apparently seeking some sort of confession of guilt — suggested a "plea bargain" to him, under which his dismissal punishment would be dropped in exchange for a confession of wrongdoing and his participation in a program of "diverse community environment living" to "re-educate" him. It would appear that Jacobowitz's rather understandable outburst required what can be defined as mind control to remedy what was judged to be at best racial "insensitivity."

The University of Pennsylvania incident was followed in the spring of 1994 by another university capitulation — this time at Brandeis University. In this instance, a small minority at the school — approximately fifty of 340 of its faculty and less than one hundred of its four thousand students — intimidated the administration into a reversal of its decision to bestow an honorary degree upon Jeane Kirkpatrick, former U.S. Ambassador to the United Nations and prominent political commentator. The protesters charged that Kirkpatrick, as a Reagan appointee, had once supported some Latin American repressive governments. The protesters failed to mention, however, that virtually all of the then-repressive regimes gradually but eventually emerged as democratic governments. Moreover, some outside observers of the Brandeis incident made the additional point that the protesters were more likely disturbed by Kirkpatrick's long record of support for the State of Israel and in particular by her outspoken reservations over Israel's agreements with the P.L.O.

In recent days, a number of U.S. intellectuals — New York Senator Daniel Patrick Moynihan, *New York Times* columnist Russell Baker and *Washington Post* political commentator Charles Krauthammer — have written and spoken about similar disturbing trends in present-day popular beliefs. In an essay in *The American Scholar*, Moynihan offered a cogent insight into such trends: What is taking place, he wrote, is that deviancy has been "defined down" to convert once-unacceptable conduct and belief into becoming normal and even agreeable. And, Baker points out, this "defining down" keeps accelerating, while we gradually adapt to this process of normalizing the crude, the tasteless and the "dumbed" public education, almost without realizing how "dumb we're becoming." Moynihan explains that it became necessary to "redefine" deviancy because its occurrence had become so widespread that contemporary society needed to set lower and lower levels of "normalcy" in order to provide some sort of legitimacy to deviancy.

In an address before the American Enterprise Institute, Krauthammer cited one of a number of shocking examples of current deviancy: Nearly 30 percent of all U.S. newborns are now born to unmarried mothers. (President Clinton estimates that within a decade this figure will rise to 50 percent). Nonetheless, this social phenomenon is being classified by many professionals, intellectuals and the media as merely "another life-style choice," scarcely pointing out that the families of teen-agers cost the U.S. around $34 billion a year in welfare benefits. And, Krauthammer continues, there is more: the lowering of standards to "normalize" such frightening social directions is being paralleled by a trend to *raise* the levels of previous standards of middle-class normalcy. As baffling as it may seem, he stresses, it has now become *deviant* to conduct oneself in conformance with such previously normal standards because they have been "redefined upward." Thus, the "Ozzie and Harriet" middle-class members of society can no longer conform to "once-innocent" behavior without the risk of being accused of aberrant conduct in such areas as so-called "political correctness" and "racism," as well as in numerous practices newly characterized as "insensitivities."

It is such examples of contemporary societal developments and trends which typify what of late has been reverberating from the "world of the streets," streets which are now found throughout America — in the major cities, in the rural small towns, on the campuses. And, most likely, before long we shall experience an invasion of electronic streets directly into our living rooms, arteries emanating from the five hundred channels of the Information Superhighway to come.

The World of Reason

We now turn to the second of the three worlds open to the Jew in his search for an environment in which one can discover the essentials of how one might live.

As I have noted in previous pages, the free exercise of human reason was the basic underpinning of the Enlightenment. From the knowledge which reason would provide, the movement's philosophers predicted, post-medieval man's lot in the world would become vastly improved.

And, indeed, that is what took place, primarily as a result of the successful investigation by the scientist of the physical world. The huge benefit which such investigation brought to the man in the street created an esteem on his part for the men of science which overshadowed the esteem once reserved for the social philosopher. For while the philosophers had introduced better ideas, the scientist had brought about a better life. As the much-heralded source of material progress and the "good life," he soon replaced the philosopher as the quintessential "man of reason" and ever since has remained the embodiment of what is rational.

Still, however satisfying it was to enjoy material prosperity, the accomplishments of science were not able to provide man with true contentment. For one thing, *The Closing* points out, "Values are not discovered by reason," nor was it found sufficiently helpful to discover one's personal goal in life. Moreover, as a tool to seek out understanding, reason was (and is) not easily practiced. Meanwhile, the current assault upon the rational process by beliefs such as the relativism of truth and openness has substantially diminished the former reliability of reason as a source of wisdom. If everything (or almost everything) has become acceptable, what meaningful role can reason play in our search for truth and understanding?

But perhaps the most important cause of the inability of science to fulfill man's innermost yearnings is the indifference to and the aloofness of science to man's "world of experience."

In his *Theories of Everything*, John Barrow pointed out that "at root" the world is mathematical; therefore, any final theory must be stated in mathematical terms. In relying on mathematics to describe the world and its events, however, science has been compelled to divorce itself from man's everyday world. As a consequence, the objectivity of mathematical theories has been gained at the cost of considerable emptiness of content. For as more physical laws are expressed in colorless and cryptic mathematical language, the wider grows the gap between such information and man's classic comprehension of the "world of experience."

For to flesh and blood man, the scientist's theories and symbols are cold, mechanistic and unfamiliar. Typical man is not endowed with the ability to relate to or understand the impersonal approach of science because he is a creature of a sensory world, a visible world of such memorable sense impressions as the majestic and awesome vista of Arizona's mile-deep, nearly three-hundred-mile-long Grand Canyon; or what John Miur in his *Travel's in Alaska* called the "sublime grandeur" of huge Alaskan glaciers whose ever-so-slow grinding action reminded Miur that "this is still the morning of creation," during which "predestined" landscapes, mountains and river channels may actually be seen in the process of "being born"; or the burnt-orange, burgundy, pale-yellow and dark-green splendor of Indian summer in the Berkshires. These are the manifestations of the world which finite man is able to grasp, while the symbolism and abstractions of the rationalistic scientist which deal with space, time, light and the mysteries of the stars and galaxies are virtually bereft of existential meaning to man and remote from his general intellect and innermost concerns.

There is still another and even more unsettling catch to the art of reason, an art which is today most widely practiced by the men of science. The catch can be expressed in several questions being asked more and more frequently by scientists themselves: Are we striving for understanding which will always be beyond our grasp? Are we foreclosed forever from knowing everything? Is the universe far too complicated for us to comprehend? As we have noted previously, the central goal of science is to discover a final theory which would establish the nature of all events and things. In the last seventy-five years this search accelerated greatly. To a large number of bright, investigative men, the Mt. Everest of all scientific goals has become the formulation of such a final theory, which many call the "Theory of Everything" or the "Answer to Everything." It would unite all of the laws of the physical world into a single, all-encompassing law enabling us to comprehend all past events, all present ones and all of those to come about in the future. Man would then attain universal understanding, and everything would be answered.

The quest for such a unified theory began in the first half of this century, when this field of investigation was the province of but a few outstanding men, primarily Hermann Weil and Sir Arthur Eddington, who later collaborated with Weil. Their efforts, however, proved non-conclusive and, as previously recounted, it was not until the 1930's that Albert Einstein took up the search for what he called a "unified field theory." This investigation occupied him to the very last years of his life. At intervals, Einstein felt that he might be close to success, only to be compelled to abandon his course a number of times and to return to a new beginning. Years later, worn and not well, he finally conceded that he was unable to come to any satisfactory conclusion.

Professor Steven Weinberg, Nobel laureate and one of today's leaders in the prestigious field of particle physics, is one of the most supportive proponents of the potential for the discovery of such a final theory. In the mid-1993 controversy over federal funding of the eight-billion-dollar Texas supercollider project, Weinberg submitted a long op-ed letter to *The New York Times*. It strongly urged that the project be continued without any congressional funding cutback. (In October 1993, Congress, greatly concerned over the steady escalation of the project's cost, voted to discontinue further supercollider construction, and the undertaking was thereupon terminated.) He held out that the supercollider would enlarge our understanding in many ways and, in turn, facilitate the culmination of a final theory, which he characterized as "one of the noblest efforts of humankind." Should such a theory be formulated, he continued, it would establish "[the greatest] . . . break in intellectual history . . . since the birth of modern science."[4]

Yet even enthusiastic proponents of a final theory do not assert that its development is a certainty nor that it will be able to encompass all answers to scientific mysteries. Thus, prominent physicist Stephen Hawking allows that, absent future modifications in our understanding of the principle of Uncertainty, any future final theory will be conditioned by this Principle. Weinberg also concedes that, following such a discovery, science will still have to come up with

4. *The New York Times,* March 8, 1993, p. A15.

explanations of "countless, complicated phenomena, from turbulence to thought...." In effect, then, the enigmas of turbulence and most especially that of thought, together with the other "countless, complicated phenomena" referred to in Weinberg's article, dampen the prospects for the discovery anytime soon of a *single* final answer.

To his credit, Dr. Weinberg entitled his *New York Times* piece "The Answer to (Almost) Everything." From the gist of the article, it is clear that he added the qualification "almost" in view of the prospective inability of one law to embrace all natural phenomena. But the word "almost" may be seen from another perspective. However grand and all-unifying a future final answer may be, can it be called grand and all-unifying if it unveils a "final" theory but only a *partial* one, limited to our physical world and which excludes the human and spiritual attributes of existence?

In his *A Brief History of Time*, Stephen Hawking writes that a final theory is "only the first step," that the aim of the scientist is to obtain "complete understanding" of our existence, pointing out that science still faces the challenge of "predicting human behavior from mathematical equations."[5] From this observation, we may assume that science hopes that someday the human component may be investigated in the quest for a scientific final theory. Yet John Barrow, in *Theories of Everything,* makes the offsetting point that while we can more correctly "approximate the truth" by adding more rules of reasoning, "[truth] can never be captured by any finite set of rules."[6] These rules and formulas, he emphasizes, cannot embrace such features of human existence as beauty and truth. These and other such "attributes of reality" cannot be overtaken by mathematics or theories, however accurate they may become.

To Barrow's specification of such attributes as beauty, truth, harmony and simplicity, I venture to name several others which I feel no final theory will be able to encompass; they are the human qualities of love, decency, hope and faith. I have added these because I believe that they too are to be counted among those human elements which exert a palpable and significant influence in the universe.

---

5. Hawking, Stephen W., *A Brief History of Time,* New York: Bantam Books, 1988, p.127.
6. Barrow, John D., *Theories of Everything,* New York: Oxford University Press, 1991, p. 209.

The deeper science probes into the universe, the more apparent it becomes that total understanding lies beyond the power of reason and rational investigation. For our brains and bodies consist of atoms and particles, just as everything else in the universe, from a glass of water to the planets and stars of the cosmos, do. And because man is a part of the universe he seeks to understand, he encounters an inevitable dilemma: How can he hope to understand the universe if he is not even able to understand himself?

When we read Stephen Hawking writing of "predicting human behavior from mathematical equations" and Steven Weinberg writing about the phenomenon of "thought," one should have in mind this inevitable dilemma and the barrier it creates. For science is becoming increasingly aware that man cannot separate himself from his world. We are creatures of the very creation we study so intently, and we cannot view creation objectively, as something totally apart from ourselves.

John Barrow put it well in an observation that applies to this dilemma and to the scientists seeking a final theory: "There is more to Everything than meets the eye." He put it equally well when he concluded his *Theories of Everything* with the opinion that no such theory "can ever provide total insight." As noted earlier, this observation is comfortably shared by Judaism, for Judaism has always held that only God can encompass all things. Judaism posits that in Him and only in Him coalesce, simultaneously and inseparably, every perfection, power and truth in the universe. Thus, Judaism stands firm in asserting that, unlike any scientific final answer, only in God can total knowledge of everything be included.

The World of Revelation

The spiritual foundation of this world is what has been frequently referred to in these pages as "Torah," which can be defined as the repository of all Judaic law, belief and wisdom. In this repository is found the precious content of Judaic writings, both ancient and recent: The Five Books of Moses, the writings of the Prophets, the *Midrash*, the *Mishna*, the Babylonian and the Jerusalem Talmuds, the *Zohar*, the *Mishna Torah*, and the commentaries of our Sages — from Saadya Gaon, Rashi, Maimonides and Nachmanides to the Soforno, Moshe Chaim Luzzatto, the Vilna Gaon and the Chofetz Chaim, among numerous other luminaries of the Jewish world of scholarship and wisdom.

For centuries, the observant Jew has plumbed the contents of this treasury, gleaning explanations to many of the deeper questions about truth and ethics. It is Judaism's conviction that without delving into the repository of Torah, precious few of these basic issues of life can be untangled; what is real, true and just can only be discerned through the prism of the Torah. It is also Judaism's position that without the guidance of Torah, a Jewish man or woman runs the risk of succumbing to mistaken "common-sense" dogmas passed along by generations of mistaken people, dogmas which often consist neither of good sense nor a sense of right or wrong — hardly the stuff out of which to build what the men and women interviewed in *Habits of the Heart* termed a "morally coherent life."

Jewish belief enables us to relinquish such "common sense" whenever it contests divine wisdom brought down to us by Scripture, prophet or sage. Rather than viewing such relinquishment as an abdication of our intellect, Jews see it as a reaffirmation of our trust in the transcendency of the Torah's truth and the wisdom of Jewish tradition over man's transient judgments. This trust, however, calls for a willingness to stretch our minds beyond strict reason and logic. We are called upon to employ the higher will with which all Jews were endowed at Sinai and to disenthrall ourselves from the earthbound dimensions of our thinking if we are to succeed in probing into the deeper meanings of our existence.

Thereby we become able to find answers and guidance in Judaism's teachings which generally are unavailable to us elsewhere. We are enlightened through the lessons learned and the wisdom gained over our three-thousand-year history and shown which course should be followed and which should be avoided if our lives are to become purposeful and fulfilled. We are counseled on every facet of our daily and overall behavior: how to elevate ourselves in intellectual and moral stature; how to help our children achieve the same goals; how to avoid stumbling into error; how to contend with adversity; how to strive for truth — all to the end of discovering how we might live.

I have emphasized the conviction in the course of these pages that, among other available choices, the embrace of Judaism offers the searching Jewish person the surest pathway to a finer, more moral life. I recognize, however, that there may be readers who may challenge this conviction as being perhaps overly positive and self-assured. To such readers, I would point out that to avoid the possibility of partisanship, I subjected my conviction to three separate evaluations — the first being statistical, the second sociological and the third scientific.

At the onset, I searched for survey material which might demonstrate statistically whether observant Jewish people differ from the general population in such behavior categories as crime, drugs, teen-age pregnancies, alcoholism, high school drop-out rate, divorce, etc. Although I contacted a number of the leading organizations and professionals engaged in researching the Jewish community, I found that no such surveys have been conducted or are in process, although several excellent but purely demographic research projects have been completed recently.

Within the discipline of sociology, however, a number of pertinent sources are available. As examples, the reader will recall the discussion in earlier pages concerning the sociological findings of the *Habits of the Heat* research team relating to the important roles of "biblical traditions" and religious heritage in one's quest for moral coherence. The five sociologists who authored *Habits* made the telling point that the possible disappearance of biblical traditions may "altogether" deprive one's existence of meaning. And Allan Bloom, although a political, not a social, scientist, made a strong case (detailed ahead in the "holy, not good" section of this chapter) in his *The Closing* for the conclusion that young people are "isolated" from truth and ethics if they do not have the support of the "moral persuasion" of the Bible and the wisdom which its great figures can impart.

One of today's prominent authorities on the subject of morality in the American culture is Dr. Robert Coles, a long-time member of the Harvard faculty. For several decades he has investigated morality trends, especially as they relate to children both in the U.S. and in other countries. He is the author of a number of books on the subject, including the award-winning *Children in Crisis*.

Dr. Coles was the subject of a recent syndicated article by David Dyhan in which Coles is quoted by Dyhan as pointing out in a symposium that among the principal forces which shape the value systems of today's children are "the secular life, a lot of it stripped of value [and] the universities' refusal to look at issues with intense seriousness," adding that "declining religious faith and family life have coarsened American culture. . ." In his article, Dyhan reports that in the symposium the following exchange took place: "A teacher pressed Coles, 'Where can the young find moral guidance?' Coles brought down the house by cracking: 'Not on the Harvard faculty.' "

As to the scientific evaluation of my observations of the committed Jewish community, I applied the guidelines which astrophysicist Sir Fred Hoyle described in his *Nature of the Universe* concerning the process of observation. "It does not matter," he wrote, "[what your idea may be] . . . *so long as it works* — that is to say, as long as . . . its consequences are found to be in agreement with observation."[7]

In this respect, my close observations over many years of committed Jewish families (granting that there were more than a few unwelcome exceptions) confirm to me that such families substantially uphold and implement for themselves and towards others highly commendable moral standards and deportment in their daily comings and goings. It has been made clear to me that the "consequences" of their lives are "in agreement with" my observations, such consequences being demonstrated by a strong interest in decency and charity and education, attachment to family and community, compliance with religious and secular law and respect for the rights of others.

As a consequence of such "agreement," I feel confident in expressing my conviction that Judaism possesses exceptional potential to provide the guidance needed to create a moral life and to resist the forces that can destroy it.

The World of Revelation is another name for the world of Torah, a world comprised of many elements. Among the most important of these are: the ethical principle of "holy, not good," the partnership of man with God in the perfection of creation, and the goal of "knowing God."

While other elements are equally important and deserving of development, I have selected these three because of their especial

---

7. Hoyle, Fred, Sir, *The Nature of the Universe*, New York: The New American Library of World Literature, 1955, p. 112 (italics suppled).

relevance to the overall theme of this final chapter. We begin with "holy, not good."

Holy, Not Good

It is most helpful to view Judaism more as a code of morality than as a system of laws and rituals, however vital law and ritual are to our religion. For the paramount purpose of Judaism is to enable man to attain the highest degree of perfection. Judaism recognizes, however, that we are not angels and does not call upon us to strive for levels of achievement which are beyond our finite capacity.

The Judaic "code of morality" is based on the principle that man is made in the image of God and thus should walk in His ways. Judaism differs from other doctrines in that it accompanies each ideal with the obligation to translate it into an action. Ideals and morals are not enough; we are asked not only to believe in His ways but to *walk* in them. We must go beyond convictions and high-minded thoughts, translating them into positive deeds.

It is also essential to note that Jewish morality and the Jewish concept of how we are to live are based on the ethical standard of "holy, not good." This standard has its source in God's instruction to the Jewish nation in *Leviticus* 30:2: "You shall be holy for I, the Lord your God, am holy." Since the finite influence of man can initiate an equivalent influence of the Infinite (a process discussed in the next subsection, "Partnership"), Judaism looks to the Jew to uphold standards of mercy, righteousness, truth and forgiveness which are especially elevated, not merely "good." The reason is easily understood. Judaism, seeking to maximize the salutary effect of the divine influence in the world, logically insists that man's triggering deeds be exemplary, to assure that the divine influences which such deeds initiate are correspondingly maximized.

Why is "good" not good enough? After all, the urge to "do good," which is present in almost all men, is an admirable and enviable quality. Judaism does not look at all patronizingly, for example, upon the non-observant Jewish person who leads an ethical life, conducting himself with honesty, kindness, charity and regard for his fellow. But the difficulty lies with the definitions of "good and evil," "fair and unfair." For these are subjective qualities which, similar to the subjective impressions of the five senses described in Chapter V, vary from person to person, society to society, generation to generation. There are no absolutes in our everyday world. There are no fixed ideals by which society can chart its course. The *Random House Dictionary of the English Language* lists sixty-two definitions of the noun, adjective and adverb "right." Charles Wilson, a former chairman of General Motors, once told a U.S. Senate committee that "what is good for General Motors is good for the United States."

Psychiatrist Erich Fromm writes in *Man for Himself* that humanistic morality is the answer, that man's inherent reasoning alone should establish his ethical criteria of good and evil. In the 1970's and 1980's such views moved a dangerous step beyond, to the ethic "If it feels good, do it." Without the objective, unvarying moral standards of Judaism, we come close to moral chaos, to an anarchy of the "good." Fromm's thinking is one of the indirect sources upon which so many recent pop-psychology books draw their flawed ideas of re-making yourself into becoming, as their titles suggest, your own best friend and thinking of yourself first.

To assert that the ethical stance of society can rest upon the reasoning and authority of individual men — that of "the streets" — is to disregard experience and to believe in the near-impossible. In a phrase originated by Viktor Frankl, it is comparable to trying to climb an Indian fakir's rope which you yourself have thrown into the air.

How does "holy" differ from "good?" Throughout Jewish history, writings and law, we find abundant distinctions between the Judaic standard of "holy" and the standard of "good" of other peoples and religions. To illustrate just a few of dozens of Judaic practices of the "holy": Stealing includes "stealing the mind" (that means, do not ask the price of an article which you do not intend to buy; do not invite someone to a celebration simply to curry favor, if you know the invitee cannot attend). Even the truth becomes unworthy if used to gain revenge. Misleading the gullible is a serious violation of the prohibition against putting a "stumbling block before the blind." A court may not show favoritism to a poor man if he is undeserving, nor may it hesitate to render unfavorable judgment against a rich or famous man for fear of embarrassing him. One may not pressure one's debtor to repay a loan while one knows the debtor is unable to do so. Circulation of information which, even if true, harms or belittles someone else is a most serious transgression. The same is true of berating someone publicly, even if you are, or believe yourself to be, in the right. If able to do so, one should lend interest-free funds to a rich man who is in financial difficulty, not as a favor but as an obligation.

Other examples are bearing no grudges, quickly forgiving one who wrongs you, not overlooking worthiness in your enemy, extending your concern and protection to every creature, being modest and avoiding pride and arrogance, never betraying another's secret, always seeking to help those in difficulty, shunning deception and unlawful practices whether by word or deed, visiting the sick and the troubled, scrupulously respecting the needs and property of the community as well as the individual and wishing for others the same well-being and success which you wish for yourself, in accordance with the Torah's admonition to love your fellow as yourself.

These qualities are but some of the numerous ways described in the Jewish writings through which a Jewish person can demonstrate the "holy," rather than simply the "good." They are illustrative of those attributes which can be seen as the finest expressions of a Jewish person's potential.

One of the many excellent exhibits in the recently restored Ellis Island complex is a display of articles brought to America by those who came in the great immigration wave of the early 1900's. Fronting the interesting display is a wall-sized enlargement of a note written by a Jewish child who recalled the family's voyage: "The most important things my mother packed for the voyage were her Bible and her Sabbath candlesticks, which reminded us most of the home we left."

Over the last two generations, however, we have been witnessing a widening indifference within the Jewish family towards our past history and traditional sources of wisdom. As Allan Bloom remarked in *The Closing*, not so long ago — in our grandparents' time — Jewish people felt that the Bible "belonged to them," "told their story" and "embodied their instinct." Then, it was a source of "primary learning" for the Jewish family; today, sadly, it is much neglected, and in many families it is virtually abandoned. As a result, all too many Jews in this generation have been left without the very knowledge and motivation which can best serve to strengthen them in withstanding the impact of current relativistic thinking and many bewildering innovations in morality.

Without the moral persuasion of the Bible, Bloom comments, and without the connectedness of past tradition but with the freedom to decide all things, the young person is left isolated from everyone else and especially isolated from the truth. For the Bible, he continues, "is closer to the truth" because it relates "the real nature of things." The heroic, ethical figures of the Bible who speak to us from the past impart the significance of the vital issues and choices facing man — what is right and wrong, true and false. Without the benefit of familiarity with the sublime deeds of the Patriarchs, the voices of the Prophets and the writings of the Psalmists, one is without hope that there is someone left out there from other times who can disclose the truth we seek. And so, one can only struggle with the inadequacies of our contemporary wisdom.

Admittedly, it is not always easy to comply with the Bible's elevated standards of "holy, not good." To do so entails overcoming our ethical and intellectual inertia, which influences us to remain content with what we already know and do, and with what we have grown comfortable. And yet, we owe it to ourselves not to allow the unwisdom and accelerating deviance of some segments of contemporary society and the New Age culture to stand in the way of our progressing towards solving the puzzle of personal existence. To so progress, we would do well to learn what believing Jews have always known — that the answers we seek can best be found in our Torah, our traditions, our historical experience and the richness of our Jewish narrative.

The Partnership

As we have noted in previous chapters, a remarkable encounter with God came about at Mt. Sinai when the Torah and its commandments were given to the Jewish people. The underlying goal of many of these commandments was the eventual achievement of perfection by both man and his fellow. In furtherance of this grand goal, the Torah encourages man to form a partnership with God for the dual purposes of attaining such perfection and completing the creation of our world, whose creation tradition teaches us was purposely left unfinished so that self-perfected man could share in the privileged process of completion. This partnership with God thus offers man the rare opportunity to bring his life onto a higher plane and to participate in the very work undertaken by the Creator Himself.

It is noteworthy that Alfred North Whitehead had a most interesting approach to this subject. This distinguished British scientist and equally prominent philosopher was a neighbor of and, in his youth, knew Sir Moses Montefiori, the noted Jewish philanthropist. In his later years, Whitehead left Cambridge for Harvard, where he became a leading intellectual figure, continuing in the famous philosophical traditions of William James and George Santayana.

Whitehead greatly admired Judaism and wrote that Jews had an "ethical perception" and a "beauty of holiness" which others did not "approach." Shortly before his death in 1947, he granted a lengthy (371-page) wide-ranging interview, the final sentences of which were related to immortality and the age-old Judaic concept of man's potential partnership with God. Here is what he had to say on that subject, after a lifetime of brilliant thought and teaching:

> God's creativity is continual and everywhere, in the "ether, water, earth, human hearts . . . Insofar as man partakes of this creative process does *he partake of the divine*, of God, and *that participation is his immortality* . . . His true destiny as a co-creator in the universe is his dignity and his grandeur."[8]

Whitehead's observations are deserving of high compliment for their clarity and expressiveness. Still, I feel they require two comments. First, the concept of co-creation and partnership between man and God originated in Jewish thought; much later, it was borrowed from Judaism by other religions. (Whitehead, known for his accuracy and objectivity, most likely would have confirmed this.) Secondly, but more importantly, Whitehead failed to give us any clue as to the workings of what he identified as the "process." Just how can man "partake of the divine"?

Nor did Eddington, notwithstanding his daring and innovative "new thinking in science," suggest how man can access the "spiritual domain" in which, he asserted, the veil is "lifted in places."

---

8. Price, Lucien, *Dialogues of Alfred North Whitehead*, Boston: Little, Brown, 1954, p. 371.

Rank also revealed a number of important psychological insights into man's need to reach out to the cosmos in order to learn who and why he is. But while he made clear what prompts this drive within man, he did not clearly specify the way in which man can accomplish such self-transcending "reaching out."

It is within Judaism, however, that we can discover the workings of the spiritual process to which such scientists refer but do not delineate. In his essay *If You Were God*, Rabbi Aryeh Kaplan, relying on a number of Judaic sources, helped us to comprehend the process. Kaplan pointed out that it is first necessary to recognize that there can be no greater good in store for man than in his drawing close to God, since God is the "greatest good."[9] Man can best achieve this closeness by "imitating" such divine qualities as righteousness and kindness. When man does so, he, in effect, "creates" good, just as God continually creates good. In this fashion, Kaplan added, man joins with God to fulfill the purpose of creation, that purpose being the bestowal of good upon others. It is in this role that man achieves the status of a co-creator with God and thereby experiences a "knowledge and understanding of God" — the closest approach one can ever make "to the 'Mind of God.' "

This, maintains Judaism, is the true "creative process"; it is the path whereby a Jewish person may participate in creation and join in the process of perfecting himself and others.

Man's partnership with God as a co-creator is that element of Judaism which was singled out in Chapter IX as belonging to all three of Judaism's streams of time, "yesterday," "today" and "tomorrow." As such, it is one of the most important components of the "case" for Judaism.

Still, without some further clarification and illustration, one might find the concepts of co-creation and partnership somewhat mystifying and vague. Just what are the dynamics of such an alliance between man and God? In what specific manner can man activate a process which enables him to participate with God in the acts of creation?

Perhaps these challenging questions can be met best by recalling both the Law of Conservation and Newton's Third Law of

---

9. This and all direct quotations or paraphrasings of Rabbi Aryeh Kaplan are taken from the pages of his book: *If You Were God,* New York: National Conference of Synagogue Youth/Union of Orthodox Jewish Congregations of America,1983.

Mechanics. The Law of Conservation maintains, in part, that nothing in the world ever disappears; it only changes form. So, too, there is a moral law of conservation in Judaism which assures us that no worthy act of man will fail to survive. And Newton's Third Law states, in summary, that for each and every action there is an equal and opposite reaction. Some eighteen hundred years ago, the *Zohar*'s text expressed precisely the same phenomenon but in spiritual rather than physical terms: "Any act below stimulates a corresponding activity above." Thus, when I initiate a *human* gesture of kindness, I activate the descent from the cosmic realm to earth of a corresponding and equivalent *divine* kindness which redounds both to my personal benefit and to humanity as well.

Does all of this sound a bit specious? If so, it will help us if, first, we rephrase the phenomenon stated in the *Zohar* by describing it as "a system in which human ethical acts trigger celestial ones." Then, we should compare it with linked "systems" in the physical world, which lately are being revealed by modern, rational investigators of a new science called "Chaos." They, too, find it difficult to explain, except in terms of cosmic influence, a number of physical phenomena which only recently have been noted.

In the past two decades, Chaos scientists, through advanced and complex computer imaging, have demonstrated that a remarkable order and pattern exist within the disorder and chaos revolving about us. Among the principles upon which these finding are based is that of "sensitive dependence on initial conditions." In an abbreviated layman's interpretation, this principle proposes that some significant events can be directly affected by and linked to preceding, seemingly unrelated, even minute, influences.

Accordingly, in respect of the difficulties encountered in long-range weather predictions, Chaos scientists identify a phenomenon which they call the "butterfly effect." They describe this effect to mean that the delicate beating of a butterfly's wings in a Brazilian rain forest can initiate a minute current of air which, in turn, is able to activate a series of subsequent currents that ultimately can have an impact on the origin and intensity of a severe tropical storm over Texas some weeks later. (James Gleick, the author of a recent, splendid book, *Chaos: Making a New Science*, when asked by a book reviewer why such effects also seem to be present in systems other than weather, replied that it "is a question for God."[10]) And, as we recall, Chapter V described the strange and extraordinary connection between photons which can bring about simultaneous communication between two fragments of a photon, even though the fragments are widely separated and traveling in opposite directions.

These illustrations of exceptional and mystifying physical interconnections should give us pause before we classify the *Zohar*'s account of a spiritual interconnection between terrestrial and heavenly moral influences as too incredible for a modern, rational Jew to accept. Once we become better able to recognize such spiritual interconnection and to accept their plausibility (just as we recognize and accept perplexing phenomena such as the "butterfly effect" and communication between photon fragments), we also become able to conceive the possibility that through profound spiritual encounters man may be able to become a co-creator with God in bringing to fruition a world in which evil, cruelty and injustice have been replaced by loving-kindness, mercy and equity.

Knowing God

We recall that the purpose of men of science is to "know the mind of God." While still in his thirties, Albert Einstein stated that his lifetime goal was to "draw the lines of God's face."

Yet, Judaism's approach toward "knowing the mind of God" is something quite different from that of the scientist. Judaism's knowledge of God has been gained through the pathway established on the morning Moses ascended Mt. Sinai. There, Moses asked of God, "Show me now Your ways, that I might know You," and again, "Show me, I pray You, Your glory" (*Exodus* 33:18).

The latter request related to a desire to glimpse God's essence, but God responds that no mortal can see His face and live. However, He grants Moses' first entreaty to be shown God's attributes, and He replies that He will cause "to pass all My Goodness before you." God then reveals, in ordinary terms which a human can grasp, a number of the attributes of His "ways" which constitute His Divine "Goodness": mercy, justice, graciousness, forbearance, righteousness, truth, forgiveness, love, compassion.

In later times, in words spoken through Jeremiah the Prophet,

---

10. *Newsweek*, December 21, 1987, p. 47.

God further defines how "to know" Him. He cautions that man should not glory in his wisdom, might or riches, but rather:

> Let him that glorieth glory in this
> That he understandeth and *knoweth* Me
> That I am the Lord Who exercises mercy, justice
> and righteousness in the earth;
> For in these things I delight, sayeth the Lord.[11]
>
> *Jeremiah* 9:23

In *The Guide* (Part III, Ch. LIV, ed. Friedlander), Maimonides stressed how "perfect and concise" are the words of Jeremiah, "Let him that glorieth glory in this, that he understandeth and knoweth Me." The words "understandeth" and "knoweth," Maimonides explained, mean that one comprehends God's "greatness, providence and perfection." *The Guide* points out, however, that Jeremiah did not regard such understanding and knowledge as sufficient to establish "the highest kind of perfection" to which man can aspire. Otherwise, Maimonides commented, the Prophet would have ended there; instead, he added:

> That I am the Lord Who exercises justice
> and righteousness in the earth;
> For in these things I delight, sayeth the Lord.

Maimonides clarifies that these additional verses were added to convey that man can "only" glory if he acquires a knowledge of God's greatness and perfection and *also* gains a knowledge of His ways, that is, His acts of justice and righteousness. Having once acquired this combined knowledge, Maimonides continues, man will then "be determined always to seek loving-kindness, justice and righteousness and thus to imitate the ways of God." Apropos of the explanation, it is interesting to note (see also *The Guide* Part I, Ch. LIV, ed. Friedlander) that our Sages implied that God encourages man to strive to so follow in His ways when they interpreted *Leviticus* 19:2 ["You shall be holy"] as meaning: "He is gracious, so be you also gracious; He is merciful, so be you also merciful."

To "know," to "understand" God, then, man is instructed to imitate the moral attributes in which God "delights." In our performance

---

11. *Jeremiah*, ed. H. Friedman, London: Soncino Press, 1973.

of His qualities of mercy, justice and righteousness, we can come closer to "knowing" the metaphorical "Face" or "Mind" of God. Thus, Judaism views "knowing" as a *qualitative* concept.

In contrast, the classical scientist's "knowing" is a *quantitative*, linear concept. To approach reality, Einstein felt he needed to sketch lines, to measure, to quantify. So too, the non-scientific man of reason, in order to "know," measures all ideas against his own finite, subjective standards and yardsticks. Yet, Eddington went to the heart of the matter when he declared during an important lecture series at Cornell in 1934 that although the world is being "remorselessly dissected" and "studied and measured," it is never "*known*" (emphasis added).

But if the world cannot be "known" by scientific dissection, is there another avenue? Judaism answers, "Yes, through the concept of *imitateo Dei,* the Jewish people possess an implemental approach towards the knowledge of the world and its Creator. This approach, entailing the practice by man of the moral qualities which are attributed to God, was designed and gifted to our people when the Revelation at Sinai took place."

In Part I, LXV of *The Guide*, Maimonides explained that by succeeding both in knowing God's greatness as well as in knowing His ways, man can arrive at "the true glorification of God." As we have noted in a previous paragraph above, Maimonides further pointed out that upon man's attainment of both of these prerequisites to God's glorification, man is informed by God, "Let him that glorieth glory in this. . ."

It would appear, then, that concomitant with man's achievement of the glorification of God, there is bestowed by God upon man a glory *all his own*, reflecting his having reached a human summit which neither his wisdom nor his power nor his wealth can reach. Implicit in this ideal of personal glory are such superlatives of human achievement as "praiseworthy," "illustrious," "distinguished," and "honorable."

Consequently, the potential triumph of being rewarded with the gift of personal glory takes on for every Jew a greater urgency and a more sought-after life-goal. To the distanced-from-religion Jewish person, such an accomplishment would effect a truly remarkable re-acquaintanceship with God. To the committed Jew, it would effect his closest approach yet to the goal of human perfection.

There is a telling parable, based on a classic story in Judaic literature, which, with slight adaptation, serves to illuminate how, through righteousness, we can gain our most sought-after rewards. The account comes from the pen of the most beloved and illustrious Jewish sage of the last century, Rabbi Israel Meir HaCohen, who was known as the "Chofetz Chaim."[12]

There once lived a man who had three friends, the first of whom he loved ardently, the second somewhat less so and the third for whom he had only slight affection. One day, he was falsely accused by the police of a serious offense. Exceedingly frightened, he called upon each of his three friends to help exonerate him from the baseless accusation at a forthcoming trial before the high court in the capital city.

The first and most beloved friend replied that he was incapable of testifying to the man's innocence and hence would not even attend the trial. The second, somewhat less beloved friend replied that he could not appear in court either but would be willing to act as escort on the long journey to the courtroom, at which point he would turn about and return home. The third and least admired of the man's friends embraced and comforted him. Unhesitatingly, the third friend agreed not only to appear at the trial but promised that his testimony would fully exonerate the prisoner and free him from the threat of lifetime imprisonment. Subsequently, the third friend did what he promised. He testified in court and won the man's total acquittal from all charges.

The first and most esteemed friend, the Chofetz Chaim explains, is man's money and material possessions. They are of no value in bringing about our innermost wishes. The second friend represents man's family and influential friends. They accompany him to the grave but then leave to return to their own lives, homes, and interests. The third friend is man's personal righteousness, to which he had given only scant attention and devotion in his lifetime. Yet this friend brought him the greatest comfort and satisfaction.

12. HaCohen, Israel Meir, *Ahavas Chesed*, trans. by Leonard Oschry, New York: Feldheim Publishers, Ltd., 1979, p. 210-211.

In conclusion, then, we come to recognize that the two questions posed at the beginning of this chapter are really one, for "moral coherence" is *the* essential quality of "How then should we live?" In fulfilling a life of true moral coherence, we thereby can achieve the most rewarding and meaningful of all possible lives in the here and now.

And the reward stretches beyond the here and now, into the long, silent time ahead. In concluding the parable, the Chofetz Chaim touched upon man's deep longing for immortality, commenting that the parable's source is in the verse (*Numbers* 5:10): "And every man's holy things shall be his" — signifying, the Chofetz Chaim noted, that man's righteous acts ". . . will stay with him forever."

It is as if, then, our wordly deeds of goodness leave indelible fingerprints on the universe which survive finitude and create for us a link with, yes, eternity — assuring that our having lived righteously shall be remembered and honored, forever.

Epilogue — A Final Word

A few thoughts for those Jewish men and women who would like to learn more about their religion. . .

At this point you may wish there were more to discover about how to gain enhanced meaning in your life. Well, there is more, lots more.

How does one go about finding that "lots more"? One of the most frequently quoted Judaic aphorisms is the great sage Hillel's reply to a heathen who asked him to describe the entire Torah in the brief time a person could remain standing on one foot. Hillel replied: "What is hateful to you, do not do to your neighbor. That is the whole Torah; the rest is commentary." This is the most frequently stated quotation.

But there are two more words omitted by many with which Hillel ended his summary: "Go learn!"[1] After years of personal exploration, I am convinced that these two words of advice form the passkey to life's enrichment.

Why is "learning" (not merely "studying") Torah so important and so effective? The Torah is more than a constitution of the Jewish nation. It is a vast sea of concepts, guidelines, teachings, insights, commandments, laws and ethics, all together forming the world-view of Judaism. The Torah illuminates *every* matter that touches man and his universe.

The Torah unfolds the entire narrative of Judaism — its traditions, history, triumphs, tragedies, mission and memories. With this narration, it bridges the generations of the past to our own generation, providing a coherence and a significance to our lives found nowhere else.

Above all, it reveals both God's benevolence and His will. Thus, "learning Torah" is deemed the finest of all man's efforts, for through Torah man carries on, so to speak, a dialogue with God Himself. In

1. Babylonian Talmud, *Tractate Shabbath,* p. 31a.

studying the sacred texts we learn how God, their Author, desires us to fulfill our roles in the world surrounding us, roles we might not otherwise have recognized or understood.

We know that man never will be able to fully isolate Ultimate Reality. But learning the wisdom of the Torah provides man with the surest and most authentic pathway towards achieving a limited knowledge of and attachment to that Reality.

Regrettably, there are a number of reasons why so few of us "learn" today. Frequently, we are influenced by the expression of cynicism towards any formal religion, a cynicism engendered by science and humanism. And in some sectors, Torah values are derided as unrealistic, irrelevant and obscurantist. Then, there is the hesitation that through belief in religion we surrender our independence of mind. In some cases we shun our religion or doubt its value because we have known some who identify themselves as "religious" but who behave shamefully or hypocritically. In other instances we are simply too preoccupied with contemporary causes and issues.

None of these reasons, however, is valid enough to stand in the way of exploring Judaic intellectual content. For Jewish education is that vibrant force which has powered and regenerated Judaism over the centuries. Torah education has been compulsory within Judaism for over two millennia, ever since the High Priest Joshua ben Gamla required every community to provide public schools for all children over the age of five. And for many centuries an adult graduate educational system functioned in Israel, in which every Jew participated in study groups held during the required pilgrimages to Jerusalem for the Festivals of Passover, Shavuoth and Succoth. Interestingly, some years back, in a French archaeological zone, a Jewish school was unearthed dating from the eighth-ninth centuries C.E. The plastered walls of one schoolroom still bore graffiti in Hebrew reciting the equivalent of "Kilroy was here." This was in an age when the reigning emperor, Charlemagne, was illiterate.

In the past few decades especially, the need for and value of Jewish education has been recognized and fostered by each of the three principal movements within Judaism, as evidenced by a burgeoning throughout America of day schools and yeshivas for the young and educational programs for adults.

In Nobel laureate S. Y. Agnon's *Days of Awe*, he recounted the legend of a wealthy father and his spendthrift son. On the father's deathbed, he tells the son that he knows the son will squander his large inheritance. The father goes on to say that part of his own inheritance was a certain marvelous garden which he cautions the son never to sell, confiding that if its owner is ever in difficult straits, the garden will bring forth his rescue.

As predicted, soon after the father's passing the son gambles away his inheritance and becomes poverty stricken. It was then that he recalls the garden. He walks within it, wondering to himself how it was conceivable that a garden could rescue him from his distress. Then, Agnon related, the son's attention is drawn to a distinguishing mark on a certain tree. Digging under it, he finds a great treasure.[2]

The moral of the tale can be adapted to the thrust of this epilogue. Most of the Jewish immigrants to America neglected or abandoned the art of learning, which for centuries had given Judaism its cohesiveness, continuity and distinction. Arriving on the shores of the New World, they pursued material or professional success and social acceptance, rationalizing away their obligation to learn Torah by leaving it to the "small remnant." (In 1933, Einstein wrote that the study of Judaism's "spiritual and ethical" content "has rightly been the sacred endeavor of the capable ones among us."[3]) Many of the new arrivals were not even familiar with the inestimable value of their treasure, thousands of Torah volumes brimming with knowledge and perception. Fortunately, the treasure is still intact, waiting for any Jewish person to unearth it.

---

2. Agnon, S. Y., *Days of Awe*, New York: Schochen Books, 1948, pp. 142-143.
3. Dukas, Helen and Hoffman, Banish, editors, *Albert Einstein: The Human Side*, Princeton: Princeton Univ. Press, 1979, p. 66.

Bibliography

Albright, William Foxwell. *From Stone Age to Christianity.* Baltimore: Johns Hopkins Press, 1946.

Albright, William Foxwell. *Archaeology and the Religion of Israel.* Baltimore: Johns Hopkins Press, 1968.

Andrade, E. N. da C. *Sir Isaac Newton.* New York: Doubleday and Company, 1938.

Barth, Aron. *The Perennial Quest.* Jerusalem: World Zionist Organization, 1984.

Becker, Ernest. *Angel in Armor.* New York: Geo. Braziller, 1969.

Becker, Ernest. *The Denial of Death*. New York: Free Press, 1973.

Becker, Ernest. *Escape From Evil*. New York: Free Press, 1941.

Berkovitz, Eliezer. *God, Man and History*. New York: Jonathan David, 1965.

Besdin, Abraham R. *Reflections of the Rav* (Translated or adapted from lectures of Rabbi Joseph B. Soloveitchik). Jerusalem: World Zionist Organization, 1981.

Bloom, Allan. *The Closing of the American Mind.* New York: Simon & Schuster Inc., 1987.

Bohr, Niels. *Atomic Theory and the Description of Nature.* London: Cambridge Univ. Press, 1934.

Born, Max. *The Restless Universe.* New York: Dover Books, 1981.

Born, Max. *The Born-Einstein Letters.* New York: Walker and Company, 1971.

Born, Max. *My life and My Views.* New York: Charles Scribner's Sons, 1968.

Bretall, R., ed. *Kirkegaard Anthology.* Princeton: Princeton Univ. Press, 1946.

Cohen, I. Bernard. *Revolution in Science.* Cambridge: Belknap Press, 1985.

Cordovero, Moses. *The Palm of Deborah.* New York: Hermon Press, 1974.

Cornell, James, ed. *Bubbles, Voids, Bumps in Time: The New Cosmology.* Cambridge: Cambridge Univ. Press, 1989.

Douglas, A. Vilbert. *The Life of Arthur Stanley Eddington,* New York: Thomas Nelson and Sons Ltd., 1957.

Dukas, Helen and Hoffman, Banish, eds. *Albert Einstein: The Human Side.* Princeton: Princeton Univ. Press, 1979.

Eddington, Arthur Stanley, Sir. *New Pathways in Science.* London: Cambridge Press, 1934.

Eddington, Arthur Stanley, Sir. *The Nature of the Physical World.* New York: McMillan Press, 1928.

Einstein, Albert and Infield, Leopold. *The Evolution of Physics.* Cambridge: Cambridge Univ. Press, 1938.

Einstein, Albert. *Out of My Later Years.* New York: Philosophical Library, 1950.

Flood, Raymond and Lockwood, Michael, ed. *The Nature of Time.* New York: Basil Blackwell Inc., 1987.

Frankl, Viktor E. *Man's Search for Meaning.* New York: Pocket Books, 1963.

Fromm, Erich. *Man for Himself.* Greenwich, Conn.: Fawcett Publications Inc., 1947.

Fromm, Erich. *Escape from Freedom.* New York: Holt, Rinehart, Winston, 1962.

Gilder, George. *Microcosm.* New York: Simon & Schuster, Inc. 1989.

Gleick, James. *Chaos: Making a New Science.* New York: Viking Press, 1987.

Hawking, Stephen W. *A Brief History of Time.* New York: Bantam Books, 1988.

Heisenberg, Werner. *Physics and Philosophy.* London: Allen & Unwin, 1959.

Heisenberg, Werner. *Across the Frontiers.* New York: Harper & Row, 1974.

Hertzberg, Arthur. *The Jews in America.* New York: Simon & Schuster, 1989.

Heschel, Abraham Joshua. *God In Search of Man.* New York: Meridian Books, 1959.

Heschel, Abraham Joshua. *The Earth is the Lord's.* New York: Harper & Row, 1966.

Hirsch, Samson Raphael. *Judaism Eternal.* London: Soncino Press, Ltd., 1956.

Hirsch, Samson Raphael. *The Nineteen Letters.* Jerusalem: Feldheim Publishers, Ltd., 1969.

Hoyle, Fred. *The Nature of the Universe.* New York: Mentor Books, 1955.

Hoyle, Fred. *Frontiers of Astronomy*. New York: Mentor Books, 1951.

Jastrow, Robert. *Until the Sun Dies.* New York: Warner Books, 1977.

Jastrow, Robert. *God and the Astronomers*. New York: Bantam Books, 1988.

Jeans, James Hopwood, Sir. *New World of Physics.* New York: McMillian Company, 1943.

Jeans, James Hopwood, Sir. *The Mysterious Universe.* New York: The MacMillian Company, 1930.

Jung, Carl G. *Modern Man in Search of a Soul.* New York: Harcourt, Brace and Company, 1957.

Jung, Carl G. *Memories, Dreams and Reflections.* London: Collins and Routledge & K. Paul, 1963.

Manuel, Frank E. *Religion of Sir Isaac Newton.* London: Oxford Univ. Press, 1974.

May, Rolls. *Existential Psychology*. New York: Random House, 1961.

Menaker, Esther. *Otto Rank.* New York: Columbia Univ. Press, 1982.

Morison, Samuel E. *European Discovery of America: The Northern Voyages, 500-1600.* New York: Oxford University Press, 1971.

Planck, Max. *The New Science.* New York: Meridian Books, 1959.

Rank, Otto. *Beyond Psychology*. New York: Dover Books, 1941.

Steinberg, Milton. *Basic Judaism*. New York: Harcourt, Brace and Company, 1947.

Weinberg, Steven. *The First Three Minutes.* London: Fontana Paperbacks, 1984.

Weyl, Hermann. *Mind and Nature*. Philadelphia: Univ. of Pennsylvania, 1934.